22.45

OSKAR SCHINDLER

D0555569

Other titles in the
People Who Made History series:

PEOPLE
WHO MADE
HISTORY

OSKAR SCHINDLER

Bruce Thompson, *Book Editor*

Daniel Leone, *President*
Bonnie Szumski, *Publisher*
Scott Barbour, *Managing Editor*
Stuart B. Miller, *Series Editor*

GREENHAVEN PRESS
SAN DIEGO, CALIFORNIA

GALE GROUP

THOMSON LEARNING

Detroit • New York • San Diego • San Francisco
Boston • New Haven, Conn. • Waterville, Maine
London • Munich

Every effort has been made to trace the owners of copy-righted material. The articles in this volume may have been edited for content, length, and/or reading level. The titles have been changed to enhance the editorial purpose. Those interested in locating the original source will find the complete citation on the first page of each article.

Library of Congress Cataloging-in-Publication Data

Oskar Schindler / Bruce Thompson, book editor.
    p. cm. — (People who made history)
    Includes bibliographical references and index.
    ISBN 0-7377-0894-8 (pbk. : alk. paper) —
    ISBN 0-7377-0895-6 (lib. : alk. paper)
    1. Schindler, Oskar, 1908–1974. 2. Righteous Gentiles in the Holocaust—Biography. 3. World War, 1939–1945—Jews—Rescue. 4. Holocaust, Jewish (1939–1945)
I. Thompson, Bruce. II. Series.

D804.66.S38 O75   2002
362.87'81'092—dc21   2001040918

Cover photo: © Bettmann/Corbis

Copyright © 2002 by Greenhaven Press,
an imprint of The Gale Group
10911 Technology Place
San Diego, CA 92127
Printed in the U.S.A.

CONTENTS

Chapter 4: Discussions of Schindler's Moral Character and Motivations

Chapter 5: Reflections on the Movie *Schindler's List*

3. Not the Last Word

FOREWORD

In the vast and colorful pageant of human history, a handful of individuals stand out. They are the men and women who have come variously to be called "great," "leading," "brilliant," "pivotal," or "infamous" because they and their deeds forever changed their own society or the world as a whole. Some were political or military leaders—kings, queens, presidents, generals, and the like—whose policies, conquests, or innovations reshaped the maps and futures of countries and entire continents. Among those falling into this category were the formidable Roman statesman/general Julius Caesar, who extended Rome's power into Gaul (what is now France); Caesar's lover and ally, the notorious Egyptian queen Cleopatra, who challenged the strongest male rulers of her day; and England's stalwart Queen Elizabeth I, whose defeat of the mighty Spanish Armada saved England from subjugation.

Some of history's other movers and shakers were scientists or other thinkers whose ideas and discoveries altered the way people conduct their everyday lives or view themselves and their place in nature. The electric light and other remarkable inventions of Thomas Edison, for example, revolutionized almost every aspect of home-life and the workplace; and the theories of naturalist Charles Darwin lit the way for biologists and other scientists in their ongoing efforts to understand the origins of living things, including human beings.

Still other people who made history were religious leaders and social reformers. The struggles of the Arabic prophet Muhammad more than a thousand years ago led to the establishment of one of the world's great religions—Islam; and the efforts and personal sacrifices of an American reverend named Martin Luther King Jr. brought about major improvements in race relations and the justice system in the United States.

Each anthology in the People Who Made History series begins with an introductory essay that provides a general overview of the individual's life, times, and contributions. The group of essays that follow are chosen for their accessibility to a young adult audience and carefully edited in consideration of the reading and comprehension levels of that audience. Some of the essays are by noted historians, professors, and other experts. Others are excerpts from contemporary writings by or about the pivotal individual in question. To aid the reader in choosing the material of immediate interest or need, an annotated table of contents summarizes the article's main themes and insights.

Each volume also contains extensive research tools, including a collection of excerpts from primary source documents pertaining to the individual under discussion. The volumes are rounded out with an extensive bibliography and a comprehensive index.

Plutarch, the renowned first-century Greek biographer and moralist, crystallized the idea behind Greenhaven's People Who Made History when he said, "To be ignorant of the lives of the most celebrated men of past ages is to continue in a state of childhood all our days." Indeed, since it is people who make history, every modern nation, organization, institution, invention, artifact, and idea is the result of the diligent efforts of one or more individuals, living or dead; and it is therefore impossible to understand how the world we live in came to be without examining the contributions of these individuals.

INTRODUCTION: A MAN OF EXCEPTIONAL VIRTUE

When one begins looking for the names of the everyday heroes who changed history by saving the Jews of Europe, no one gets all the credit. But one name does stand out among the others. Oskar Schindler saved over a thousand Jewish lives by providing sanctuary for them directly under the noses of the German executioners. He took grave personal risks and spent a vast fortune to protect people, most of whom he barely knew. While Schindler schemed and struggled to save Jewish lives, most Germans looked away and did little or nothing to help. Many even encouraged the Holocaust. Why did Schindler do so much while ordinary, decent Germans did so little? Perhaps Schindler was a man of exceptional virtue. Many aspects of his life suggest just the opposite. He was not religious; he drank heavily; he cheated on and neglected his wife; he was unscrupulous and dishonest in his business dealings; he loved fast cars and fine clothes. He was hardly a moral paragon.

Schindler is a person well worth trying to understand. In trying to understand Schindler, we confront one of the darkest moments in human history and ask how such tragedies can occur. We ask what psychological traits make someone a hero at such moments; we even ask what it means to be moral. In short, we ask some of the most important questions possible.

THE SUDETENLAND

When Oskar Schindler was born on April 28, 1908, the region where he lived, known as Moravia, was part of the Austrian Empire. The Austrian Empire and the kingdom of Hungary together formed a country known as Austria-Hungary. The ruler of Austria-Hungary was the Austrian emperor, Franz Josef. Moravia had been part of the Austrian

11

Empire since the Late Middle Ages, so it is not surprising that many German-speaking Austrians had settled there, especially in the Sudeten Mountains in northern Moravia. (Schindler's ancestors arrived sometime during the sixteenth century.) The heavily German-speaking regions of Moravia and neighboring Bohemia came to be known as the Sudetenland.

In 1914, when Schindler was six years old, an ethnic Serb murdered Archduke Franz Ferdinand, Franz Josef's nephew and heir to the Austrian and Hungarian thrones. In response, Austria-Hungary declared war on the neighboring country of Serbia, and the conflict escalated quickly into what came to be called World War I. Germany sided with Austria-Hungary, but France, England, and eventually the United States sided with Serbia, and four years later Austria-Hungary was defeated. After the war, Austria-Hungary was divided into various smaller pieces. Moravia and Bohemia, including the Sudetenland, became part of a new country called Czechoslovakia; the majority population was made up of two groups of Slavic-speaking people, the Czechs (who lived primarily in Moravia and Bohemia) and the Slovaks (who lived primarily in a neighboring region known, appropriately, as Slovakia). In an instant, the German-speaking Sudetenlanders went from being the ruling ethnic group in the land they had inhabited for hundreds of years to being a foreign minority. Thus, it is perhaps not surprising that when Adolf Hitler, in the 1930s, began promising to reunify the German-speaking regions of Europe, the Sudetenlanders were (typically) among his most ardent supporters.

A DASHING YOUNG MAN

There is no evidence that the Schindler family paid much attention to politics during these tumultuous times. Oskar Schindler's father, Hans Schindler, was a salesman (he sold motor-driven machinery such as farm equipment and electrical generators), and his business depended on being on good terms with everyone. The Schindlers' neighbors were Jewish, and young Oskar frequently played with the children of that family. The town of Zwittau, where Oskar grew up, was an ethnically mixed, but friendly, community.

As a teenager, Oskar developed an interest in cars and motorcycles. His father encouraged—even indulged—this interest. Perhaps the senior Schindler imagined that his son's interest in motors indicated an interest in the family business. Oskar's car, a red Galloni, was the envy of his friends. Oskar also had a 250-cc Moto-Guzzi motorcycle, a professional-quality racer. He loved motorcycle racing, and he was good at it. He could hold his own against the best racers in Europe, and as a young man he must have dreamed of making this his career.

When he was nineteen years old, Oskar met Emilie Peltzl and married her, despite the objections of both their families. Unlike the dashing, fun-loving Oskar, Emilie was a quiet, serious girl. Everyone seemed to realize how poorly suited they were for each other—everyone except Oskar and Emilie. Once they were married, the young couple moved in with Oskar's parents, and lived with them for seven years, until 1935. The young Schindlers lived on the upper floor, and the senior Schindlers lived on the ground floor. It was an uncomfortable arrangement. Emilie did not get along well with her in-laws, and (as everyone knew he would) Oskar quickly tired of his new bride.

A SPY FOR THE THIRD REICH

In 1935 Hans Schindler's business went bankrupt. That year was the heart of the Great Depression, which affected Europe as badly as it did the United States. Unable to support his family, Hans Schindler abandoned them. Oskar loudly denounced his father, and it was many years before the two men were on speaking terms again. The rift was made worse by the fact that Oskar's mother, Louisa Schindler, died soon afterward.

No longer supported by the family business, Oskar took a job as a sales manager for Moravian Electrotechnic. The job involved quite a bit of travel. Occasionally, it even took him to Krakow, Poland, only 150 miles to the east. There, he met a woman who put him in touch with the German Counterintelligence Service, which recruited him to be a spy for the German government. Thereafter, his sales job was primarily just a front for his intelligence-gathering activities.

Schindler was an ethnic German, but he was not, of course, a citizen of Germany. As a citizen of Czechoslovakia, his work for the German Counterintelligence Service put him in the dangerous position of being a spy for a foreign government. And not just *any* foreign government: He was a spy for Nazi Germany.

The years of the Great Depression had been good for the Nazis in Germany. In 1930 Hitler's National Socialist Party—the Nazis—won 107 seats in Germany's parliament, called the Reichstag. In 1932 they won 229 seats. Six months later, on January 30, 1933, Hitler was named chancellor of Germany in a coalition government in which he shared power with two opposition parties, the Social Democratic Party and the German Nationalist Party. Then, on February 27, 1933, a fire destroyed the Reichstag building. Hitler blamed the Communists and put fellow Nazi Party member Hermann Göring in charge of investigating the incident. The Nazis used the burning of the Reichstag as a pretext for brutal political repression, and they were soon in complete control of the German government. On March 23, 1933, with no building in which to meet, the Reichstag disbanded, granting its governing powers directly to Hitler's cabinet, which, however, still included some opposition members. In June, the opposition parties were dissolved and their members purged from the cabinet. The final consolidation of power came a year later, on August 19, 1934, when German president Paul von Hindenburg died. Hitler took over as president, while still retaining the office of chancellor. This gave Hitler the powers of an absolute dictator.

Having consolidated power in Germany, Hitler began making plans to extend German authority to other parts of Europe, including Poland and Czechoslovakia. To prepare for this expansion, the German government needed people to gather information about Poland and Czechoslovakia for them. Someone like Oskar Schindler, an ethnic German with an excuse to travel in those regions and meet people, was just what they needed.

Schindler loved being a spy. He loved the travel that it involved; he loved the intrigue and danger; he loved the theatrics of pretending to be someone he was not—perhaps someone more elegant and sophisticated than his rather middle-class upbringing would otherwise have suggested. Schindler was also a talented spy. The work primarily involved meeting people from whom he could collect information, getting them drunk enough to become talkative, and holding his own liquor well enough to pay attention when they did. Schindler could be charming even with people he did not like, and he could hold his liquor. For the remainder of his life, these were his two chief talents. At times they served him very well indeed.

Schindler's work for the German Counterintelligence Service was so impressive that he was made section chief in Mahrisch-Ostrau (Ostrava), the regional capital. He and Emilie took an apartment there, and she assisted him by typing reports, answering the phone, and running errands. As she describes it, their apartment "became the permanent meeting place for spies and informers."[1] Eventually, however, the Czech authorities caught on. The Schindlers' apartment was ransacked, incriminating papers were found, and Oskar Schindler was arrested and sentenced to death.

MANUFACTURING POTS AND PANS

However, Schindler was not executed. On March 14, 1939, Germany took control of Czechoslovakia. Undoubtedly, Schindler's intelligence work had played some role in laying the groundwork for the takeover. Naturally, Schindler was released from prison by the new German administration. He needed a new job, and because of his work for the Germans, he had excellent contacts. If any interesting business opportunities were to come up, he would be sure to hear of them.

On September 30, 1939, Germany and Russia engaged in a joint invasion of Poland, splitting the country between them. Hitler hoped that this invasion, like the March 1938 invasion of Austria and the recent acquisition of Czechoslovakia, would be tolerated by other countries in Europe. It was not. In response to the invasion, France and Britain declared war on Germany.

For Oskar Schindler, the invasion of Poland opened up just the opportunity he had been looking for. The city of Krakow, less than a hundred miles east of Mahrisch-Ostrau, was part of German-occupied Poland. It was German policy to "Aryanize" its occupied territory by taking businesses and manufacturing away from Poles and Jews—especially Jews— and leasing them to German *Treuhanders* (managers). In most cases, the previous owner or manager would continue to work as an employee of the German *Treuhander*—at least until he was no longer needed. A month after the invasion, Schindler was in Krakow making inquiries about a company called Rekord, which manufactured metal products. The company was currently bankrupt, but Schindler thought that perhaps it could be retooled to turn out military mess kits and other enamel cookware. If it could, he knew he could get lucrative military contracts.

Schindler sought out the advice of a Jewish accountant named Itzhak Stern, who was working for a *Treuhander* named Aue. It was Aue who introduced Schindler to Stern. Stern knew of the Rekord company, since his brother worked for a Swiss banker to whom Rekord owed money. Stern gave the company a good review. Its troubles arose from poor management, not from more fundamental causes, he said.

Schindler arranged to take over the company as its *Treuhander*. The company was renamed Deutsche Email-waren Fabrik (German Enamelware Factory), and it began producing enamel-coated cookware sometime during December 1939. It employed only a hundred workers, of whom only seven were Jewish. As was customary, the company's previous manager, Abraham Bankier, was retained, but in other respects, this was not a typical "Aryanization" of a Jewish business. Bankier had not been demoted from owner to employee. To Bankier, Schindler's takeover of the company meant only that he would be working for an economically viable business rather than one that was bankrupt. Moreover, in January 1940, a month after taking over as *Treuhander*, Schindler arranged to purchase the factory outright. As owner he was less subject to German supervision, and for some reason Schindler wanted to avoid close supervision.

Soon after going into production, Schindler hired Stern as his accountant. In Steven Spielberg's movie *Schindler's List*, Stern is represented as Schindler's best friend, confidante, and right-hand man. In fact, this cinematic character is a composite of Stern and Bankier. Stern was Schindler's friend and confidante, but it was Bankier who ran the business. The history of Schindler's enamelware factory can probably best be understood in terms of the progressively worsening situation of its Jewish workers. From December 1939, when the factory opened, until 1944, when it closed, Schindler's enamelware factory evolved into a haven for Polish Jews at the very epicenter of the Holocaust.

THE KRAKOW GHETTO

As soon as the Germans were in control of Krakow, they began the process of clearing Jews out. The first *Aktion*, or raid aimed at encouraging Jewish emigration, in Krakow took place on December 4, 1939. Somehow Schindler found out about it in advance and warned Stern the night before.

At the time, Schindler and Stern had only just met (Schindler had not yet taken over the Rekord factory), and Stern did not entirely trust Schindler. Nevertheless, he passed the word along, and some Jewish families managed to be safely absent during the *Aktion*. The fact that Schindler's warning turned out to be accurate convinced Stern that Schindler was someone who could be trusted.

Similar raids were also taking place in the Polish countryside. Many dispossessed families had no choice but to move to the city. Jews fleeing Nazi persecution in other Polish cities also moved to Krakow. Hence, the initial effect of efforts to rid Krakow of its Jews was to swell the Jewish population.

By November 1940, less than a year after Schindler's enamelware factory began operations, the Jews of Krakow—excepting only those who were in hiding or getting by on false papers—had been herded into a designated Jewish ghetto surrounded by fences and barbed wire. Residents of the ghetto were allowed to leave only with a valid work permit. In order to reduce the population of the ghetto to tolerable levels, residents who lacked useful skills (useful, that is, for German war production) were sorted out and shipped to nearby concentration camps. This included intellectuals, the sick, and the elderly. On one occasion, several of Schindler's workers, including Abraham Bankier, were chosen to be sent away. Schindler barely managed to rescue them before the train pulled out. Despite this winnowing, the population of the Krakow ghetto, when it was sealed off in November 1940, was approximately seventy thousand. This was more than Krakow's prewar Jewish population had been.

Because Jews could leave the ghetto only with a work permit, Stern asked Schindler to hire more Jewish workers. Schindler was happy to comply. For one thing, it made economic sense. Jews were essentially slave labor. To employ them, Schindler only had to pay a modest fee to the SS (Schutzstaffel), who oversaw the Jewish relocation effort, and, of course, he had to make sure they were getting something to eat. These costs were significantly less than the wages he paid to his Polish workers. Even so, it is unlikely that Schindler used Jewish workers only because they were cheap labor. Many German *Treuhander*s who used Jewish labor cut costs still further by feeding their workers as little as possible. Schindler's Jewish workers ate extremely well by comparison. Schindler was not the only German employer who made sure his Jewish workers were adequately fed, but he was one of a small group. Also, the fact that Schindler used his intelligence-gathering skills to keep Stern and the Jewish community informed about German activities suggests that he already disapproved of German policies and was working with Stern and Bankier to thwart them.

Figures concerning the number of Jewish workers at the enamelware factory vary somewhat, but sources agree that the number rose steadily. According to author Luitgard Wundheiler, "The number of Jewish workers rose from seven in 1939 to 190 in 1941, and to 550 in 1942."[2] By contrast, Herbert Steinhouse, the only journalist ever to have interviewed Schindler, claims that in 1942 the enamelware factory employed roughly 800 workers, of whom only 370 were Jewish. Whichever figures are correct, it is clear that Schindler was adding Jewish workers rather than "Aryanizing" the factory.

SCHINDLER'S PERSONAL AFFAIRS

While Oskar was living in Krakow, running the enamelware factory, his wife, Emilie, continued to live in Mahrisch-Ostrau. However, being less than a hundred miles apart, they saw each other frequently. Oskar made regular visits home to see friends and family. Emilie made regular visits to Krakow and claims to have been quite familiar with the factory.

Oskar had two steady mistresses in Krakow. One was his Polish secretary, Viktoria Klonowska. The other was a German woman he had known through his work with the German Counterintelligence Service. Like Schindler, she had become a *Treuhander*, and she ran her own business in Krakow. She and Oskar were together so much that she was often addressed as "Frau Schindler," a fact that caused considerable embarrassment for the real Mrs. Schindler when she came to visit.

Meanwhile, thanks largely to the efforts of Stern and Bankier, Schindler's business was flourishing, and he was becoming extremely rich. On the surface, at least, the profits of Schindler's enamelware factory came primarily from government contracts to supply mess kits to the German military. These contracts were awarded by the German Armaments Inspectorate, which was run by a man named Julius Schindler. There was, in fact, no familial relation between General Schindler and Oskar, but because of the coincidence of having the same last name, Oskar tried to get to know General Schindler. The general was so charmed by Oskar that he treated him like a favorite nephew. When other German officials made the mistake of presuming that there was a familial relation between the two men, Oskar did not always bother to correct them.

Beyond the Armaments Inspectorate contracts, much of the profit from the enamelware factory came from selling on the black market. As with any criminal enterprise, black marketeering naturally requires operating outside the purview of the police and courts. Since disputes cannot be settled in court, they have to be settled by violence, or at least by threats of violence. There is a story that on at least one occasion Schindler had a Jewish black market contact beaten for removing more enamelware from the loading dock than had been paid for. Ironically, this story survives because the victim of the alleged beating was later put on "Schindler's list" and was thereby saved from the gas chambers of Auschwitz. Thomas Keneally, who tells this story in his book *Schindler's List*, does not reveal the name of the alleged victim.

On one occasion, Schindler was arrested on suspicion of black marketeering. Someone—perhaps the person who was beaten—had reported him to the German authorities. It was here that his contacts with high government officials—people such as General Schindler and former colleagues of the German Counterintelligence Service—paid off. He was released after only one night in custody.

Despite being a successful industrialist, Schindler still regarded himself as an intelligence agent. However, now he was working against the Germans rather than for them. Schindler was aware that members of the Zionist underground, a Jewish resistance movement, were among his workers at the enamelware factory. They apparently gave his name to leaders in the Zionist movement headquartered in Budapest, Hungary. A Zionist agent named Sedlacek visited Schindler in Krakow. Schindler was eager to pass along what he knew about the German mistreatment of Jews. He even arranged to visit Budapest—smuggled across the border on a freight train—so that he could give the information in person. He was afraid the information would be so shocking that it would not be believed unless he were present to vouch for it himself. Meanwhile, the Zionists began funneling money to their members in Poland by sending it through

Schindler. Schindler could have kept some of this money as a fee or to cover his expenses. Other agents employed by the Zionists did this as a matter of course. Schindler, apparently, kept none of the money.

PLASZOW

In 1943, soon after Schindler returned from his visit to Hungary, conditions for the Krakow Jews became much worse. The Germans were ready to shut down the ghetto and move its residents into a concentration camp. For that purpose, a new concentration camp was built outside Krakow at a place known as Plaszow. Part of the camp sat on the remains of a centuries-old Jewish cemetery, and the paths of the camp were paved with the headstones of that cemetery. The captain (*Hauptsturmführer*) in charge of the concentration camp was an SS officer named Amon Goeth (pronounced "girt"). By most accounts, Goeth was a pathological sadist and killer with few social graces. Emilie Schindler describes him as "the most despicable man I have ever met,"[3] and his Jewish prisoners were, of course, terrified of him. Schindler, who was always good at charming people he did not like, immediately made it his business to become Goeth's closest friend. This was not difficult to do. The two men shared a number of common interests. Goeth had a reputation as a man of refined tastes. He had a discriminating ear for music, which he especially loved. He also enjoyed good brandy and appreciated beautiful jewelry. Schindler brought him frequent "gifts" on the pretext of catering to Goeth's renowned sensibilities. However, this man of "refined tastes" was also a brutal and indiscriminate killer. Early in the construction of the Plaszow camp, Goeth had the Jewish engineer who was overseeing the work, a woman named Diana Reiter, summarily shot merely for contradicting the opinion of a less experienced German engineer. He occasionally shot Jewish laborers from the veranda of his villa simply for target practice.

On March 13, 1943, the Krakow ghetto was liquidated. Many ghetto residents were sent directly to Auschwitz, some were shot outright, and the remainder were moved to Plaszow. Schindler's workers were among those moved to Plaszow. Goeth's original plan was that factories using large numbers of Jewish workers would move to Plaszow as an integral part of the camp. The largest factory to make this move was a textile factory that produced military uniforms.

This factory, run by Julius Madritsch, employed roughly three thousand workers. Madritsch, like Schindler, sympathized with his Jewish workers and did what he could to protect them. However, he lacked Schindler's imagination and daring.

Schindler knew that he would not be able to control the working conditions in his factory if he moved it to Plaszow. Claiming that his factory's heavy metal presses would be too difficult to move, Schindler insisted on keeping his factory in town. Using a combination of charm, brandy, and expensive jewelry, he persuaded Goeth to allow his workers to be transported each day under guard from Plaszow to the factory and back again. However, Schindler quickly realized that this arrangement would not be sufficient to protect his workers, for as long as they were in Plaszow there was no guarantee that Goeth would not use one of them for target practice.

To overcome this problem, Schindler asked Goeth to allow him to build a "subcamp" adjoining the enamelware factory. Schindler purchased the necessary land, and at his own expense had the barracks, guard towers, and wire enclosures built. On paper, the subcamp was nominally part of Plaszow, under the authority of Amon Goeth. In practice, Schindler did everything he could to minimize intrusions by SS guards and officers. The guards were kept outside the compound, and inspectors were usually waylaid at the office with an offer of brandy. For this reason, many inspections never took place at all; if they did, the inspector was often too cheerfully drunk to understand much of what he saw.

The enamelware factory with its adjoining subcamp was regarded as almost a paradise on earth by the residents of Plaszow. There was enough food to eat, there were enough blankets to keep warm, and there was not the constant threat of being shot for minor or imagined infractions. Residents of the subcamp were even permitted to observe Sabbath. The Jewish workers referred to the enamelware factory as "Emalia," a name that translates, roughly, as "the enamelry." They began to refer to themselves as *Schindlerjuden*, "Schindler's Jews." Schindler referred to them as *meine Schutzlinge*, usually translated as "my children."

THE LIST

In July 1944, matters took another ugly turn for the worse. The war was turning against Germany, and its armies were in retreat. Plaszow might soon be overrun by the Russians. As a result, orders were issued for the Plaszow concentration camp, along with the small subcamp adjoining Schindler's factory, to be dismantled. The residents were to be relocated to Auschwitz and Gross-Rosen for "special treatment" (that is, the gas chambers).

Schindler was distraught. In desperation he devised a plan so daring that it is a wonder it succeeded. He announced that he would close the enamelware factory in Krakow and open a munitions factory near his home in Czechoslovakia. The workers at this new factory would be none other than his old employees from the Emalia, who would be transported to the new location at Schindler's expense. Moreover, the new factory would be *even larger* than the old Emalia, so he would need other workers as well.

Extremely complex arrangements had to be made to pull off this desperate scheme. Schindler had to locate a facility—a vacant factory or warehouse—that could be converted to munitions production. He eventually found one in the town of Brinnlitz (Brnenec) in Moravia, not far from his hometown, Zwittau. Then he had to overcome local opposition to the opening of what the local residents saw as a "prison" housing "criminals." He had to land military contracts to justify the opening of such a factory. He had to get approval from the German authorities to use Jewish workers. He had to buy machinery and have it transported to the factory. He had to arrange transportation for the workers. He had to have the factory surrounded with barbed wire and guard towers so that it could function as a concentration camp. Last, but not least, he had to draw up a list of names of those individuals—roughly seven hundred men and three hundred women, from among the twenty-five thousand residents of Plaszow—who would be spared the gas chambers of Auschwitz and Gross-Rosen.

In order to save more lives, Schindler pleaded with Julius Madritsch to join him in this venture. Madritsch turned him down, not because he was less compassionate than Schindler or even less courageous. He just could not imagine that the scheme might succeed.

From the point of view of the residents of Plaszow, the list of those who would be relocated to Brinnlitz became a matter of supreme importance. It was, after all, a list of those who had a chance to live. The original list was drawn up with the help of Raimond Titsch, the manager at Madritsch's textile factory. For this reason, it included the names of many of Madritsch's workers as well as the workers at the Emalia factory. Once the list was drawn up, it was maintained by Schindler's personnel clerk, Marcel Goldberg. Goldberg was not above taking bribes, and it is known that he removed some names from the original list in order to make room for those who paid him in diamonds to be put on the list instead. This was done without Schindler's knowledge or approval.

THE MUNITIONS FACTORY IN BRINNLITZ

The move to Brinnlitz did not go smoothly. One trainload of workers was mistakenly diverted to the Gross-Rosen concentration camp. Another train on which the women were loaded was sent to Auschwitz. The men who were sent to Gross-Rosen were returned to Schindler in fairly short order. It was a much more difficult matter to free the women from Auschwitz. Schindler tried bribes and appeals to his friends in the German bureaucracy. Nothing worked. After a number of weeks, Schindler sent a woman to Auschwitz to bargain for their release. Emilie Schindler identifies this woman as a childhood friend of Oskar's named Hilde, probably one of his former mistresses. She was, in any case, a beautiful woman, and Emilie remarks demurely that her "great beauty"[4] probably played a decisive role in obtaining the women's release. Other sources are more blunt, claiming that Hilde probably traded sex with German officials for the women's release and that Schindler probably sent her to Auschwitz with that in mind. In any case, Hilde's mission was successful. The women were released from Auschwitz and shipped by train to Brinnlitz.

The factory at Brinnlitz was an elaborate hoax from the outset. Schindler never intended for the factory to produce usable munitions, and it did not. Instead, Schindler purchased munitions at black market prices from other factories and resold them, often at a loss, to the German Armaments Ministry. This created the illusion that the factory was in production. The illusion had to be maintained even within the factory itself. Security at the factory was still technically maintained by the SS, under *Untersturmführer* (Second Lieutenant) Josef Leipold. Leipold was not, like Goeth, a pathological killer, but he was a loyal Nazi who had to be kept ignorant of the factory's true nature. To that end, the factory turned out a steady supply of defective and unusable shell casings that wasted the time and slowed the production of the other factories to which they were sent for completion.

Schindler kept steady pressure on the German authorities to send him more Jewish workers on the pretext that the factory was shorthanded. This was a plausible claim. Because of the war, there was in fact a severe labor shortage in the region. Schindler managed to have as many as three thousand Jewish women transferred from Auschwitz to various textile mills throughout Moravia. Additional workers were also occasionally transferred to the Brinnlitz factory.

In January 1945, a trainload of 250 workers was transferred to a Polish mine near the city of Goleschau. When the train arrived, the mine operator refused to accept them on the grounds that their physical condition was too poor for them to be useful workers: They were little more than human skeletons covered in skin. Rather than return them to Dachau, the engineer brought them to the Brinnlitz factory. The weather had been bitterly cold, and several had frozen to death in the boxcars. The arrival of the train from Goleschau, and the unloading of the frozen corpses, left vivid memories in the minds of those who were there that night. Emilie Schindler had those who were still alive brought into the factory. There, the survivors were slowly nursed back to health.

Somehow the factory and its residents managed to survive the winter of 1944–1945. On May 9, 1945, Germany officially surrendered. Brinnlitz would soon be occupied by Russian soldiers. Schindler knew, of course, that the Russians would not know that his factory was a hoax any more than the Germans had. He would be considered a German collaborator and arrested or even shot. Hence, on the day the armistice was signed, he and his wife fled to the west in the company of several of the Jewish workers, who came along in part to provide the Schindlers with cover. The party managed to find their way to the American lines, but along the way their car was confiscated by Czech soldiers. With the car went the last of Schindler's fortune: a large diamond hidden under the seat.

THE AVENUE OF THE RIGHTEOUS

After the war, Schindler and his wife found their options limited. They could not return to their home in Czechoslovakia since ethnic Germans, now the *victims* of discrimination, were being expelled from the Sudetenland. For several years, the Schindlers tried to find a home in Germany. During this period, they often shared housing with their many Jewish friends. However, their pro-Jewish sympathies did not make them popular among their fellow Germans. Oskar Schindler testified at the war crimes trials of captured Nazi officers, including Josef Leipold. As one would expect of a former intelligence agent with inside information, his testimony was detailed, well organized, and damning. He did not testify against Amon Goeth, but Goeth's Jewish secretary, Mietek Pemper, who had been on Schindler's list, did, along with many other Plaszow survivors. Goeth was executed for his crimes.

Eventually, the Schindlers immigrated to Argentina, where they tried their hand at raising chickens. Not content with the modest living this provided, Schindler insisted, over his wife's objections, that they try raising nutria, a fur-bearing weasel related to the mink, instead. This venture was not successful. With the failure of the nutria business, Schindler left his wife in Argentina and returned to Germany, where he tried running a cement factory. This venture never actually began production, however.

In 1961, Schindler was invited to visit Israel, where he was greeted as a celebrity. He was invited to plant a tree along the Avenue of the Righteous in Jerusalem and was honored with the title "Righteous Among the Nations," perhaps the single greatest honor bestowed by the Jewish community on non-Jews.

By this time, many of the former *Schindlerjuden* had made new lives for themselves, in the United States, Israel, and elsewhere. Among themselves they elected to donate a portion of their incomes to Schindler, and he lived on this stipend for the remainder of his life. This money allowed him to make long visits to Israel nearly every year, where he spent time drinking and visiting with old friends. Schindler died on October 9, 1974, in his small apartment in Frankfurt of a heart attack. He was buried in the Latin Cemetery in Jerusalem.

In the minds of many whose lives he touched, Schindler is now associated with a saying from the Talmud: "He who saves one life saves the world entire." There is a widely told story that makes the same point. The original source of the story is unknown, but one variation goes like this:

It was a breezy day on the beach and there were very few people braving the weather. One man, however, came upon a child kneeling determinedly in the sand. Watching, he observed the child stand, walk a few feet while looking down, then every few feet she would stop. Bending down, she would carefully cradle something in her hands, then gently toss it into the ocean. The man walked over and asked what kind of game this was.

The little girl smiled as she looked up. "I'm saving starfish."

The man was amused. "Are you kidding? Just look at all of these! There are too many! Why, honey, you would have to spend all day and all night out here, tossing starfish back into the ocean. And why? You'll never save them all. Besides . . ." the man patted her head kindly, "in the grand scheme of life, they're just starfish. It doesn't matter if they live or die."

The child thought for a minute, then scooped another starfish up from the sand, considered it briefly, then gently placed the small creature into the ocean.

"It mattered to that one."[5]

NOTES

1. Emilie Schindler, *Where Light and Shadow Meet: A Memoir.* New York: W.W. Norton, 1996, p. 31.
2. Luitgard N. Wundheiler, "Oskar Schindler's Moral Development During the Holocaust," *Humboldt Journal of Social Relations*, vol. 13, 1985–1986, p. 337.
3. Schindler, *Where Light and Shadow Meet*, p. 59.
4. Schindler, *Where Light and Shadow Meet*, pp. 68–69.
5. Haldago Bay Original Artwork, "The Starfish," http://haldago. org/starfish.htm.

CHAPTER 1

THE BACKGROUND OF GERMAN ANTI-SEMITISM

PEOPLE
WHO MADE
HISTORY

OSKAR SCHINDLER

Pre-War Persecution of Jews: The World Must Know

Michael Berenbaum

Michael Berenbaum is a distinguished scholar in the field of Holocaust studies. He has a Ph.D. in philosophy from Florida State University. He served as head of Washington's Jewish Community Council and assisted in the founding of the United States Holocaust Museum. He has since become president and chief executive officer of the Survivors of the Shoah Visual History Foundation, which is the foundation started by Steven Spielberg using funds generated by the movie *Schindler's List.* This selection, based on materials at the United States Holocaust Museum, provides a summary of the early years of the Holocaust in Germany.

Racism was the central and pervasive theme of Nazi ideology. It shaped social policy in Germany between 1933 and 1939, was a major factor in Nazi conduct of World War II, motivated German policy in occupied countries, and, when carried to its ultimate conclusion, resulted in the Holocaust.

Hitler's obsession with racial purity, his hatred of both Marxism and democracy, his beliefs in German racial supremacy, and the notion of an Aryan master race that would take over the world should have come as no surprise when they became state policy after March 1933. He had stated them clearly not only in his speeches, but in his book, *Mein Kampf (My Struggle)*, which was first published in 1925. It was the "sacred mission of the German people . . . to assemble and preserve the most valuable racial elements . . . and raise them to a dominant position."

The Nazis regarded the Germans as racially superior, and considered Slavs, Gypsies, and blacks to be inferior. At the bottom of this scale were the Jews, the most dangerous of races, in part because they parasitically lived off the other races and weakened them.

"All who are not of a good race are chaff," Hitler wrote. As a young man, he had been repelled by the cosmopolitan diversity of Vienna: a mixture of "Czechs, Poles, Hungarians, Ruthenians, Serbs and Croats, and . . . the eternal mushroom of humanity—Jews." The Aryan race was destined to be superior, therefore the German people "are the highest species of humanity on earth." In the racial struggle of history, the "master race" would dominate if it preserved its purity. Otherwise, it would be polluted, corrupted, and destroyed by inferior races.

It was necessary for Germans to "occupy themselves not merely with the breeding of dogs, horses and cats but also with care for the purity of their own blood." These notions were not original. Hitler simplified racial doctrines propounded in the nineteenth century, particularly in the writings of the French aristocrat Joseph Arthur de Gobineau and the English-born disciple of Wagner, Houston Stewart Chamberlain.

Whatever the theoretical underpinnings of Hitler's racial beliefs, Nazi racism under his direction was far from theoretical. Blood mixture was abhorrent. Procreation by inferior races was to be discouraged, at first through forced sterilization, later by systematic murder.

BOYCOTT

Official persecution of Jews began on April 1, 1933. At ten o'clock on that Saturday morning, the Nazis initiated a boycott of Jewish businesses and shops in cities and towns throughout Germany. Until then, violence against Jews had been individual and sporadic. The boycott was the first salvo in a nationwide campaign against the entire German Jewish community.

Storm troopers were stationed menacingly in front of Jewish-owned shops. The Star of David was painted in yellow and black across thousands of doors and windows. Signs were posted saying: "Germans! Defend Yourselves! Don't Buy from Jews," "The Jews Are Our Misfortune," or simply "*Jude.*"

The boycott was Hitler's response to foreign criticism of his regime. Reports of Nazi violence against Jews and Jewish businesses in Germany had prompted talk of an American boycott of German goods. On March 26, Hitler summoned

Joseph Goebbels, now the minister of Public Enlightenment and Propaganda. Goebbels described Hitler's instructions: "We must . . . proceed to a large-scale boycott of Jewish businesses in Germany. Perhaps the foreign Jews will think better of the matter when their racial comrades in Germany begin to get it in the neck."

The boycott was a Nazi party operation. Julius Streicher, the master Jew-baiter, was given the title of leader of the Central Committee for Counteracting Jewish Atrocity Tales and Boycotts. When the boycott began, the police were instructed not to hinder it in any way, but rather to "view the boycott with magnanimity."

The reaction of non-Jews was mixed. In some cities, the boycott inspired greater eruptions of violence against Jews, but some Germans made it a point of honor to enter Jewish shops or telephone their Jewish friends. Some German Jews were quick to see the boycott as a sign of things to come. A few fled; others took their lives in despair. But many Jews were more optimistic and appealed to the German public's sense of justice through leaflets and advertisements, urging them not to respect the boycott.

Still others were openly defiant. Robert Weltsch, the editor of a German-language Jewish newspaper, refused to accept the Nazis' use of the Star of David as a sign of shame. German Jews, he said, should wear the yellow badge with pride.

The boycott, which was scheduled to last for five days, was called off after twenty-four hours. The boycott committee remained in existence and the boycott was made compulsory for Reich agencies and party members. A week later, the government announced the first of a series of laws singling out Jews. The Civil Service Law of April 7, 1933, dismissed all non-Aryans from the civil service, including notaries and teachers in state schools. (Communists were removed four days later.) It was the first of four hundred separate pieces of legislation enacted between 1933 and 1939 that defined, isolated, excluded, segregated, and impoverished German Jews.

Soon after Hitler came to power, Leo Baeck, the most prominent rabbi in Germany, wrote: "The end of German Jewry has arrived." Baeck's words were prophetic, although many German Jews found this impossible to imagine in the spring of 1933.

Before the advent of Nazi rule, Jews felt comfortable as Germans. They were active and successful in theater and the arts, science and literature, industry and the professions. Ever since the late eighteenth century, Germany had represented culture and freedom to the European Jewish community. Germany had epitomized the best of Western civilization.

Although they encountered social discrimination and were often restricted in their professional careers, Jews were confident of their future as Germans. Many Jews converted to Christianity, and even more had shed their ancestral religious practices. Intermarriage with non-Jews was common. Their language was German, and they identified with the German nation. It was their home.

German Jews had demonstrated their loyalty to the fatherland during World War I. More than one hundred thousand—one of every six Jews in the population—served in the army, 80 percent in combat roles. Thirty-five thousand were decorated for bravery, and twelve thousand lost their lives. Under the Weimar Republic, Jews served in high office, held important places in the civil service and the judiciary, and studied and taught in Germany's great universities. Their influence in German intellectual life was enormous considering their relatively small proportion of the population. Of the thirty-eight Nobel Prizes won by Germans between 1905 and 1936, fourteen were received by Jews. . . .

The Nuremberg Race Laws

The end of German Jewry came gradually. In the spring of 1933, Jews were removed from the civil service; in the fall, non-Aryan editors were dismissed from German newspapers; and by year's end, Jewish artists, musicians, filmmakers, and writers were expelled from the guilds set up under the Reich Chamber of Culture by Goebbels in order to make sure artists were politically acceptable to the Reich.

Martin Heidegger, the renowned existential philosopher who served as rector of the University of Freiburg, set an example of obedience to Nazism, first by publicly swearing to support Hitler, then by hastening to dismiss Jews from the faculty.

In 1935, German Jews were stripped of their citizenship. Two laws promulgated at the annual Nazi party rally in Nuremberg on September 15—the Law for the Protection of German Blood and the Reich Citizenship Law—became the centerpiece of Hitler's anti-Jewish legislation. Those laws, which were soon known throughout the world as the

Nuremberg Laws, restricted citizenship in the Reich to those of "German or kindred blood." Only citizens, racial Germans, were entitled to civil and political rights. Jews were merely subjects of the state.

In order to "protect German blood and honor," the marriage of Jews and "citizens of German or kindred blood" was forbidden. So were sexual relations between Jews and Aryans. Women under the age of forty-five could not work in Jewish households. Jews could not fly the German flag. Categorization had consequences. Definition was the first step toward destruction.

For the first time in history, Jews were persecuted not for their religious beliefs and practices, but because of their so-called racial identity, irrevocably transmitted through the blood of their grandparents. (Once resolved, the question of definition was closed, and a precedent had been set.) The Nuremberg Laws were later imposed on lands occupied by the Nazis and served as a model for the treatment and eventual extermination of the Gypsies.

But who was a Jew? Although the Nuremberg Laws divided the German nation into Germans and Jews, neither the term *Jew* nor the phrase *German or kindred blood* was defined. Since the laws contained criminal provisions for noncompliance, the bureaucrats had the urgent task of spelling out what the words meant. The civil service and the Nazi party were at loggerheads in their efforts to define a Jew. The civil service wanted to protect the "German" part of the half-Jew, while the party viewed part-Jews as even more abhorrent than full Jews.

It was the notion of the mixing of blood that had driven Hitler into the frenzy expressed in *Mein Kampf* and, as Führer, in nationally broadcast speeches telling Germans they would triumph only if their blood was pure. The mongrelization of the Germanic race "has robbed us of world domination," he said. From now on, the German nation must be protected from racial contamination.

Two basic Jewish categories were established. A full Jew was anyone with three Jewish grandparents. That definition was fairly simple. Defining part-Jews—*Mischlinge* (mongrels)—was more difficult, but they were eventually divided into two classes. First-class *Mischlinge* were people who had two Jewish grandparents, but did not practice Judaism and did not have a Jewish spouse. Second-class *Mis-*

chlinge were those who had only one Jewish grandparent.

In the end, the bureaucratic contortions were immaterial: anyone who had even one Jewish grandparent was technically Jewish and for all practical purposes no longer had full rights as a German citizen. According to the Nuremberg Laws, even Roman Catholic priests and nuns and Protestant clergy who were converts to Christianity, or whose parents had converted, were considered Jews. Jewish emancipation in Germany had ended.

Seven documents were required to prove German descent: a birth or baptismal certificate, certificates for both parents, and certificates of all four grandparents. Church offices, which had registered all births until 1875, were besieged with requests for documents proving German ancestry. A new cottage industry sprang up as hordes of "licensed family researchers" offered their services to an anxious clientele of Germans afraid of a skeleton in the family closet.

In the United States, the public thought the legislation was unfair, but few believed there was anything their government could do to challenge it. American Jewish organizations could not agree on how to respond. While working behind the scenes to help individual Jewish refugees enter the country, some of the major groups were opposed to either launching a public protest or lobbying for liberalizing the restrictive US. immigration laws. They were afraid of stirring up anti-semitism, both in Germany and at home.

Commentary in the international press condemned the Nuremberg Laws, but most reporters did not understand that the laws marked a new and ominous departure in Nazi treatment of the Jews. An editorial in the *Los Angeles Times* claimed that the laws did not signify much of a new problem for Jews because "generally speaking, nobody has any civil rights in Germany." Church leaders also criticized the Nuremberg Laws, but had little success in arousing the Christian conscience.

Neither President Roosevelt nor the State Department made any public comment on the Nuremberg Laws. Before the Nazi party meeting, the American ambassador to Germany, William Dodd, had alerted FDR that new laws would be issued ensuring "complete subordination for the Jews." Dodd wanted the American, French, and British ambassadors to boycott the rally. The State Department rejected his proposal. Nevertheless, Dodd did not attend. He warned Washington that soon even more severe measures would be aimed at the "complete separation of the Jews from the German community."

Those who predicted that the new laws heralded even worse persecution were right. After Nuremberg, the pace of ostracism was stepped up. Signs saying *Juden unerwünscht* (Jews unwelcome) were posted on public facilities—shops, theaters, restaurants, hotels, even pharmacies. Jews were forbidden to sit on park benches restricted to Aryans; they could sit only on benches set aside for them.

The regime then set out to deprive Jews of any means of livelihood. All Jewish property was registered in 1937. In 1938, all Jewish businesses still in existence were Aryanized: Jewish workers and managers were dismissed, and Jewish stockholders disfranchised. The German business and banking community, which benefited richly, cooperated fully with the dismantling of Jewish firms.

Within a year, Germans had taken over the ownership of four out of five Jewish businesses, acquiring them at bargain prices prescribed by the Nazi Ministry of Economics. German banks made enormous profits from these forced transactions, first in commissions on the transfers, then through loans to the buyers and subsequent business contracts with the new firms. Many Jewish businesses were liquidated.

In July 1938, Jewish physicians were forbidden to treat non-Jews; in September, Jewish lawyers were forbidden to practice; and in October, at the request of the Swiss, who were fearful of being overrun by Jews fleeing Germany, Jewish passports were marked with the letter *J*, for *Jude*. On August 17, 1938, Jews had to take new middle names: all Jewish men were to be called Israel; all Jewish women, Sara. . . .

NIGHT OF BROKEN GLASS

On the night of November 9, 1938, anti-Jewish violence erupted throughout the Reich, which now included Austria and the Sudetenland. What appeared to be a spontaneous outburst of national anger sparked by the assassination of a minor German embassy official in Paris at the hands of Herschel Grynszpan, a seventeen-year-old Jewish youth, was carefully orchestrated by the Nazi regime. Grynszpan's parents were Polish Jews living in Germany. They had been deported from Germany to Poland, but because Poland refused to accept its Jewish citizens, they were stranded in limbo. From the border town of Zbyngyn they wrote to their son in desperation. His immediate response was to seek revenge.

Just before midnight on November 9, Gestapo Chief Heinrich Müller sent a telegram to all police units letting them know that "in shortest order, actions against Jews and especially their synagogues will take place in all Germany. These are not to be interfered with." Rather, the police were to arrest the victims. Fire companies stood by synagogues in flames with explicit instructions to let the buildings burn. They were to intervene only if a fire threatened adjacent Aryan properties.

Within forty-eight hours, over one thousand synagogues were burned, along with their Torah scrolls, Bibles, and prayer books. Seven thousand Jewish businesses were trashed and looted, ninety-six Jews were killed, and Jewish cemeteries, hospitals, schools, and homes were destroyed. The attackers were often neighbors. Thirty thousand Jews were arrested. To accommodate so many new prisoners, the concentration camps of Dachau, Buchenwald, and Sachsenhausen were expanded.

When the fury subsided, the pogrom was given a fancy name: *Kristallnacht*—crystal night, or night of broken glass. It came to stand for the final shattering of Jewish existence in Germany. In the aftermath of *Kristallnacht*, the regime made sure that Jews could no longer survive in their country.

The cost of the broken window glass alone came to five million marks, the equivalent of well over two million dollars. Jews of German nationality, unlike Jewish-owned corporations from abroad, could not file for damages. Any compensation claims paid to Jews by insurance companies were confiscated by the Reich. The rubble of ruined synagogues had to be cleared by the Jewish community. A fine of one billion Reichmarks ($400 million) was imposed collectively on the Jewish community. After assessing the fine, Goring remarked: "The swine won't commit another murder. Incidentally ... I would not like to be a Jew in Germany." On November 15, Jews were barred from schools. Two weeks later, local authorities were given the right to impose a curfew, and by December Jews were denied access to most public places. All remaining Jewish businesses were Aryanized.

The *Kristallnacht* pogrom was the last occasion of street violence against Jews in Germany. It appeared that Jews could leave and enter their homes in safety. But they no longer had any illusions. Life in the Reich was no longer possible.

The Holocaust: Tell Them We Remember

Susan D. Bachrach

Susan D. Bachrach works for the education department of the United States Holocaust Museum in Washington, D.C. Her book, *Tell Them We Remember*, includes many reproductions of photographs taken during the Holocaust, and pictures of other artifacts kept at the museum. It covers the worst period of the Holocaust, from the inception of the extermination camps until the camps were liberated by allied forces at the end of the war.

THE KILLING BEGINS

After the German army invaded the Soviet Union on June 22, 1941, a new stage in the Holocaust began. Under cover of war and confident of victory, the Germans turned from the forced emigration and imprisonment of Jews to the mass murder of them. Special action squads, or *Einsatzgruppen,* made up of Nazi (SS) units and police, moved with speed on the heels of the advancing German army. Their job was to kill any Jews they could find in the occupied Soviet territory. Some residents of the occupied regions, mostly Ukrainians, Latvians, and Lithuanians, aided these German mobile killing squads by serving as auxiliary police.

The mobile killing units acted swiftly, taking the Jewish population by surprise. The killers entered a town or city and rounded up all Jewish men, women, and children. They also took away many Communist party leaders and Gypsies. Victims were forced to surrender any valuables and remove their clothing, which was later sent for use in Germany. Then the killing squad members marched their victims to open fields and ravines on the outskirts of conquered towns and cities. There they shot them and dumped the bodies into mass graves.

On September 21, 1941, the eve of the Jewish New Year, a mobile killing squad entered Ejszyszki, a small town in what is now Lithuania. The killing squad members herded four thousand Jews from the town and the surrounding region into three synagogues, where they were held for two days without food or water. Then, in two days of killing, Jewish men, women, and children were taken to cemeteries, lined up in front of open pits, and shot to death. Today there are no Jews in Ejszyszki. It was one of hundreds of cities, towns, and shtetls [small villages] whose Jews were murdered during the Holocaust. The rich culture of most of these Jewish communities was lost forever.

The killing squads murdered more than a million Jews and hundreds of thousands of other innocent people. At Babi Yar, near Kiev, about 34,000 Jews were murdered in two days of shooting. Only a few people in the general population helped their Jewish neighbors escape. Most people were afraid that they, too, might be killed.

The massacres of innocent men, women, and children in Babi Yar and other towns were not the crimes of hoodlums or crazy men. The executioners were "ordinary" men who followed the orders of their commanding officers. Many of the killers had wives and children back in Germany. Propaganda and training had taught many members of the mobile killing squads to view their victims as enemies of Germany. Some killers drank heavily to dull their thoughts and feelings. In addition, when they described their actions they used code words like "special treatment" and "special action" instead of "killing" or "murder" to distance themselves from their terrible crimes.

On January 20, 1942, fifteen high-ranking Nazi party and German government leaders gathered for an important meeting. They met in a wealthy section of Berlin at a villa by a lake known as Wannsee. Reinhard Heydrich, who was SS Chief Himmler's head deputy, held the meeting for the purpose of discussing the "final solution to the Jewish question in Europe" with key non-SS government leaders, including the Secretaries of the Foreign Ministry and Justice, whose cooperation was needed.

The "final solution" was the Nazis' code name for the deliberate, carefully planned destruction, or *genocide*, of all European Jews. The Nazis used the vague term "final solution" to hide their policy of mass murder from the rest of the world. In fact, the men at Wannsee talked about methods of killing, about liquidation, about "extermination."

The Wannsee Conference, as it became known to history, did not mark the beginning of the "final solution." The mobile killing squads were already slaughtering Jews in the occupied Soviet Union. Rather, the Wannsee Conference was the place where the "final solution" was formally revealed to non-Nazi leaders who would help arrange for Jews to be transported from all over German-occupied Europe to SS-operated "extermination" camps in Poland. Not one of the men present at Wannsee objected to the announced policy. Never before had a modern state committed itself to the murder of an entire people.

THE CONCENTRATION CAMPS

In the months following the Wannsee Conference, the Nazi regime continued to carry out their plans for the "final solution." Jews were "deported"—transported by trains or trucks to six camps, all located in occupied Poland: Chelmno, Treblinka, Sobibór, Belzec, Auschwitz-Birkenau, and Majdanek-Lublin.

The Nazis called these six camps "extermination camps." Most of the deportees were immediately murdered in large groups by poisonous gas. The Nazis changed to gassing as their preferred method of mass murder because they saw it as "cleaner" and more "efficient" than shooting. Gassing also spared the killers the emotional stress many mobile killing squad members had felt shooting people face to face. The killing centers were in semi-rural, isolated areas, fairly well hidden from public view. They were located near major railroad lines, allowing trains to transport hundreds of thousands of people to the killing sites.

Many of the victims were deported from nearby ghettos, some as early as December 1941, even before the Wannsee meeting. The SS began in earnest to empty the ghettos, however, in the summer of 1942. In two years' time, more than two million Jews were taken out of the ghettos. By the summer of 1944, few ghettos remained in eastern Europe.

At the same time that ghettos were being emptied, masses of Jews and also Gypsies were transported from the many distant countries occupied or controlled by Germany, including France, Belgium, Holland, Norway, Hungary, Romania, Italy, North Africa, and Greece.

The deportations required the help of many people and all arms of the German government. The victims in Poland were already imprisoned in ghettos and totally under German control. The deportation of Jews from other parts of Europe, however, was a far more complex problem. The German Foreign Ministry succeeded in pressuring most governments of occupied and allied nations to assist the Germans in the deportation of Jews living in their countries. . . .

After the trains arrived at the camps, guards ordered the deportees to get out and form a line. The victims then went through a selection process. Men were separated from women and children. A Nazi, usually an SS physician, looked quickly at each person to decide if he or she was healthy and strong enough for slave labor. This SS officer then pointed to the left or to the right; victims did not know that individuals were being selected to live or to die. Babies and young children, pregnant women, the elderly, the handicapped, and the sick had little chance of surviving this first selection.

Those who had been selected to die were led to gas chambers. In order to prevent panic, camp guards told the victims that they were going to take showers to rid themselves of lice. The guards instructed them to turn over all their valuables and to undress. Then they were driven naked into the "showers." A guard closed and locked the steel door. In some killing centers, carbon monoxide was piped into the chamber. In others, camp guards threw "Zyklon B" pellets down an air shaft. Zyklon B was a highly poisonous insecticide also used to kill rats and insects.

Usually within minutes after entering the gas chambers, everyone inside was dead from lack of oxygen. Under guard, prisoners were forced to haul the corpses to a nearby room, where they removed hair, gold teeth, and fillings. The bodies were burned in ovens in the crematoria or buried in mass graves.

Many people profited from the pillage of the corpses. Camp guards stole some of the gold. The rest was melted down and deposited in an SS bank account. Private business firms bought and used the hair to make many products, including ship rope and mattresses.

Auschwitz-Birkenau was the largest of the Nazi death camps, located near Cracow, Poland. More than one million people lost their lives at this camp, nine out of ten of them

Jewish. The four largest gas chambers could each hold 2,000 people at one time.

A sign over the entrance to Auschwitz-Birkenau read *Arbeit Macht Frei,* which means "work makes one free." In the camps, however, the opposite was true. Labor became another form of genocide that the Nazis called "extermination through work."

Victims who were spared immediate death by being selected for labor were systematically stripped of their individual identities. They had their hair shaved off and a registration number tattooed on their left forearm. Men were forced to wear ragged, striped pants and jackets, and women wore work dresses. Both were issued ill-fitting work shoes, sometimes clogs. They had no change of clothing and slept in the same clothes they worked in.

Each day was a struggle for survival under unbearable conditions. Prisoners were housed in primitive barracks that had no windows and were not insulated from the heat or cold. There was no bathroom, only a bucket. Each barrack held about thirty-six wooden bunkbeds, and inmates were squeezed in five or six across on the wooden plank. As many as 500 inmates lodged in a single barrack.

Inmates were always hungry. Food consisted of watery soup made with rotten vegetables and meat, a few ounces of bread, a bit of margarine, tea, or a bitter drink resembling coffee. Diarrhea was common. People weakened by dehydration and hunger fell easy victim to the contagious diseases that spread through the camp.

Some inmates worked as forced laborers inside the camp, in the kitchen or as barbers, for example. Women often sorted the piles of shoes, clothes, and other prisoner belongings, which would be shipped back to Germany for use there. The storage warehouses at Auschwitz-Birkenau, located near two of the crematoria, were called "Canada," because the Poles regarded that country as a place of great riches. At Auschwitz, as at hundreds of other camps in the Reich and occupied Europe where the Germans used slave laborers, prisoners were also employed outside the camps, in coal mines and rock quarries, and on construction projects, digging tunnels and canals. Under armed guard, they shoveled snow off roads and cleared rubble from roads and towns hit during air raids. A large number of slave laborers eventually were used in factories that produced weapons and other goods that supported the German war effort. Many private companies, such as I.G. Farben and Bavarian Motor Works (BMW), which produced automobile and airplane engines, eagerly sought the use of prisoners as a source of cheap labor.

Escape from Auschwitz-Birkenau was almost impossible. Electrically charged barbed-wire fences surrounded both the concentration camp and the killing center. Guards, equipped with machine guns and automatic rifles, stood in the many watchtowers. The lives of the prisoners were completely controlled by their guards, who on a whim could inflict cruel punishments on them. Prisoners were also mistreated by fellow inmates who were chosen to supervise the others in return for special favors by the guards.

Cruel "medical experiments" were conducted at Auschwitz-Birkenau. Men, women, and children were used as subjects. SS physician Dr. Josef Mengele carried out painful and traumatic experiments on dwarfs and twins, including young children. The aim of some experiments was to find better medical treatments for German soldiers and airmen. Other experiments were aimed at improving methods of sterilizing people the Nazis considered inferior. Many people died during the experiments. Others were killed after the "research" was completed and their organs removed for further study.

Most prisoners at Auschwitz-Birkenau survived only a few weeks or months. Those who were too ill or too weak to work were condemned to death in the gas chambers. Some committed suicide by throwing themselves against the electric wires. Others resembled walking corpses, broken in body and spirit. Yet other inmates were determined to stay alive.

LIBERATING THE CAMPS

Near the end of the war, when Germany's military force was collapsing, the Allied armies closed in on the Nazi concentration camps. The Soviets approached from the east, and the British, French, and Americans from the west. The Germans began frantically to move the prisoners out of the camps near the front and take them to be used as slave laborers in camps inside Germany. Prisoners were first taken by train and then by foot on "death marches," as they became known. Prisoners were forced to march long distances in bitter cold, with little or no food, water, or rest. Those who could not keep up were shot.

The largest death marches took place in the winter of 1944–1945, when the Soviet army began its liberation of Poland. Just hours before the Soviets arrived at Auschwitz, the Germans marched 60,000 prisoners out of the camp toward Wodzislaw, a town thirty-five miles away, where they were put on freight trains to other camps. About one in four died on the way.

The Nazis often killed large groups of prisoners before, during, or after marches. During one march, seven thousand Jewish prisoners, six thousand of them women, were moved from camps in the Danzig region bordered on the north by the Baltic Sea. On the ten-day march, seven hundred were murdered. Those still alive when the marchers reached the shores of the sea were driven into the water and shot.

Soviet soldiers were the first to liberate concentration camp prisoners in the final stages of the war. On July 23, 1944, they entered the Majdanek concentration camp in Poland, and later overran several other killing centers. On January 27, 1945, they entered Auschwitz-Birkenau and there found hundreds of sick and exhausted prisoners. The Germans had been forced to leave these prisoners behind in their hasty retreat from the camp. Also left behind were victims' belongings: 348,820 men's suits, 836,255 women's coats, and tens of thousands of pairs of shoes.

British, Canadian, American, and French troops also freed prisoners from the camps. The Americans were responsible for liberating Buchenwald and Dachau, while British forces entered Bergen-Belsen. Although the Germans had attempted to empty the camps of surviving prisoners and hide all evidence of their crimes, the Allied soldiers came upon thousands of dead bodies "stacked up like cordwood," according to one American soldier. The prisoners who were still alive were living skeletons.

Bill Barrett, an American army journalist, described what he saw at Dachau: "There were about a dozen bodies in the dirty boxcar, men and women alike. They had gone without food so long that their dead wrists were broomsticks tipped with claws. These were the victims of a deliberate starvation diet. . . ."

Allied troops, physicians, and relief workers tried to provide nourishment for the surviving prisoners, but many of them were too weak to digest the food and could not be saved. In spite of the liberators' efforts, many camp sur-

vivors died. Half of the prisoners discovered alive in Auschwitz died within a few days of being freed.

Survivors had mixed reactions to their newfound freedom.
While a few looked forward to being reunited with other
family members, some felt guilty for surviving when so
many of their relatives and friends had died. Some felt overwhelmed, as one survivor, Viktor Frankl, a psychiatrist, expressed: "Timidly, we looked around and glanced at each
other questioningly. Then we ventured a few steps out of the
camp. This time no orders were shouted at us, nor was there
any need to duck quickly to avoid a blow or a kick. 'Freedom,'
we repeated to ourselves, and yet we could not grasp it."

Hitler's Willing Executioners

Daniel Jonah Goldhagen

Daniel Jonah Goldhagen teaches in the department of government and social studies at Harvard University. His book, *Hitler's Willing Executioners*, is based on his Ph.D. dissertation, which won the American Political Science Association's award for best dissertation in the field of comparative politics for 1994.

The common view among historians is that ordinary Germans went along with the Holocaust only because the policy of exterminating Jews seemed to be entrenched in a governmental system that they felt too weak to oppose. Goldhagen argues that anti-Semitism was regarded as a "common sense" attitude among ordinary Germans, and that German citizens actively supported the Holocaust.

GERMAN ANTI-SEMITISM

When the fateful day of Hitler's assumption of the office of German Chancellor came on January 30, 1933, the Nazis found that they did not have to remake Germans at least on one central issue—arguably the most important one from their point of view—the nature of Jewry. Whatever else Germans thought about Hitler and the Nazi movement, however much they might have detested aspects of Nazism, the vast majority of them subscribed to the underlying Nazi model of Jews and in this sense (as the Nazis themselves understood) were "Nazified" in their views of Jews. It is, to risk understatement, no surprise that under the Nazi dispensation the vast majority of Germans continued to remain antisemitic, that their antisemitism continued to be virulent and racially grounded, and that their socially shared "solution" to the "Jewish Problem" continued to be eliminationist. *Nothing* occurred in Nazi Germany to undermine or erode the cultural cognitive model of Jews that had for decades underlain German attitudes and emotions towards the despised minority among them. Everything publicly said or done worked to reinforce the model.

In Germany during the Nazi period, putative Jewish evil permeated the air. It was discussed incessantly. It was said to be the source of every ill that had befallen Germany and of every continuing threat. The Jew, *der Jude,* was both a metaphysical and an existential threat, as real to Germans as that of a powerful enemy army poised on Germany's borders for the attack. . . .

During its Nazi period, German antisemitism took predictable turns. Harnessed now to a state occupied by the most virulent and dedicated anti-semites ever to assume the leadership of a modern nation, anti-Jewish hatreds and yearnings previously confined to civil society by states that would not organize the burning sentiments into systemic persecution became during the Nazi period the guiding principles of state policy, with a number of unsurprising results:

1. The enactment of extensive, severe legal restrictions upon Jewish existence in Germany.
2. Physical and increased verbal attacks upon Jews, both spontaneous ones from ordinary Germans and ones orchestrated by governmental and party institutions.
3. A further intensification of antisemitism within society.
4. The transformation of Jews into "socially dead" beings.
5. A society-wide consensus on the need to eliminate Jewish influence from Germany.

All of these characterized not just the Nazi leadership but the vast majority of the German people, who were aware of what their government and their countrymen were doing to Jews, assented to the measures, and, when the opportunity presented itself, lent their active support to them.

SOCIAL OSTRACISM OF JEWS

The litany of German anti-Jewish policies and legal measures began with the almost instantaneous, yet sporadic, physical attacks upon Jews, their property, burial sites, and houses of worship, and with the establishment of "wild" concentration camps for them and for the political left. The regime's and the public's highly injurious verbal attacks aside, the first large-scale and potently symbolic organized assault upon German Jewry came just two months after

Hitler's assumption of power. The nationwide boycott of Jewish businesses on April 1, 1933, was a signal event, announcing to all Germans that the Nazis were resolute. The Jews would be treated in accordance with the oft-stated conception of them: as aliens within the German body social, inimical to its well-being. Rhetoric was to be turned into reality. How did Germans react to the boycott? One Jew recounts that a few Germans defiantly expressed their solidarity with the beleaguered Jews. Yet "such protests were not very common. The general attitude of the public was reflected in an incident which occurred at a chemist's shop. A lady, accompanied by two uniformed Nazis, had entered. She brought with her some goods she had purchased a few days before, and demanded that the chemist should return her money. 'I did not know that you were a Jew,' she declared, 'I don't want to buy anything of Jews.'" Here was the

AN ALTERNATE VIEW OF GERMAN ANTI-SEMITISM

Daniel Jonah Goldhagen's argument that the German people were willing participants in the Holocaust has drawn considerable criticism. Distinguished German historian Hans Mommsen disagrees with some of Goldhagen's claims.

Goldhagen believes that he can demonstrate, in Emile Durkheim's sense, a specific collective consciousness and speaks of "the German cultural cognitive model of the Jew." However, he avoids corroborating this with source material, and he instead refers to a few works on the history of anti-Semitism in Germany whose findings he not infrequently takes out of context and generalizes in a one-sided manner. . . .

Goldhagen's view that anti-Semitism swept Hitler into power—or was successfully used by him for mass mobilization—is therefore incorrect. In the decisive electoral campaigns of 1930 and 1932, which gave the NSDAP its breakthrough as a mass party, anti-Semitic agitation proved, if anything, more of a hindrance, so that the Reich-level campaign leadership consciously played it down. In the decision to vote for the NSDAP, anti-Semitism played a subordinate role, however regrettable it is that many NSDAP sympathizers were hardly disturbed by its extreme anti-Semitism and—in the conservative camp—viewed it as a mere childhood disease that would peter out in time. . . .

By his emphasis on the violence, sadism, and pleasure taken in murder, Goldhagen diverts attention from the peculiarity of sight of the German *Volk,* organized by the German state, collectively boycotting an entire group of German citizens, because this group allegedly, in cahoots with racial brethren abroad, was harming Germany. The Nazis signaled repeatedly and clearly, the boycott having been but one instance, that the era of Jews in Germany would soon come to a close.

Following upon this boycott, which was devastating to the social position of Jews, who were now publicly, officially proclaimed to be, and treated as, a pariah people, was a series of anti-Jewish legal measures that began what was to become the systematic elimination of Jews from German economic, social, and cultural life, from a public and social existence in Germany. The Nazis passed the Law for the Restoration of the Professional Civil Service just a few days after the boycott, which led to the immediate dismissal of thousands of Jews, because it mandated "race" as a qualifi-

---

the National Socialist persecution and extermination of the Jews. It was qualitatively different from earlier anti-Semitic outbursts and pogroms, which arose out of a surplus of emotionality but also exhausted themselves therein. Among the Jewish Councils of eastern Europe, the traditional pogrom experience elicited an erroneous appraisal of the persecutors, whom they attempted to bring to reason by passivity and compliance. It was characteristic of National Socialism, by contrast, that the "wild" assaults on the Jews were replaced by planned and bureaucratically perfected segregation, by casting out into pariah status, and ultimately by extermination. That corruption, murderous delight, and sadism would also turn up—although Heinrich Himmler disavowed this and Oswald Pohl as chief of the concentration camp system attempted (in vain) to restrain the use of force in the camps—was hardly surprising under the circumstances and was certainly not a specific feature of the Holocaust. . . .

The corrosive sharpness with which Goldhagen charges the Germans with a will to "demonic anti-Semitism"—and to make them out not as accomplices but as generally pleased perpetrators—is certainly ill suited to quiet resentments, and it is anything but helpful in gaining a sober confrontation with the past in the light of the present.

Hans Mommsen, "The Thin Patina of Civilization: Anti-Semitism Was a Necessary, but by No Means a Sufficient, Condition for the Holocaust," in *Unwilling Germans?: The Goldhagen Debate.* Ed. Robert R. Shandley. Trans. Jeremiah Riemer. Minneapolis: University of Minnesota Press, 1998.

cation for civil service employment. Again, the symbolism was quite clear. This law, one of the first that the Nazis promulgated on any matter, was directed at the Jews, producing a "purification" of the state, an elimination of the Jewish presence in the institution perhaps most identified with the common and collective welfare of the people, most identified with serving the people. By definition, Jews could not serve (because serving implies helping) the German people. Although there were Germans who voiced criticism towards the open violence against Jews and towards the boycott (which was deemed to hurt Germany's standing abroad and was accompanied by great brutality), the criticism generally betrayed neither dissent from the conception of Jews underlying these measures nor solidarity with the beleaguered Jews. The law excluding Jews from the civil service, being unaccompanied by public displays of brutality, was, not surprisingly, widely popular in Germany. It was especially popular among the Jews' civil service colleagues. Working closely for years with the Jews did not, as would have ordinarily been expected, engender among the Germans feelings of camaraderie and sympathy. Thomas Mann, who had already long been an outspoken opponent of Nazism, could nevertheless find some common ground with the Nazis when it came to eliminating Jewish influence in Germany: ". . . it is no great misfortune after all that . . . the Jewish presence in the judiciary has been ended." The dominant cultural cognitive model of Jews and the eliminationist mindset that it spawned was dominant in Germany.

For the next two years, Germans inside and outside the government succeeded in making life for Jews in Germany— who suffered under a plethora of laws, measures, and assaults upon their livelihoods, social positions, and persons— all but unbearable. During this period, the society-wide attack upon the Jews proceeded in an uncoordinated manner. Some of its aspects were mandated from above, some initiated from below, the latter generally, though not always, by avowed Nazis. The main, though not sole, initiators of assaults upon Jews were the men of the SA, the brown shirt shock troops of the regime. During the middle part of 1933, they unleashed physically destructive and symbolic attacks against Jews all across Germany. The assaults ran the gamut of what was to become the standard German repertoire. Verbal assaults were so common as to be "normal" actions, unworthy of special notice. The Jews' pariah status was publicly declared in Germany on explicit, unequivocal public signs. For example, all over Franconia, at the entrances to many villages and in restaurants and hotels, Germans posted signs with proclamations like "Jews Not Wanted Here" or "Entry Forbidden to Jews." Munich, already in May 1933, also boasted signs on its outskirts that declared "Jews Not Wanted.". . .

PHYSICAL ATTACKS ON JEWS

Supplementing the verbal assaults were physical attacks of fearsome symbolic content that began in the first months of the Nazi period and continued until its end. They included Germans forcibly cutting Jews' beards and hair.

One Jewish refugee recalls having seen, in a Berlin hospital in early 1933, an old Jewish man with unusual facial wounds: "He was a poor rabbi from Galicia, who had been stopped in the street by two men in uniform. One of them gripped him by the shoulders, the other held his long beard. Then the second man took a knife from his pocket, and cut off the old man's beard. To remove it thoroughly, he had cut off several pieces of skin." Upon being asked by the physician whether or not the perpetrator had said anything, the man responded, "I don't know. He screamed at me: 'Death to the Jews!'" Attacks upon Jewish businesses, synagogues, and cemeteries were perpetrated both by individuals and by organized groups. In Munich in 1934, for example, a man who had no Nazi affiliation provoked crowds of Germans to demonstrate against Jewish store owners, a demonstration that eventually erupted in violence. Beatings, maimings, and killings of Jews also became an all too "normal" occurrence during these years. An illustrative episode was recounted by the daughter of an unsuspecting cattle dealer from a small town in East Prussia, who was set upon by five heavily armed SA men in the middle of the night in March 1933. The "SA-man first beat my father, then my mother, and finally myself with a rubber truncheon. My mother received a deep cut on her head, and my forehead was also lacerated. . . . Outside the front door all of my father's competitors had gathered, and they behaved in such an indecent manner that I, as a young girl, cannot relate of this to you. . . ." Attacks against Jews during this period were by no means confined to cities. Jews living in the countryside and in small towns throughout Germany were so persecuted by their non-Jewish neighbors and were subjected to so much violence in the first years of the regime that they by and large fled their homes to larger and more anonymous cities or abroad. Such neighborly attacks, coming from people who had lived, worked, given birth, and buried parents, side by side with them, were intense. What took place in two nearby small towns in Hesse was by no means out of the ordinary.

Forty Jewish families were living in one of the Hessen towns, Gedern, upon the Nazis' assumption of power. Already, less than two months into the Nazi era, on the night of March 12, 1933, Germans broke into the houses of the town's Jews and brutalized them. They bludgeoned one Jew so badly that he had to spend a year in a hospital. When, on the occasion of the one national election that took place during the Nazi period, graffiti urging a vote for the (forbidden) leader of the Communist Party was discovered, Germans of the town marched some Jews in drill step to the bridge and forced them to wash it clean. They then beat the Jews. During this period, one Jewish boy was assaulted on the street, losing his eye to his assailant. A little while later, the Germans forced two Jewish men to parade in front of the town, beating them with whips which they had procured from a prosperous farmer. They communicated their desire to be rid of Jews with another unmistakably symbolic act, common to Germany at the time—the overturning of the gravestones in the Jewish cemetery. All of the Jews fled their intolerable existence in this town well before *Kristallnacht,* the last Jew leaving on April 19, 1937. Upon his departure, this apparently destitute man was denied food by his erstwhile neighbors.

A second town, Bindsachen, was yet another home to an early assault on Jewish existence. On the evening of the attack, March 27, 1933, immediately before it commenced, a large part of the town assembled in order to witness SA men bludgeon the chosen Jewish victim, who was known to everyone in the town. The townspeople, enthusiastic at the sight of their suffering neighbor, urged on the SA man with cheers.

A chronicle of Germans' attacks of all varieties upon Jews during this period (uncoordinated by state or Party offices) would fill many volumes. The instances recounted here were anything but atypical. Attacks of these sorts were a "normal," quotidian part of Germany once Nazism was in a position to unleash the pent-up antisemitic passion. . . .

ANTI-SEMITISM AT ALL LEVELS OF SOCIETY

The attacks upon Jews during this period, the attempts to hasten the eliminationist program, came by no means only from the "rabble" of German society, that 10 percent at the lower end of the socioeconomic scale, all too blithely dismissed by interpreters of this period as immoral or amoral people from whom one could not expect better conduct. The initiative to eliminate Jews from social contact with Germans was also taken by municipalities and heterogeneous groups of Germans of all classes well before the state demanded such action, such as when, on their own, cities and towns began to bar Jews as early as 1933 from using swimming pools or public bathing facilities. So many measures and assaults against Jews were initiated by small businessmen during this early period that this social stratum appears to have been the font of the majority of attacks originating from private German citizens. Yet the initiative to eliminate Jewish influence from society was also taken by the most prestigious and best-educated professionals. German medical institutions and groups, for example, giving expression to their hatred of Jews, on their own began to exclude their Jewish colleagues, even before the government mandated the measures. University administrators, faculty, and students across Germany similarly applauded and contributed to driving their Jewish colleagues out from their ranks. . . .

The unsystematic nature of the legal measures taken against the Jews during the first few years of Nazism, and particularly the uncoordinated and often wild attacks upon Jews which, according to the government's own reports, occurred in every administrative district and in almost every locality, did cause many Germans to feel unsettled. Some objected to the wanton violence, and many, in and out of government and the Party, were unsure what sorts of action against the Jews were to be taken or tolerated. The Nuremberg Laws of September 1935 and subsequent legislation brought order to the uncoordinated state of affairs, defining precisely who was to be considered a Jew, or a partial Jew, and enacting a broad set of prohibitions that provided a good measure of coherence to the eliminationist program. Above all else, the Nuremberg Laws made explicit and to a great extent codified the elimination of Jews from a civil or social existence in Germany, going a long way towards creating an insuperable separation between Jews and members of the

Volk. Its two measures, the Reich Citizenship Law and the Law for the Protection of German Blood and German Honor, stripped Jews of their citizenship and forbade new marriages and sexual relations outside of existing marriages between Jews and Germans. The laws were very popular among the German people. Germans welcomed the laws because of the coherence that they imposed in this most pressing of spheres, and more so because of the content of the measures. A Gestapo report from Magdeburg captured well the popular mood when it noted that "the population regards the regulation of the relationships of the Jews as an emancipatory act, which brings clarity and simultaneously greater firmness in the protection of the racial interests of the German people." The eliminationist program had received at once its most coherent statement and its most powerful push forward. The Nuremberg Laws promised to accomplish what had heretofore for decades been but discussed and urged on *ad nauseam.* With this codifying moment of the Nazi German "religion," the regime held up the eliminationist writing on the Nazi tablets for every German to read. All were literate in its language. And many wanted the implementation of its program to be hastened, as a Gestapo report from Hildesheim covering February 1936, a few months after the laws' promulgation, conveys: "It is said by many that the Jews in Germany are still treated much too humanely."

The Righteous Gentiles

Leon W. Wells

Leon W. Wells survived the Holocaust by hiding
with other Jews in a cellar on the property of a non-
Jewish farmer in Poland. Drawing primarily on
Philip Friedman's book *Their Brothers' Keepers*, as
well as on his personal experiences, Wells recalls
some of the courageous people who tried to protect
Jews during the Holocaust. It is interesting that this
discussion, written before the release of the movie
Schindler's List, does not even mention Oskar
Schindler, whose story was not widely known prior
to the release of the movie.

The best-known story of a righteous Gentile, one that has
been the subject of several books and a television documentary, is that of the Swede, Raoul Wallenberg. Born in 1912 to
a distinguished Swedish family (his grandfather had been
ambassador to Japan and to Turkey; his father was a prominent banker), Wallenberg was a partner in an import-export
firm and only thirty-two years old when he was recruited for
a special mission to rescue Hungarian Jews facing deportation after March 19, 1944. When the situation of the Jews of
Hungary became extremely precarious, Herschel Johnson,
the U.S. ambassador to Stockholm, asked the Swedish Ministry of Foreign Affairs to find a prominent Swede who would
be prepared to carry on rescue work in Budapest.

Wallenberg's selection may have come by sheer accident,
because his partner's offices were adjacent to those of Ivar
C. Olsen, who was the financial attaché at the U.S. embassy
in Stockholm. Dr. Karl Laurer, the Jewish partner of Wallenberg, described him as one who was disturbed about the
predicament of Hungarian Jews and who wanted to be of assistance. Wallenberg was a suitable choice, but the mission
was delicate and dangerous.

In order that he might have diplomatic immunity in Bu-

Excerpted from Leon W. Wells, "The Righteous Gentiles," in *Holocaust Literature: A
Handbook of Critical, Historical, and Literary Writings,* edited by Saul S. Friedman.
Copyright © 1993 by Saul S. Friedman. Used with permission of Greenwood Publish-
ing Group, Inc., Westport, CT.

dapest, he was appointed an attaché of the Swedish embassy in the Hungarian capital. He arrived on July 9, 1944, with only an attaché case containing the list of the Jews to be given rescue priority and the names of Hungarian anti-Nazis whose assistance he might seek. From 20 volunteer workers in the embassy the staff grew to 660 persons, including their families. For the most part Jewish, they enjoyed a precarious immunity as employees of the Swedish embassy. The safety of his staff was not the only concern of Wallenberg. He wanted to save as many Jews as he could. He issued hundreds of passports to Hungarian Jews with relatives or business ties in Sweden. He devised the "protective passport," a certificate emblazoned with Swedish colors, with which he protected more than a thousand Jews. In this he was also a pioneer, as other countries followed suit, including the papal nuncio and the Swiss, Portuguese, and Spanish embassies.

On one occasion Jews were assembled at the railroad station awaiting deportation. Wallenberg drove there at high speed, summoned the commander, and said, "I have it on good authority that among the people arrested by you for deportation are persons protected by the Kingdom of Sweden. This is an outrage. I demand that you instantly release them or I will complain to your superiors!"

This was 1944, and many Hungarian collaborators already saw the handwriting on the wall and wanted to be on good terms with a country like Sweden. The Germans were bewildered, and most of the Jews were released. Wallenberg also established a number of centers for children, which he placed under the protection of the Red Cross and so saved some 8,000 Jewish children. He also promised some Hungarian officials passports after the war. He bribed other officials with cash. All told, he saved from 30,000 to 100,000 Jews. There are many more stories about Wallenberg's heroic actions that deserve telling, but space does not permit. In any case, the Jews in Hungary thought of him as a modern Moses.

On January 17, 1945, shortly after the Russian army liberated Budapest, Wallenberg was taken away by an armed Russian guard, never to be heard from again. There were rumors through the years, carried by people who had been in Soviet prisons, of a prisoner fitting Wallenberg's description. One report said that he died in 1957 in a Russian prison, but others claim to have seen him in Siberia. Wallenberg became a forgotten man for the Jews. All over the world there were Jews who had been saved by Wallenberg, but the general public knew little, if anything, about him. There were no concerted efforts by Jewish organizations calling for pressure to be exerted on the Soviet Union to release him, and there were no Jewish efforts to locate him, such as were made to locate Adolf Eichmann, the war criminal who was very active in Hungary.

Finally, in 1978, some thirty-four years after he disappeared, Congressman Tom Lantos of California introduced a bill to make Raoul Wallenberg an honorary citizen of the United States, so that on this basis one might begin negotiations with the Russians to find out if he still lived, and, if so, what might be done to help him. Congressman Lantos and his wife had both been saved by Wallenberg in Hungary. . . .

THE KALWINSKI FAMILY: A PERSONAL REMINISCENCE

I can personally testify to the courage demonstrated by Polish Christians. On November 19, 1943, I escaped from the "Death Brigade" (Sonderkommando 1005) of the small concentration camp at Janowska near Lvov, Poland. Our task had been to erase the signs of German atrocities. We dug up mass graves, unearthed the bodies, and burned them on a huge pyre in a pit, where old Jewish grave stones were used as the base for the flaming timbers. As the end of the grisly work drew near, we knew that we would be killed and our bodies likewise burned to eliminate the last witnesses to the atrocities, so we planned and executed a breakout from our quarters.

As I fled down a road, I met another escapee from the Brigade, a Mr. Korn, then in his early thirties. I was eighteen. He had been a horse trader before the war and knew a family, the Kalwinskis, to whom he had sold some horses. He hoped that we might find refuge with them. Although I was a complete stranger to them, without any hesitation they took me in along with Korn. When he saw me, Mr. Kalwinski simply shook his head and said in Polish, "Why, he's only a baby," using the English word "baby." His children overheard him and, not knowing any English words, thought that "Baby" was my real name, so they called me "Baby" throughout the nine months of my stay. After the war, one of the sons of Kalwinski came to visit me in Lvov, and arriving at my apartment building, asked where "Baby" lived. He was surprised to learn that it was not my real name.

We were taken to the stable and shown a small opening in the floor of the pigsty, where one or two pigs were always present. In one corner of the stable was a cow, in the other a horse. Over the top of the pigsty was a sleeping place for Kalwinski's son Kazik, who was then fifteen years old. His sleeping there was not considered unusual, for it was assumed that he was there to watch out for thieves who might steal the animals. The sounds of the pigs covered any sounds that we made, and so the sty proved to be an excellent cover for our hiding place.

We crawled through the opening and found our home for the next nine months. It was a space about ten feet wide, twelve feet long, and six feet high, dug out under the stable. We had come through the only entrance. In one corner there was a small cubicle, about three feet high, under a platform bed that stood two feet below the ceiling. The cubicle was our toilet area, with a curtain for privacy hanging in front of a pot and a bucket for emptying the pot. The only piece of furniture was a cot on one side. The rest of the floor was made into one big bed.

Twenty-one other Jews were already there. There was the Holtz family. Mr. Holtz had owned the neighborhood pub. It was not a Jewish neighborhood. His sons and daughters, already grown up, were part of this neighborhood. The Kalwinskis, like so many others, were regular customers at the pub, where they spent many an evening and Sunday afternoons. When the Germans took Lvov and started their "actions" against Jews, the Holtzes got together with their neighbors the Kalwinskis, and so the "basement" was dug. Holtz, a sixty-year-old widower, came with two sons, his married daughter and her husband, and his second daughter and her fiancé. Mr. Holtz slept on the single cot.

There were Mr. and Mrs. Herches and their daughter, and Dr. Prokoczimer and his wife, and a lawyer and his wife, Mr. and Mrs. Kessler. The Kesslers had a small daughter who was hidden with another Polish family, because a crying child might have led to the discovery of the whole group. One day the Kalwinskis came to tell us that she had been discovered and taken away to the crematorium. Of course the Kesslers were shocked, and for days they argued and fought over their tragic decision. We were so hardened by the general calamity that we never asked what had happened to the Poles who hid her. But we were in a similar danger because of the youngest of the Kalwinski boys.

One day a policeman came to the house and took a walk around the outside of the house with Mrs. Kalwinski. Staszek, then nine years old, trailed along. At one point he said within earshot of the policeman, "Mother, it seems the electric meter is running." We had a light in the basement that we would turn on briefly during the day to find our way to the toilet. To our good fortune, the policeman paid no attention to the boy. But the whole episode became a matter for a family conference that evening. It was decided to send Staszek to a farm some three hundred kilometers away. The cover story was that the boy was terrified of planes and bombing, which was not at all the case, and so was sent away for his own good. It was actually a great hardship for him and his family.

My space for my life in the basement was on the platform bed, which I shared with the Kesslers. The routine of our days was organized around the relatively "safe times" for our stirring, which meant late evening into the night. The Kalwinski children hauled away our filth at night and carried our food and clothes back and forth to Mrs. Kalwinski, who cooked for us and washed our clothes at night. The cot where Mr. Holtz slept also served as a sitting couch when any member of the Kalwinski family came to visit us. Mr. Kalwinski came down every night after eight to talk to us, passing on the news of the day and the neighborhood gossip. He was a portly man who had to be helped to squeeze through the narrow opening in the stable floor, where the pigs sometimes urinated, causing some consternation.

Every Sunday, Kalwinski's daughter Marysia came down to spend the afternoon with us, sitting on Holtz's cot and telling us stories of the neighborhood. The Holtz children were especially eager for the news. Very often we protested to her that she, as a girl in her early twenties, should be with her own companions and perhaps a boyfriend on this day. Otherwise her friends might become suspicious, wondering where she spent her Sundays.

Her answer was "How can I enjoy myself, knowing that you are sitting in this hiding place? My place is with you here." So Marysia would help her mother all week with the cooking and the washing of our underwear, which was all that we could wear under the circumstance of the heat generated by so many bodies in that small space. The cooking and washing chores included chopping wood for the wood-burning stove to heat the food and the wash water. Marysia and her mother had to go shopping for the whole group in many different places, including the black market, so as not to attract attention by the amount of food they purchased. We were fortunate that the Kalwinskis were small "city farmers" who had some vegetable crops of their own and beef to slaughter. The Germans required the registration of every animal to prevent meat being sold on the black market, but this posed no problem for the Kalwinskis, who kept the meat in the family.

February, March, and April 1944 were terrifying months for us. The German army requisitioned many rooms in the neighborhood to quarter its soldiers. It took over several rooms in the Kalwinski house for its headquarters and even put a couple of horses in the stable above our hiding place. During its stay we were fed only once a day in the dead of night.

In April twelve Jews who were hiding in the home of a nearby cattle dealer by the name of Juzefek were tragically exposed. A quarrel broke out between the parents and a sixteen-year-old daughter. In a rage at her parents, she ran out of the house screaming that they were hiding Jews. Everyone heard about it. The Germans came and found Jews in the hiding place. Juzefek and his wife were hanged publicly, and their bodies were left on the gallows for forty-eight hours as an example.

The Kalwinskis simply carried on as usual, although the execution of their friends and neighbors caused them pain and grief. For some weeks we discussed the danger to the Kalwinskis among ourselves, coming to the conclusion that we should offer to leave, since we had no right to risk their lives. When we did so, their answer was "What God wants to happen to you, it will happen to us, too." Like most Poles, the Kalwinskis were religious people. We held out for three more months until August 1944, when the Russians liberated Lvov, and we were able to don our street clothes for the first time and walk out into the sunlight.

After the war the Kalwinskis moved to Gliwice from Lvov, which became part of Russia. Marysia, their only daughter, died in childbirth in 1947. The elder Kalwinskis died of old age, the father in 1967 and the mother in 1978. Their sons are still alive. . . .

THE STORY OF THE NACHTS

Perhaps the most surprising story of rescue during the Holocaust . . . is that of Fascist Italy. . . . There were some 57,000 Jews in Italy, according to the census of 1938. About 40,000 of them survived the war years because the Italian government, the army, and the people simply did not share the Nazis' anti-Semitic outlook. Jews had held high public office, including a prime minister, a minister of war, and a mayor of Rome. It was well known that Mussolini himself "frowned on racialism, calling it un-Italian." The Duce had said in 1924 that anti-Semitism "is an alien weed that cannot strike roots in Italy where Jews are citizens with full equality."

The first anti-Jewish laws in Italy came in 1938 as a result of the Italian-German alliance. Mussolini apparently came to the realization that an Italian anti-Jewish campaign was part of the price of the alliance, and he was willing to pay it. But fortunately for Italian Jews, many government officials and the people were not willing to concur with the anti-Jewish decrees in 1938. No Italian Jews were required to wear a badge. There were no ghettos, no Italian-managed deportations to death camps. Still, some 4,500 Jews converted to Christianity after the anti-Jewish laws were passed. But wherever the Italian army was in control, in southern France, Yugoslavia, and Greece, Jews were spared deportation until, toward the end of the war, the Germans took the matter into their own hands and began rounding up Jews in Italy itself.

The story of a young Jewish couple from Lvov, Poland, who were studying medicine in Belgrade, Yugoslavia, when the Germans attacked Belgrade is illustrative of the experience of Jews under the Italians. Mr. and Mrs. Nacht left Belgrade on April 6, 1941, when the first German bombs fell upon the city. They made their way to Montenegro, where they took a train to Split (Croatia), which was under Italian Fascist rule.

One day the Italian government made the announcement that any refugees who would like to come to Italy would be allowed to do so. There was a general fear among the refugees because of reports of hunger in Italy, and of course because of Mussolini's cooperation with Hitler's policies. The Nachts felt that hunger was not to be feared, as there was not too much food where they were, so they were among the first to register for Italy.

With a group of about two hundred they were put into railroad cars. The men were separated from the women and children and loosely handcuffed. When they arrived at the station in Trieste, the Nazis photographed the men as they were led in handcuffs from the train and gave the pictures to be published in newspapers. With the proper publicity behind them, the refugees were taken to Italian boats, where they were given wonderful treatment. They were served good food at tables properly set with white cloths.

In Italy they were transferred to trains, and the Nachts were taken with twenty-five other Jews to the small village of Crespano del Grappa near Venice and Padua. The Italians gave them eight lire a day for food and fifty lire a month for a room. Of course, food was rationed, but the Italians often sold the refugees food without ration coupons at the official prices, much lower than those of the black market. The relations between the Jewish refugees and the Italian villagers were very good, with much visiting back and forth. Most of them had never met Jews before, and they enjoyed the new social contacts very much.

One day the Nachts were informed that they would have to move from the house because the landlady's sister had come from Turino after her house was bombed. They were supposed to go to another village, but the local people did not want them to leave. The pharmacist's wife, with whom they had not been particularly close, came and offered them a beautifully furnished room in her house, which they were happy to accept. The local grocer sent them gifts of food. The Nachts lived there for two years.

Early in 1943 there was a knock at their door. An Italian girl had come to warn them, "The Germans are here!" Italian neighbors came with a car to take the Nachts to the railroad station at Bassano, some ten miles away. When they tried to pay them, they refused, saying, "When you come back, and when Mussolini will be hanged, we will drink wine together."

The Nachts kept moving toward the south, hoping to reach the Allied lines. On foot, carrying their suitcases through the countryside, they were met by a young girl who asked them where they were going. When they told her, she informed them that they were headed toward the Germans. The girl offered to help with the suitcases, even to store a couple of them until after the war, which the Nachts were happy to allow, because of their weight. The girl, who was the daughter of an Italian police commissioner, gave them her address, where they came to claim their cases after the war and found everything just as it had been.

The Nachts were indeed strangers in Italy, but the hospitality that they experienced could not have been warmer under the circumstances. They were the beneficiaries of a tradition of Italian humaneness that neither Mussolini's fascism nor Hitler's state terrorism could erase. Of course, such was also the case in France and in Belgium, Holland, and Denmark, wherever the rescue of Jews was considered an obligation that could not be avoided. The Nachts' story bears witness to the operative presence of the values of truth, justice, and human dignity in a time when barbarism reigned, and the policies of hatred and conquest by a people driven by the doctrine of "might makes right" brought chaos and destruction upon all of Europe.

The part of the Italian story that has received the most attention, and so has overshadowed the good record of the Italian people, is that of the pope during the period of the Holocaust. Rolf Hochhuth's controversial play *The Deputy* dramatized the problem of the pope's silence about the process of genocide taking place in Europe. While there has been much speculation about the reasons for the pope's silence, such as that the pope's official statements would have only given the impression of papal weakness and lack of influence in international affairs, there is no doubt about the real efforts taken by the pope and the clergy to rescue Jews who lived in their territories. The chief rabbi of the Jewish community of Rome, Dr. Israel (Eugene) Zolli, was hidden by the pope during the Nazi occupation. After the war he converted to Christianity. Philip Friedman describes in detail how priests and churches helped Jews in Italy, how the pope was involved with helping Italian Jews, and how he even contributed a large sum of money to the Jewish synagogue in Rome. . . .

HELP FROM ANTI-SEMITES

Another group of people who quite surprisingly appeared among the rescuers of Jews and sometimes paid with their lives were former anti-Semites. Friedman lists quite a number of them in *Their Brothers' Keepers*. There was Jan Mosdorf, who before the war was the leader of the anti-Semitic youth movement in Poland. He carried letters to a woman inmate at Birkenau, where he worked, and brought food to Jews in prison. He was eventually shot by the Nazis. Stanislaw Piasecki, who had been the editor of an anti-Semitic journal, *Prosto z mostu* (Straight from the shoulder), and an outspoken admirer of Hitler, was so shocked by the events following the German invasion that he repented of his anti-Semitism. A group of Polish anti-Semitic lawyers refused, when invited by the Nazi officials, to make public statements as to their attitude toward the Jews. "Witold Rudnicki, a member of the anti-Semitic National Democratic party . . . ordered the execution of four Polish blackmailers who threatened to inform the Germans of Jews hidden in the village of Pustelnik, near Warsaw. His apartment in Warsaw eventually became a shelter for Jews who escaped from the ghetto. He was killed during the revolt in Warsaw in the autumn of 1944."

Aleksander Witaszewicz, a wealthy landowner and a member of the National Democratic party, hid nine Jews for two years on his estate and helped five of them to find a hiding place in Warsaw, where he continued to supply them with food. He was assassinated on his estate in 1943. It was thought that he was the victim of an anti-Semitic guerilla unit. Friedman reports the statement of Dr. Franciszek Kowalski, a lawyer from Zakopane: "I was an anti-Semite before the war. Hitler's bestiality toward the Jews changed me. I had not imagined that human debasement as displayed by the Germans could sink to such depths."

While these actions of former anti-Semites are commendable, they should force us to reflect on the nature of human prejudice and its role in generating violence. While these converts away from anti-Semitism were shocked by the violence and were made to consider the moral implications of their prejudice, there were many others, perhaps persons who were converted to anti-Semitism by some of the propaganda efforts of these leaders and publicists, who used their former statements as a rationale for the violence. If there is a lesson to be learned from all this, it is that one may not ignore any prejudicial statements or behavior on the grounds that all human beings are prejudiced in some way. The prejudicial statements and discriminatory acts of today, however bland they might appear, may very well contribute to a social process that generates violence against the discriminated tomorrow. If we take this seriously, it should lead us to the conviction, upon which we should always be willing to act, that there is no such thing as a mild or harmless statement or act of prejudice.

Perhaps the hardest thing to accept about the story of the righteous Gentiles of the period of the Holocaust is that there were, relatively speaking, so few of them. We now know that one cannot take it for granted that most people place a high value on morality and human rights. These are values that must be cultivated, taught, and reinforced by public examples and by the stories that we tell our children to prepare them for the hard decisions of life. When one considers the fact that our youth today are literally bombarded with stories of violence and vengeance in movie theaters and television, it seems that what is being reinforced today is the philosophy of force and counterforce, whether at the level of street gangs or that of international diplomacy. But shouldn't we now consider the consequences of this type of negative reinforcement and seek out and tell stories of rescuers, of persons who risked everything to save lives, and promote these stories for the purpose of cultivating a keen sense of humanity, so that our children may learn, as did the righteous of Europe during the Holocaust, to resist the prevailing barbarism of their day?

CHAPTER 2

SCHINDLER'S EFFORTS TO SAVE JEWISH LIVES

Oskar Enters My Life

Emilie Schindler

Emilie Pelzl married Oskar Schindler in 1928, and although the marriage was not particularly successful, she remained married to him until his death in 1974, chiefly because of her Catholic disapproval of divorce. She and Oskar immigrated to Argentina after the war, and she continued to live there until her death in October 2001 at the age of ninety-three. Emilie knew Oskar's private side, and her memoir is an important counterbalance to the adulatory accounts of other witnesses. Although her memory for specific places, names, and dates is frequently mistaken, this passage contains important clues to Schindler's personality and motivations. She tells of her meeting with Oskar and of their life before he began running the enamelware factory in Krakow in 1939.

It was a Thursday in autumn. The countryside had begun to turn yellow, orange, green, and brown, and the fallen leaves covered the ground with a thick carpet that the wind swirled into different places and shapes, like an optical illusion. I was keeping my grandmother company; we were picking cherries, storing potatoes for the winter, and making plum preserves.

I was already twenty years old, and although I had my feet on the ground and was used to hard work, I was still dreaming of a first great love. And there I was, lost in my thoughts, when I saw a huge butterfly fluttering among the leaves of a lemon tree. It looked so magnificent, its colors so bright, and it flapped its wings in such an amazing way that it seemed to invite me to go out and look at it closely.

As I stepped out I noticed, a short distance from the house, two men who were eyeing me with curiosity. One was over fifty, tall and robust looking, and his companion was a slender youth with broad shoulders, blond hair, and deep blue eyes.

I greeted them, and the older man came closer to me and explained the reason for their visit. He and his son had come from Brünn [Brno], the capital of Moravia, to try to sell us some new motors that could supply our house with electricity. They were a brand-new product of Czechoslovakia. He started to explain all about the advantages of having these generators, and how they operated. He assumed that I had no idea what he was talking about, but I had been informing myself about this invention for several months. I have always been very inquisitive and am always asking questions about everything, a vice or a virtue, depending on how you look at it. This is a habit I have kept even into my old age.

While the man was telling me things I almost knew by heart, I noticed that his son did not take his eyes off me. There was nothing special about him, with the exception of a certain aloofness and a particularly dignified stance unusual for someone his age. He seemed bored with what his father was saying, a long spiel about technology, electricity, and progress. He soon tried to engage my complicity by means of suggestive glances and half smiles.

I thought the situation was funny and could not help laughing, though I blushed and quickly covered my mouth. When the man had finished his sales pitch, I only asked him curtly to come another day to talk with my father because there was nobody else at home. I could not then imagine that, very shortly afterward, that aloof and likable youth would become my husband.

On subsequent visits, Oskar Schindler remained silent, but I always felt his deep blue eyes caressing me. It was a virile look, dark and penetrating, that I could not get out of my mind for days. I later realized that what had fascinated me, besides his looks, was the way he fixed his gaze upon me and the intimation of his mysterious, undefinable nature. I was also impressed by his discreet and never fully explicit way of speaking, with the promise of a deeper meaning beyond words being held back.

At first I had rejected him, though, not wanting anything to do with him. But with the excuse of promoting the electric generators, his visits became more and more frequent, until I could no longer resist. One day he stayed late at the farm, and when the blue September moon rose over the plum trees, he kissed me for the first time.

Although I did not completely trust Oskar, his passionate

kisses and embraces swept away all my doubts. After some time, his mother and sister visited us. One evening he asked to speak to my parents because, as he said, he had "something important to tell them." Taking me by the hand, and fixing his beautiful blue eyes on my parents, he addressed first my father and then my mother, and in a deep voice made a statement I shall never forget, because it was later proven to be both quite truthful and totally impractical.

"I want to unite my life to Emilie's, so that we can build a future together."

At the same time Oskar was asking for my hand, I began to analyze my situation: my father was always sick and bad tempered, my grandmother was suffering from the ailments of old age, and my mother, overwhelmed by taking care of them and keeping house, had no time even to talk with her children. Besides, my brother was becoming more and more independent from our family life. In view of these circumstances, Oskar's proposal to share his life with me sounded almost irresistible.

It was then, in fact, not a very difficult decision at all. I think that today I would act very differently, but at twenty I was ready to believe everything my heart was telling me: the words fully expressed and the others that were not, the special light in his eyes and the promised warmth that seemed to emanate from him, my emotional response to his kisses and caresses, the protectiveness of his broad shoulders, and his passionate being.

THE ASCETIC AND THE SYBARITE

We were married a short time afterward. The wedding celebration took place on March 6, 1928, in an inn on the outskirts of Zwittau, Oskar's hometown and where he was still living with his family. There were many guests and no shortage of food or wine. While I was dancing in my short white wedding dress, my grandmother did not tire of telling everybody that in that dress I looked like Sleeping Beauty, just awakened from her long sleep by a handsome prince.

We went to live in Zwittau, then an important industrial city. We moved in with my in-laws on Iglau Street, in the family house that Oskar's mother had bought long before. They stayed on the ground floor, while we settled on the floor above.

I was never happy there, because of my very frequent disagreements with Oskar's father. My mother-in-law was practically confined to her bed, and I remember one occasion when I was keeping her company, with my sheepdog lying at my feet. Suddenly my father-in-law stumbled into the house, totally drunk, carrying in one hand a cake and with the other holding on to any support he could find along his way. He noticed my look of disapproval—for that he was sober enough—and when he was about to say something to me, I cut him off. He was furious, and since he could not throw me out, he kicked my dog out of the house while repeating over and over, in his drunken babble, that animals belonged on the street, well aware that this would annoy me no end.

Oskar's mother—whose name was Francisca Luser and whom everybody called Fanny—was an elegant and pleasant woman. She had been sick for a long time and died at fifty-three. Her husband, in contrast, was a completely uneducated man who had started off as an insurance salesman and, after going bankrupt, had ventured into the electric generator business. Hans Schindler was always traveling, but nobody seemed to miss him.

Oskar had a younger sister, Elfriede, thirteen at the time and a replica of her father: she was ugly, with dark hair and bulgy brown eyes, and nobody seemed to be paying much attention to her. Maybe that is why she became attached to me right away. I helped her with her homework and talked with her in the little free time I had left, as I had to take care of not only my own home but also that of my mother-in-law, who was in no condition to do any kind of housework.

My first trip to Prague, in the Fall of 1928, was to arrange for some documents Oskar needed. I was fascinated by everything: the church steeples rising proudly like needles painted on the blue sky, the stores, the streets full of people, the evenings when the city was fully lit up and reflected in the peaceful waters of the Moldau River. . . .

Prague, however, marked the end of the romantic period in my life. Imperceptibly, from that time on everything turned increasingly sad and somber. . . .

My father had given Oskar a dowry of one hundred thousand Czech crowns, a very considerable sum in those days. With that money Oskar bought a luxury car and squandered the rest on outings or unimportant things. When I protested, he replied, "Emilie, you are too austere, a real ascetic. While, on the other hand, I am by nature a sybarite!"

For months I struggled trying to understand his attitude and concluded that it was the result of his upbringing. His mother had pampered him, and his father, busy with his so-called business deals, was seldom home.

In spite of his flaws, Oskar had a big heart and was always ready to help whoever was in need. He was affable, kind, extremely generous and charitable, but at the same time, not mature at all. He constantly lied and deceived me, and later returned feeling sorry, like a boy caught in mischief, asking to be forgiven one more time. . . . And then we would start all over again.

My days in Zwittau were spent cooking, sewing, knitting, and listening to my mother-in-law, who never stopped repeating, "Oskar is now married, and it is his wife's obligation to educate him, my dear Emilie."

She would throw these words into the air and then stare into space motionless for a long time. Resigned, I kept silent.

A short time later, fortunately, we moved into a huge house that had belonged to a wealthy Zwittau family. The mansion was full of luxurious carpets, beautiful furniture, all lit in the evenings by crystal chandeliers. The place itself was the symbol of a time of splendor that was soon to disappear. . . .

SPIES FOR THE THIRD REICH

In 1935 Oskar visited Cracow, where he met a woman with whom he began a conversation that probably, as was his habit, ended up in some secluded place. That woman worked for the German Counterintelligence Service (Abwehrdienst), and she got him a recommendation with her superiors. Oskar really liked this new job, which consisted of locating and persecuting foreign spies in Poland.

The chief of the Counterintelligence Service, headquartered in Berlin, was Commander Hartmut, while Major von Kohrab was in charge of the Polish section. Von Kohrab belonged to the Hungarian nobility, but he had a dark secret: he was the son of a Jewish woman.

Von Kohrab managed to keep his secret for quite some time, until one of his nephews, perhaps more out of stupidity than malice, reported the major's Jewish origin in connection with some bureaucratic procedure. The counterintelligence chief in Poland had to pay dearly for this: he lost his rank and honors and then disappeared completely, without our ever hearing another word concerning his fate. I still remember him, blond and Apollonian in his elegant uniform: a man who, despite his Jewish origin, physically represented better than most, including the Führer himself, the paragons of race and beauty that Nazism was championing.

After some time the Counterintelligence Service decided to send Oskar to Mährisch Ostrau, the capital of Moldavia, to be in charge of the local section.

We had to abandon the huge house into which we had moved after living with Oskar's parents for a few years. It was very difficult to take our belongings with us. Everything was meticulously and carefully controlled: packed, loaded onto a moving van, and taken to our new home, some two hundred and fifty miles from Zwittau.

The apartment that the Counterintelligence Service had assigned to us was located at 24 Parkstrasse, right in the center of Mährisch Ostrau, facing the German army barracks, from which soldiers were continually being dispatched to patrol the streets. We had two large rooms with windows overlooking the garden. The kitchen was very comfortable, and in time it turned out to be the coziest place in the house. One of the rooms became our bedroom, while the other was made into an office.

I tried to help Oskar in his counterintelligence work. I would answer the telephone, receive messages, run errands, and type, while at the same time taking care of my domestic chores. The Parkstrasse apartment became our headquarters. There we received, processed, and concealed information, making sure it was out of the reach of any other foreign agent. In one corner of the closet we kept a Luger pistol, German army issue, always loaded. . . .

We had four co-workers, one of them a woman of Czech origin with whom Oskar also had an affair, in his now seemingly inevitable pattern.

One afternoon, on my return from a trip, I found our apartment in shambles: clothes out of their drawers, papers strewn all over the floor, broken lamps, a truly devastating sight. The only sound to be heard was that of the telephone, off the hook and thrown on the floor, under a layer of clothes, torn papers, busted pillows and feathers, shards from porcelain vases and dishes that apparently had been thrown furiously against the walls by our desperate visitors, frustrated because they did not find any of the things they supposedly had come for.

Nothing important had been stolen. The only thing missing was a watch my mother had given me, and which I later discovered in a pawnshop.

The second episode linked to Oskar's counterintelligence work could have ended tragically. One night, after one of our many quarrels about his extramarital affairs, I was sleeping on a couch in the office while he slept in the bedroom. Suddenly there was a noise by the window.

Ever since Oskar started in this job I found it difficult to fall asleep, and then, even in my sleep, I remained in a near-alert state. I could not get used to this almost wartime lifestyle and felt completely overwhelmed with anxiety.

The noise at the window was followed by the sound of footsteps, and a beam of light, probably from a flashlight, lit up my face for a few seconds. I got up right away and, as silently as possible, went into the bedroom, where Oskar was sleeping peacefully in our large bed. I looked for the Luger in the dark closet, walked up to the window, drew open the heavy curtain, and fired two shots in the air. I saw a shadow running, as if disoriented, toward the barracks. Apparently the soldier on duty had fallen asleep. The shadow ran well past the checkpoint and disappeared into the darkness of night.

Days later we found out that the men trying to break into our house in search of information were Polish agents.

The following is an example of the activities we had gotten involved in. A Polish soldier was paid to get us a Polish army uniform. It was then sent to Germany to serve as a pattern for manufacturing more Polish uniforms that spies of the Third Reich would wear as camouflage. When Germany invaded Poland, the SS were wearing these uniforms in the attack on the Cracow radio station but then blamed the Polish resistance for acts of sabotage.

Our Parkstrasse apartment became the permanent meeting place for spies and informers. One day the police came and started to turn the apartment upside down, looking for certain documents that Oskar had hidden behind a bedroom mirror. They finally found them, and Oskar was arrested. He had been betrayed by a Czech agent who pretended to be his friend.

Oskar was condemned to death for his offense. The German invasion of Czechoslovakia in 1939 saved his life.

The Man Who Saved a Thousand Lives

Herbert Steinhouse

As a young Canadian journalist in post-war France, Herbert Steinhouse came across Schindler's story by talking to Itzhak Stern and other surviving *Schindler-juden* in 1949. At that time Oskar and Emilie Schindler were living in Munich, waiting for permission to immigrate to Argentina. Steinhouse is the only journalist fortunate enough to have interviewed Schindler himself before his death. As a result, the following selection contains accounts of incidents that cannot be found in other sources. At first Steinhouse considered the story to be "farfetched," but he finally became convinced of its truth as he talked to witnesses and found their accounts to match. He decided to write an article on the subject.

Having written his article, Steinhouse tried to find a publisher for it. Unfortunately, at the time stories about "good Germans" were not particularly fashionable, and he was unable to get the article printed. Hence the article remained unread in his files for over forty years. With the release of the movie *Schindler's List*, Steinhouse realized he would finally be able to find a publisher. The version that appeared in the magazine, *Saturday Night*, was slightly revised to bring it up to date.

ITZHAK STERN REMEMBERS

It was from the accountant Itzhak Stern that I first heard of Oskar Schindler. They had met in Cracow in 1939. "I must admit now that I was intensely suspicious of Schindler for a long time," Stern confided, beginning his story. "I suffered greatly under the Nazis. I lost my mother in Auschwitz quite early and I was very embittered."

Excerpted from Herbert Steinhouse, "The Real Oskar Schindler," *Saturday Night*, vol. 109, no. 3 (April 1994), pp. 40–48. Used by permission.

At the end of 1939, Stern directed the accountancy section of a large Jewish-owned export-import firm, a position he had held since 1924. After the occupation of Poland in September, the head of each important Jewish business was replaced by a German trustee, or *Treuhander*, and Stern's new boss became a man named Herr Aue. The former owner, as was the requirement, became an employee, the firm became German and Aryan workers were brought in to replace many of the Jews.

Aue's behaviour was inconsistent and immediately aroused Stern's curiosity. Although he had begun Aryanizing the firm and firing the Jewish workers in accordance with his instructions, he nevertheless left the discharged employees' names on the social-insurance registry, thus enabling them to maintain their all-important workers' identity cards. As well, Aue secretly gave these hungry men money. Such exemplary behaviour could only impress the Jews and astonish the wary and cautious Stern. Only at the end of the war was Stern to learn that Aue had been Jewish himself, that his own father was murdered in Auschwitz in 1942, and that the Polish he pretended to speak so poorly actually was his native tongue.

Not knowing all this, Stern had no reason to trust Aue. Certainly he could not understand the man's presumption when, only a few days after having taken charge of the export-import firm, Aue brought in an old friend who had just arrived in Cracow to see Stern saying, quite casually, "You know, Stern, you can have confidence in my friend Schindler." Stern exchanged courtesies with the visitor, and answered his questions with care.

"I did not know what he wanted and I was frightened," Stern continued. "Until December 1, we Polish Jews had been left more or less alone. They had Aryanized the factories, of course. And if a German asked you a question in the street it was compulsory for you to precede your answer with "I am a Jew. . . ." But it was only on December 1 that we had to begin wearing the Star of David. It was just as the situation had begun to grow worse for the Jews, when the Sword of Damocles was already over our heads, that I had this meeting with Oskar Schindler.

"He wanted to know what kind of Jew I was. He asked me many questions, like was I a Zionist or assimilated or what have you. I told him what everyone knew, that I was vice president of the Jewish Agency for Western Poland and a member of the Zionist Central Committee. Then he thanked me politely and went away."

On December 3, Schindler paid another visit to Stern, this time at night and to his home. They talked chiefly of literature, Stern remembers, and Schindler revealed an unusual interest in the great Yiddish writers. And then suddenly, over some tea, Schindler remarked: "I hear that there will be a raid on all remaining Jewish property tomorrow." Recognizing the intended warning, Stern later passed the word around and effectively saved many friends from the most ruthless "control" the Germans had thus far carried out. Schindler, he realized, had been attempting to encourage his confidence, although he could still not fathom why.

THE FACTORY IN CRACOW

Oskar Schindler, a Sudeten industrialist, had come to Cracow from his native town of Zwittau, just across what had been a border a few months earlier. Unlike most of the carpetbaggers who joyously rushed into prostrate Poland to gobble up the nation's production, he received a factory not from an expropriated Jew but from the Court of Commercial Claims. A small concern devoted to the manufacture of enamelware, it had lain idle and in bankruptcy for many years. In the winter of 1939–1940 he began operations with 4,000 square metres of floor space and a hundred workers, of whom seven were Jewish. Soon he managed to bring in Stern as his accountant. Production started with a rush, for Schindler was a shrewd and tireless worker, and labour—by now semi-slave—was as plentiful and as cheap as in any industrialist's fondest dream. During the first year the labour force expanded to 300, including 150 Jews. By the end of 1942, the factory had grown to 45,000 square metres and employed almost 800 men and women. The Jewish workers, of whom there were now 370, all came from the Cracow ghetto the Germans had created. "It had become a tremendous advantage," says Stern, "to be able to leave the ghetto in the daytime and work in a German factory."

Relations between Schindler and the Jewish workers began and continued on a circumspect plane. In these early days he had little contact with all save the few who, like Stern, worked in the offices. But comparing their lot with that of the Jews trapped in the ghetto, from which deporta-

tions had by now begun, or even with those who slaved for
other Germans in neighbouring factories, Schindler's Jewish workers grew to appreciate their position. Although they
could not understand the reasons, they recognized that
Herr Direktor was somehow protecting them. An air of
quasi-security grew in the factory and the men soon sought
permission to bring in families and friends to share in their
comparative haven.

Word spread among Cracow's Jews that Schindler's factory was the place to work. And, although the workers did
not know it, Schindler helped his Jewish employees by fal-
sifying the factory records. Old people were recorded as being twenty years younger; children were listed as adults.
Lawyers, doctors, and engineers were registered as metal-
workers, mechanics, and draughtsmen—all trades considered essential to war production. Countless lives were
saved in this manner as the workers were protected from
the extermination commissions that periodically scruti-
nized Schindler's records.

At the same time, most of the workers did not know that
Schindler spent his evenings entertaining many of the local
SS and Wehrmacht [war administration] officers, cultivating
influential friends and strengthening his position wherever
possible. His easy charm passed as candour, and his personality and seeming political reliability made him popular
in Nazi social circles in Cracow.

Stern remained unimpressed by the air of security. They
were all perched on a volcano's edge, he knew. From behind
his high book-keeper's table he could see through the glass
door of Schindler's private office. "Almost every day, from
morning until evening, officials and other visitors came to
the factory and made me nervous. Schindler used to keep
pouring them vodka and joking with them. When they left
he would ask me in, close the door, and then quietly tell me
whatever they had come for. He used to tell them that he
knew how to get work out of these Jews and that he wanted
more brought in. That was how we managed to get in the
families and relatives all the time and save them from deportation." Schindler never offered explanations and never
revealed himself as a die-hard antifascist, but gradually
Stern began to trust him.

Schindler maintained personal links to "his Jews," each of
whom worked in the factory's office. One was Itzhak Stern's

brother, Dr. Nathan Stern, a man who is a respected member of Poland's small Jewish community. Magister Label Salpeter and Samuel Wulkan, both old ranking members of the Polish Zionist movement, were the other two. Together with Stern, they were part of a group that served as a link with the outside underground movement. And in this work they were soon joined by a man named Hildegeist, the former leader of the Socialist Workers' Union in his native Austria, who, after three years in Buchenwald, had been taken on in the factory as an accountant. A factory worker, the engineer Pawlik, subsequently to reveal himself as an officer in the Polish underground, led these activities.

Schindler himself played no active role in all this, but his protection served to shelter the group. It is doubtful that these few men did effective resistance work, but the group did provide the *Schindlerjuden* with their first cohesiveness and a semblance of discipline that later was to prove useful.

PLASZOW CONCENTRATION CAMP

While friends and parents in the ghetto were being murdered in the streets or were dying of disease or were being sent to nearby Auschwitz, daily life in the factory continued in this minor key until 1943. Then, on March 13, came the orders to those in the Cracow ghetto. All Jews were moved to the forced-labour camp of Plaszow, outside the city. Here, in a sprawling series of installations that included subordinate camps throughout the region, conditions even for the graduates of the terrible Cracow ghetto were shocking. The prisoners suffered and by the hundreds either died in camp or were moved to Auschwitz. The order to complete the extermination of Jewry had already been given and willing hands on all sides cooperated to carry out the command as efficiently and quickly as possible.

Stern along with Schindler's other workers had also been moved to Plaszow from the ghetto but, like some 25,000 other inmates who inhabited the camp and worked outside, they continued spending their days in the factory. Falling deathly ill one day, Stern sent word to Schindler urgently pleading for help. Schindler came at once, bringing essential medicine, and continued his visits until Stern recovered. But what he had seen in Plaszow had chilled him.

Nor did he like the turn things had taken in his factory.

Increasingly helpless before the frenetic Jew-haters and

Jew-destroyers, Schindler found that he could no longer joke easily with the German officials who came on inspections. The double game was becoming more difficult. Incidents happened more and more often. On one occasion, three SS men walked onto the factory floor without warning, arguing among themselves. "I tell you, the Jew is even *lower* than an animal," one was saying. Then, taking out his pistol, he ordered the nearest Jewish worker to leave his machine and pick up some sweepings from the floor. "Eat it," he barked, waving his gun. The shivering man choked down the mess. "You see what I mean," The SS man explained to his friends as they walked away. "They eat anything at all. Even an animal would never do that."

Another time, during an inspection by an official SS commission, the attention of the visitors was caught by the sight of the old Jew, Lamus, who was dragging himself across the factory courtyard in an utterly depressed state. The head of the commission asked why the man was so sad, and it was explained to him that Lamus had lost his wife and only child a few weeks earlier during the evacuation of the ghetto. Deeply touched, the commander reacted by ordering his adjutant to shoot the Jew "so that he might be reunited with his family in heaven," then he guffawed and the commission moved on. Schindler was left standing with Lamus and the adjutant.

"Slip your pants down to your ankles and start walking," the adjutant ordered Lamus. Dazed, the man did as he was told.

"You are interfering with all my discipline here," Schindler said desperately. The SS officer sneered.

"The morale of my workers will suffer. Production for *der Vaterland* [the Fatherland] will be affected." Schindler blurted out the words. The officer took out his gun.

"A bottle of *schnapps* if you don't shoot him," Schindler almost screamed, no longer thinking rationally.

"*Stimmt!*" To his astonishment, the man complied. Grinning, the officer put the gun away and strolled arm in arm with the shaken Schindler to the office to collect his bottle. And Lamus, trailing his pants along the ground, continued shuffling across the yard, waiting sickeningly for the bullet in his back that never came.

The increasing frequency of such incidents in the factory and the evil his eyes had seen at the Plaszow camp probably were responsible for moving Schindler into a more active antifascist role. In the spring of 1943, he stopped worrying about the production of enamelware appliances for Wehrmacht barracks and began the conspiring, the string-pulling, the bribery, and the shrewd outguessing of Nazi officialdom that finally were to save so many lives. It is at this point that the real legend begins. For the next two years, Oskar Schindler's ever-present obsession was how to save the greatest number of Jews from the Auschwitz gas chamber only sixty kilometres from Cracow.

A DOZEN DARING SCHEMES

His first ambitious move was to attempt to help the starving, fearful prisoners at Plaszow. Other labour camps in Poland, such as Treblinka and Majdanek, had already been shut down and their inhabitants liquidated. Plaszow seemed doomed. At the prompting of Stern and the others in the "inner-office" circle, Schindler one evening managed to convince one of his drinking companions, General Schindler—no relative, but well placed as the chief of the war-equipment command in Poland—that Plaszow's camp workshops would be ideally suited for serious war production. At that time they were being used only for the repair of uniforms. The general fell in with the idea and orders for wood and metal were given to the camp. As a result, Plaszow was officially transformed into a war-essential concentration camp. And though conditions hardly improved, it came off the list of labour camps that were then being done away with. Temporarily at least, Auschwitz's fires were cheated of more fuel.

The move also put Schindler in well with Plaszow's commander, the Hauptsturmfuhrer Amon Goeth, who, with the change, now found his status elevated to a new dignity. When Schindler requested that those Jews who continued to work in his factory be moved into their own sub-camp near the plant "to save time in getting to the job," Goeth complied. From then on, Schindler found that he could have food and medicine smuggled into the barracks with little danger. The guards, of course, were bribed, and Goeth never was to discover the true motives in Schindler's request.

Schindler began to take bigger risks. Interceding for Jews who were denounced for one "crime" or another was a dangerous habit in fascist eyes, but Schindler now started to do this almost regularly. "Stop killing my good workers," was his usual technique. "We've got a war to win. These things can always be settled later." The ruse succeeded often enough to save dozens of lives.

One August morning in 1943, Schindler played host to two surprise visitors who had been sent to him by the underground organization that the American Jewish welfare agency, the Joint Distribution Committee, then operated in occupied Europe. Satisfied that the men indeed had been sent by Dr. Rudolph Kastner, head of the secret JDC apparatus, who was at the time leading a shadowy existence in Budapest with a sizable price on his head, Schindler called for Stern. "Speak frankly to these men, Stern," he said. "Let them know what has been going on in Plaszow."

"We want a full report on the anti-Semitic persecutions," the visitors told Stern. "Write us a comprehensive report."

"Go ahead," urged Schindler. "They are Swiss. It is safe. You can rely on them. Sit down and write."

To Stern the risk was purposeless and foolhardy, and he flared up. Turning angrily to Schindler, he asked, "Schindler, tell me frankly, isn't this a provocation? It is most suspicious."

Schindler in turn became angry at Stern's sudden mistrust. "Write!" he ordered. Stern had little choice. He wrote everything he could think of, mentioned names of those living and those dead, and penned the long letter that, years later, he discovered had been circulated widely and helped to settle uncertainties in the hearts of the prisoners' relatives scattered around the world outside Europe. And when the underground subsequently brought him answering letters from America and Palestine, any doubts he still might have had of the integrity or judgment of Oskar Schindler vanished.

Life in the Schindler factory went on. Some of the less hardy men and women died, but the majority continued doggedly at their machines, turning out enamelware for the German army. Schindler and his "inner-office" circle had become taut and apprehensive, wondering just how long they could continue their game of deception. Schindler himself still entertained the local officers but, with the change of tide that followed Stalingrad and the invasion of Italy, tempers were often out of control. A stroke of a pen could send the Jewish workers to Auschwitz and Schindler along with them. The group moved cautiously, increased the bribes to the guards at the camp and the factory, and, with Schindler's smuggled food and medicines, fought for survival. The year 1943 became 1944. Daily, life ended for thousands of Polish

Jews. But the *Schindlerjuden*, to their own surprise, found themselves still alive.

THE MOVE TO BRINNLITZ

By the spring of 1944, the German retreat on the Eastern Front was on in earnest. Plaszow and all its sub-camps were ordered emptied. Schindler and his workers had no illusions about what a move to another concentration camp implied. The time had come for Oskar Schindler to play his trump card, a daring gamble that he had devised beforehand.

He went to work on all his drinking companions, on his connections in military and industrial circles in Cracow and in Warsaw. He bribed, cajoled, pleaded, working desperately against time and fighting what everyone assured him was a lost cause. He got on a train and saw people in Berlin. And he persisted until someone, somewhere in the hierarchy, perhaps impatient to end the seemingly trifling business, finally gave him the authorization to move a force of 700 men and 300 women from the Plaszow camp into a factory at Brnenec [Brinnlitz] in his native Sudetenland. Most of the other 25,000 men, women, and children at Plaszow were sent to Auschwitz, there to find the same end that several million other Jews had already discovered. But out of the vast calamity, and through the stubborn efforts of one man, a thousand Jews were saved temporarily. One thousand half-starved, sick, and almost broken human beings had had a death sentence commuted by a miraculous reprieve.

The move from the Polish factory to the new quarters in Czechoslovakia, it turned out, was not uneventful. One lot of a hundred did go out directly in July, 1944, and arrived at Brnenec safely. Others, however, found their train diverted without warning to the concentration camp of Gross-Rosen, where many were beaten and tortured and where all were forced to stand in even files in the great courtyard, doing absolutely nothing but putting on and taking off their caps in unison all day long. At length Schindler once more proved successful at pulling strings. By early November all of the *Schindlerjuden* were again united in their new camp.

And until liberation in the spring of 1945 they continued to outwit the Nazis at the dangerous game of remaining alive. Ostensibly the new factory was producing parts for V2 bombs, but, actually, the output during those ten months between July [1944] and May [1945] was absolutely nil.

Jews escaping from the transports then evacuating Auschwitz and the other easternmost camps ahead of the oncoming Russians found haven with no questions asked. Schindler even brazenly requested the Gestapo to send him all intercepted Jewish fugitives: "in the interest" he said, "of continued war production." A hundred additional people were saved in this way, including Jews from Belgium, Holland, and Hungary. "His children" reached the number of 1,098: 801 men and 297 women.

The *Schindlerjuden* by now depended on him completely and were fearful in his absence. His compassion and sacrifice were unstinting. He spent every bit of money still left in his possession, and traded his wife's jewellery as well, for food, clothing, and medicine and for *schnapps* with which to bribe the many SS investigators. He furnished a secret hospital with stolen and black-market medical equipment, fought epidemics, and once made a 300-mile trip himself carrying two enormous flasks filled with Polish vodka and bringing them back full of desperately needed medicine. His wife, Emilie, cooked and cared for the sick and earned her own reputation and praise.

In the factory some of the men began turning out false rubber stamps, military travel documents, and the special official papers needed to protect the delivery of food bought illicitly. Nazi uniforms and guns were collected and hidden, along with ammunition and hand grenades, as all eventualities were prepared for. The risks mounted and the tension grew.

Schindler, however, seems to have maintained an equilibrium throughout this period that was virtually unshakable. "Perhaps I had become fatalistic," he says now. "Or perhaps I was just afraid of the danger that would come once the men began to lose hope and acted rashly. I had to keep them full of optimism."

But two real frights did disturb his normal calm during the constant perils of these months. The first was when a group of workers, lost for some means of expressing their pent-up gratitude, foolishly told him that they had heard the illegal radio broadcast a promise to name a street in postwar Palestine "Oskar Schindler Strasse." For days he waited for the Gestapo to come around. When the hoax was finally admitted he could no longer laugh.

The other occurred during a visit from the local SS commandant. As was customary, the SS officer sat around

Schindler's office drinking glass after glass of vodka and getting drunk rapidly. When he lurched perilously near an iron
staircase leading to the basement, Schindler, suddenly yield-
ing to temptation, made one of his rare unpremeditated acts.
A slight push, a howl, and a dull thud from the bottom. But
the man was not dead. Climbing back into the room with
blood pouring from his scalp, he bellowed that Schindler
had shot him. Cursing with rage, he flung over his shoulder
as he ran out: "You will not live until any liberation,
Schindler. Don't think you fool us. You belong in a concentration camp yourself, along with all your Jews!"

THE END OF THE WAR

Schindler understood "his children" and catered to their
fears. Near the factory he had been given a beautifully furnished villa that overlooked the length of the valley where
the small Czech village lay. But since the workers always
dreaded the SS visits that might come late at night and spell
their end, Oskar and Emilie Schindler never spent a single
night at the villa, sleeping instead in a small room in the
factory itself.

When the Jewish workers died they were secretly buried
with full rites despite Nazi rulings that their corpses be
burned. Religious holidays were observed clandestinely and
celebrated with extra rations of black-market food.

Perhaps the most absorbing of all the legends that
Schindlerjuden on four continents repeat is one that graphi-
cally illustrates Schindler's self-adopted role of protector
and saviour in the midst of general and amoral indifference.
Just about the time the Nazi empire was crashing down, a
phone call from the railway station late one evening asked
Schindler whether he cared to accept delivery of two railway
cars full of near-frozen Jews. The cars had been frozen shut
at a temperature of 5[degrees]F and contained almost a hundred sick men who had been locked inside for ten days, ever
since the train had been sent off from Auschwitz ten days
earlier with orders to deliver the human cargo to some willing factory. But, when informed of the condition of the prisoners, no factory manager would hear of receiving them.
"We are not running a sanatorium!" was the usual word.
Schindler, sickened by the news, ordered the train sent to his
factory siding at once.

The train was awesome to behold. Ice had formed on the

locks and the cars had to be opened with axes and acetylene torches. Inside, the miserable relics of human beings were stretched out, frozen stiff. Each had to be carried out like a carcass of frozen beef. Thirteen were unmistakably dead, but the others still breathed.

Throughout that night and for many days and nights following, Oskar and Emilie Schindler and a number of the men worked without halt on the frozen and starved skeletons. One large room in the factory was emptied for the purpose. Three more men died, but with the care, the warmth, the milk, and the medicine, the others gradually rallied. All this had been achieved surreptitiously, with the factory guards, as usual, receiving their bribes so as not to inform the SS commandant. The men's convalescence also had to be effected secretly lest they be shot as useless invalids. Later they became part of the factory labour force and joined the others in the motions of feigning war production.

Such was life at Brnenec until the arrival of the victorious Russians on May 9 put an end to the constant nightmare. The day before, Schindler had decided that they would have to get rid of the local SS commander just in case he suddenly remembered his drunken threat and got any desperate last-minute ideas. The task was not difficult, for the guards had already begun pouring out of town in panic. Unearthing their hidden weapons, a group slipped out of the factory late at night, found the SS officer drinking himself into oblivion in his room, and shot him from outside his window. In the early morning, once certain that his workers finally were out of danger and that all was in order to explain to the Russians, Schindler, Emilie, and several of his closest friends among the Jewish workers discreetly disappeared and were not heard from until they turned up, months later, deep in Austria's U.S. Zone. For the Nazis, he had known all the answers. But at the end he had decided that, as an owner of a German slave-labour factory, he would take no chances on Russian troops casually shooting him before asking for character references or his particular views on the fascist system.

The List

Thomas Keneally

Thomas Keneally is an Australian novelist whose
works often have historical themes. The following selection is taken from Keneally's best-known book,
Schindler's List, which was the basis for the 1993
movie of the same title directed by Steven Spielberg.
Keneally's book is classified as fiction, but it is based
on extensive research, including interviews with
many of the surviving *Schindlerjuden*. It is therefore
considered by historians to be an accurate account of
the events in question. This brief selection concerns
the compiling of the list itself, an event of monumen-
tal importance to the people whose names appeared
on the list, and, by most accounts, a turning point in
Schindler's efforts to protect his "children."

A VISION OF SAFETY

At some point in any discussion of Schindler, the surviving
friends of the *Herr Direktor* will blink and shake their heads
and begin the almost mathematical business of finding the
sum of his motives. For one of the commonest sentiments of
Schindler Jews is still "I don't know why he did it." It can be
said to begin with that Oskar was a gambler, was a senti-
mentalist who loved the transparency, the simplicity of doing good; that Oskar was by temperament an anarchist who
loved to ridicule the system; and that beneath the hearty
sensuality lay a capacity to be outraged by human savagery,
to react to it and not to be overwhelmed. But none of this, jot-
ted down, added up, explains the doggedness with which, in
the autumn of 1944, he prepared a final haven for the graduates of Emalia.

And not only for them. In early September he drove to
Podgórze and visited [industrialist Julius] Madritsch, who at
that point employed more than 3,000 prisoners in his uniform factory. This plant would now be disbanded. Madritsch

would get his sewing machines back, and his workers would vanish. If we made a combined approach, said Oskar, we could get more than four thousand out. Mine and yours as well. We could relocate them in something like safety. Down in Moravia.

Madritsch would always and justly be revered by his surviving prisoners. The bread and chickens smuggled into his factory were paid for from his pocket and at continuous risk. He would have been considered a more stable man than Oskar. Not as flamboyant, and not as subject to obsession. He had not suffered arrest. But he had been much more humane than was safe and, without wit and energy, would have ended in Auschwitz.

Now Oskar presented to him a vision of a Madritsch-Schindler camp somewhere in the High Jeseniks; some smoky, safe little industrial hamlet.

Madritsch was attracted by the idea but did not rush to say yes. He could tell that though the war was lost, the SS system had become more instead of less implacable. He was correct in believing that, unhappily, the prisoners of Plaszow would—in coming months—be consumed in death camps to the west. For if Oskar was stubborn and possessed, so were the SS Main Office and their prize field operatives, the commandants of the Concentration Camps.

He did not say no, however. He needed time to think about it. Though he couldn't say it to Oskar, it is likely he was afraid of sharing factory premises with a rash, demonic fellow like Herr Schindler.

IT WILL TAKE SOME MONEY

Without any clear word from Madritsch, Oskar took to the road. He went to Berlin and bought dinner for Colonel Erich Lange. I can go completely over to the manufacture of shells, Oskar told Lange. I can transfer my heavy machinery.

Lange was crucial. He could guarantee contracts; he could write the hearty recommendations Oskar needed for the Evacuation Board and the German officials in Moravia.

Later, Oskar would say of this shadowy staff officer that he had given consistent help. Lange was still in that state of exalted desperation and moral disgust characteristic of many who had worked inside the system but not always for it. We can do it, said Lange, but it will take some money. Not for me. For others.

Through Lange, Oskar talked with an officer of the Evacuation Board at OKH on Bendler Street. It was likely, said
this officer, that the evacuation would be approved in principle. But there was a major obstacle. The Governor *cum*
Gauleiter of Moravia, ruling from a castle at Liberec, had followed a policy of keeping Jewish labor camps *out* of his
province. Neither the SS nor the Armaments Inspectorate
had so far persuaded him to change his attitude. A good man
to discuss this impasse with, said the officer, would be a
middle-aged *Wehrmacht* engineer down in the Troppau office of the Armaments Inspectorate, a man named Sussmuth. Oskar could talk to Sussmuth too about what relocation sites were available in Moravia. Meanwhile, Herr
Schindler could count on the support of the Main Evacuation Board. "But you can understand that in view of the pressure they are under, and the inroads the war has made on
their personal comforts, they are more likely to give a quick
answer if you could be considerate to them in some way. We
poor city fellows are short of ham, cigars, liquor, cloth, coffee . . . that sort of thing."

The officer seemed to think that Oskar carried around
with him half the peacetime produce of Poland. Instead, to
get together a gift parcel for the gentlemen of the board, Oskar had to buy luxuries at the Berlin black-market rate. An
old gentleman on the desk at the Hotel Adlon was able to acquire excellent schnapps for Herr Schindler for a discount
price of about 80 RM. [reichsmarks, the currency issued by
Nazi Germany] a bottle. And you couldn't send the gentlemen of the board less than a dozen. Coffee, however, was
like gold, and Havanas were at an insane price. Oskar
bought them in quantity and included them in the hamper.
The gentlemen might need a head of steam if they were to
bring the Governor of Moravia around. . . .

Sussmuth told Oskar that he had already proposed that
some small Jewish work camps be set up in the border
towns of Moravia to turn out goods for the Armaments Inspectorate. Such camps would, of course, be under the central control of either Auschwitz or Gröss-Rosen, for the areas
of influence of the big concentration camps crossed the
Polish-Czechoslovak border. But there was more safety for
prisoners in little work camps than could be found in the
grand necropolis of Auschwitz itself. Sussmuth had got
nowhere, of course. The Castle at Liberec had trampled on

the proposal. He had never had a lever. Oskar—the support Oskar had from Colonel Lange and the gentlemen of the Evacuation Board—*that* could be the lever.

THE FACTORY IN BRINNLITZ

Sussmuth had in his office a list of sites suitable to receive plants evacuated from the war zone. Near Oskar's home-town of Zwittau, on the edge of a village called Brinnlitz, was a great textile plant owned by the Viennese brothers Hoffman. They'd been in butter and cheese in their home city, but had come to the *Sudetenland* behind the legions (just as Oskar had gone to Cracow) and become textile magnates. An entire annex of their plant lay idle, used as a storehouse for obsolete spinning machines. A site like that was served from the rail depot at Zwittau, where Schindler's brother-in-law was in charge of the freight yard. And a railway loop ran close to the gates. The brothers are profiteers, said Sussmuth, smiling. They have some local party backing—the County Council and the District Leader are in their pockets. But you have Colonel Lange behind you. I will write to Berlin at once, Sussmuth promised, and recommend the use of the Hoffman annex.

Oskar knew the Germanic village of Brinnlitz from his childhood. Its racial character was in its name, since the Czechs would have called it Brnenec, just as a Czech Zwittau would have become Zvitava. The Brinnlitz citizens would not fancy a thousand or more Jews in their neighborhood. The Zwittau people, from whom some of Hoffman's workers were recruited, would not like it either, this contamination, so late in the war, of their rustic-industrial backwater.

In any case, Oskar drove down to take a quick look at the site. He did not approach Hoffman Brothers' front office, since that would give the tougher Hoffman brother, the one who chaired the company, too much warning. But he was able to wander into the annex without being challenged. It was an old-fashioned two-story industrial barracks built around a courtyard. The ground floor was high-ceilinged and full of old machines and crates of wool. The upper floor must have been intended as offices and for lighter equipment. Its floor would not stand the weight of the big pressing machines. Downstairs would do for the new workshops of DEF, as offices and, in one corner, the *Herr Direktor's* apartment. Upstairs would be barracks for the prisoners.

He was delighted with the place. He drove back to Cracow yearning to get started, to spend the necessary money, to talk to Madritsch again. For Sussmuth could find a site for Madritsch too—perhaps even floor space in Brinnlitz. . . .

A week after Oskar spoke to Sussmuth, the gentlemen of the Berlin Armaments Board instructed the Governor of Moravia that Oskar's armaments company was to be allocated the annex of Hoffman's spinning mill in Brinnlitz. The Governor's bureaucrats could do nothing more, Sussmuth told Oskar by telephone, than slow the paperwork down. But Hoffman and other Party men in the Zwittau area were already conferring and passing resolutions against Oskar's intrusion into Moravia. The Party *Kreisleiter* [a county-level leader] in Zwittau wrote to Berlin complaining that Jewish prisoners from Poland would be a peril to the health of Moravian Germans. Spotted fever would very likely appear in the region for the first time in modern history, and Oskar's small armaments factory, of dubious value to the war effort, would also attract Allied bombers, with resultant damage to the important Hoffman mills. The population of Jewish criminals in the proposed Schindler camp would outweigh the small and decent population of Brinnlitz and be a cancer on the honest flank of Zwittau.

A protest of that kind didn't have a chance, since it went straight to the office of Erich Lange in Berlin. Appeals to Troppau were quashed by honest Sussmuth. Nonetheless, the posters went up on walls in Oskar's hometown: "KEEP THE JEWISH CRIMINALS OUT."

And Oskar was paying. He was paying the Evacuation Committee in Cracow to help speed up the permits for the transfer of his machinery. The Department of the Economy in Cracow had to be encouraged to provide the clearances of bank holdings. Currency wasn't favored these days, so he paid in goods—in kilos of tea, in pairs of leather shoes, in carpets, in coffee, in canned fish. He spent his afternoons in the little streets off the market square of Cracow haggling at staggering prices for whatever the bureaucrats desired. Otherwise, he was sure, they would keep him waiting till his last Jew had gone to Auschwitz.

It was Sussmuth who told him that people from Zwittau were writing to the Armaments Inspectorate accusing Oskar of blackmarketeering. If they're writing to me, said Sussmuth, you can bet the same letters are going to the police chief of

Moravia, *Obersturmführer* [first lieutenant] Otto Rasch. You should introduce yourself to Rasch and show him what a charming fellow you are.

Oskar had known Rasch when he was SS police chief of Katowice. Rasch was, by happy chance, a friend of the chairman of Ferrum AG at Sosnowiec, from which Oskar had bought his steel. But in rushing down to Brno to head off informers, Oskar didn't rely on anything as flimsy as mutual friendships. He took a diamond cut in the *brilliant* style which, somehow, he introduced into the meeting. When it crossed the table and ended on Rasch's side of the desk, it secured Oskar's Brno front.

Oskar later estimated that he spent 100,000 RM.—nearly $40,000—to grease the transfer to Brinnlitz. Few of his survivors would ever find the figure unlikely, though there were those who shook their heads and said, "No, *more!* It would have to have been more than that."

COMPILING THE LIST

He had drawn up what he called a preparatory list and delivered it to the Administration Building. There were more than a thousand names on it—the names of all the prisoners of the backyard prison camp of Emalia, as well as new names. Helen Hirsch's name was freshly on the list, and Amon was not there to argue about it.

And the list would expand if Madritsch agreed to go to Moravia with Oskar. So Oskar kept working on Titsch, his ally at Julius Madritsch's ear. Those Madritsch prisoners who were closest to Titsch knew the list was under compilation, that they could have access to it. Titsch told them without any ambiguity: You must get on it. In all the reams of Plaszow paperwork, Oskar's dozen pages of names were the only pages with access to the future.

But Madritsch still could not decide whether he wanted an alliance with Oskar, whether he would add his 3,000 to the total.

There is again a haziness suitable to a legend about the precise chronology of Oskar's list. The haziness doesn't attach to the existence of the list—a copy can be seen today in the archives of the *Yad Vashem*. There is no uncertainty as we shall see about the names remembered by Oskar and Titsch at the last minute and attached to the end of the official paper. The names on the list are definite. But the circumstances encourage legends. The problem is that the list is remembered with an intensity which, by its very heat, blurs. The list is an absolute good. The list is life. All around its cramped margins lies the gulf.

Some of those whose names appeared on the list say that there was a party at Goeth's villa, a reunion of SS men and entrepreneurs to celebrate the times they'd had there. Some even believe that Goeth was there, but since the SS did not release on bail, that is impossible [Amon Goeth had been arrested on charges of black marketeering]. Others believe that the party was held at Oskar's own apartment above his factory. Oskar had for more than two years given excellent parties there. One Emalia prisoner remembers the early hours

THE HAND OF FATE

Schindler's story is known to millions because of the film by Steven Spielberg. Spielberg based his movie on the book by Thomas Keneally. Keneally heard the story from Leopold (Poldek) Pfefferberg, who changed his name to Leopold Page after immigrating to the United States.

Page believes that some power might have sent him Thomas Keneally. The Australian was on his way home from Italy and awaiting a connecting flight in Los Angeles when his briefcase came unhinged. He walked into Page's shop to buy a new one. It was a Saturday, and it took a while to process the foreigner's credit card.

Leather goods have been Page's livelihood since he came to the United States. He settled first in New York, where he got a job repairing handbags, then moved to Los Angeles and opened his own store.

Over the years, as he worked to make his business a success, Page has been driven to spread the story of the man he says gave him this new life in a new land.

The two men talked, and Page learned his customer was an author. And so he told Keneally the story of Oskar Schindler, as he had laid it out for countless other writers.

"I approached anybody with a pen in their hand," Page says. But no one would write the book.

Keneally also had reservations, but Page convinced him to postpone his flight and spend the weekend in Los Angeles. By Monday morning, Keneally agreed to write the book.

Clark Brooks, "The Hand of Fate: He Was Saved from Hell to Tell the World About Unsung Hero," *San Diego Union-Tribune*, August 16, 1994.

of 1944 when he was on night watch duty and Oskar had wandered down from his apartment at one o'clock, escaping the noise upstairs and bringing with him two cakes, two hundred cigarettes, and a bottle for his friend the watchman.

At the Plaszow graduation party, wherever it took place, the guests included Dr. Blancke, Franz Bosch, and, by some reports, *Oberführer* Julian Scherner, on vacation from his partisan-hunting. Madritsch was there too, and Titsch. Titsch would later say that at it Madritsch informed Oskar for the first time that he would not be going to Moravia with him. "I've done everything I can for the Jews," Madritsch told him. It was a reasonable claim; he would not be persuaded although he said Titsch had been at him for days.

Madritsch was a just man. Later he would be honored as such. He simply did not believe that Moravia would work. If he had, the indications are that he would have attempted it.

What else is known about the party is that an urgency operated there, because the Schindler list had to be handed in that evening. This is an element in all the versions of the story survivors tell. The survivors could tell and expand upon it only if they had heard it in the first place from Oskar, a man with a taste for embellishing a story. But in the early 1960s, Titsch himself attested to the substantial truth of this one. Perhaps the new and temporary Commandant of Plaszow, a *Hauptsturmführer* [captain] Büscher, had said to Oskar, "Enough fooling around, Oskar! We have to finalize the paperwork and the transportation." Perhaps there was some other form of deadline imposed by the *Ostbahn* [railroad], by the availability of transport.

At the end of Oskar's list, therefore, Titsch now typed in, above the official signatures, the names of Madritsch prisoners. Almost seventy names were added, written in by Titsch from his own and Oskar's memories. Among them were those of the Feigenbaum family—the adolescent daughter who suffered from incurable bone cancer, the teen-age son Lutek with his shaky expertise in repairing sewing machines. Now they were all transformed, as Titsch scribbled, into skilled munitions workers. There was singing in the apartment, loud talk and laughter, a fog of cigarette smoke, and, in a corner, Oskar and Titsch quizzing each other over people's names, straining for a clue to the spelling of Polish patronyms.

In the end, Oskar had to put his hand on Titsch's wrist.

We're over the limit, he said. They'll balk at the number we already have. Titsch continued to strain for names, and to-morrow morning would wake damning himself because one had come to him too late. But now he was at the limit, wrung out by this work. It was blasphemously close to cre-ating people anew just by thinking of them. He did not be-grudge doing it. It was what it said of the world—that was what made the heavy air of Schindler's apartment so hard for Titsch to breathe.

The list was vulnerable, however, through the personnel clerk, Marcel Goldberg. Büscher, the new Commandant, who was there merely to wind the camp down, himself could not have cared, within certain numerical limits, who went on the list. Therefore Goldberg had the power to tinker with its edges. It was known to prisoners already that Goldberg would take bribes. The Dresners knew it. Juda Dresner—uncle of red Genia, husband of the Mrs. Dresner who'd once been refused a hiding place in a wall, and father of Janek and of young Danka—Juda Dresner knew it. "He paid Gold-berg," the family would simply say to explain how they got on the Schindler list. They never knew what was given. Wulkan the jeweler presumably got himself, his wife, his son on the list in the same way.

Poldek Pfefferberg was told about the list by an SS non-commissioned officer named Hans Schreiber. Schreiber, a young man in his mid-twenties, had as evil a name as any other SS man in Plaszow, but Pfefferberg had become some-thing of a mild favorite of his in that way that was common to relationships—throughout the system—between individ-ual prisoners and SS personnel. It had begun one day when Pfefferberg, as a group leader in his barracks, had had re-sponsibility for window cleaning. Schreiber inspected the glass and found a smudge, and began browbeating Poldek in the style that was often a prelude to execution. Pfefferberg lost his temper and told Schreiber that both of them knew the windows were perfectly polished and if Schreiber wanted a reason to shoot him, he ought to do it without any more delay. The outburst had, in a contradictory way, amused Schreiber, who afterward occasionally used to stop Pfefferberg and ask him how he and his wife were, and sometimes even gave Poldek an apple for Mila. In the sum-mer of 1944, Poldek had appealed to him desperately to ex-tricate Mila from a trainload of women being sent from Plaszow to the evil camp at Stutthof on the Baltic. Mila was already in the lines boarding the cattle cars when Schreiber came waving a piece of paper and calling her name. Another time, a Sunday, he turned up drunk at Pfefferberg's barracks and, in front of Poldek and a few other prisoners, began to weep for what he called "the dreadful things" he had done in Plaszow. He intended, he said, to expiate them on the Eastern Front. In the end, he would.

Now he told Poldek that Schindler had a list and that Poldek should do everything he could to get on it. Poldek went down to the Administration Building to beg Goldberg to add his name and Mila's to the list. Schindler had in the past year and a half often visited Poldek in the camp garage and had always promised rescue. Poldek had, however, become such an accomplished welder that the garage supervisors, who needed for their lives' sake to produce high-standard work, would never let him go. Now Goldberg sat with his hand on the list—he had already added his own name to it—and this old friend of Oskar's, once a frequent guest in the apartment in Straszewskiego, expected to have himself written down for sentiment's sake. "Do you have any diamonds?" Goldberg asked Pfefferberg.

"Are you serious?" asked Poldek.

"For this list," said Goldberg, a man of prodigious and accidental power, "it takes diamonds."

A Phoenix from the Ashes

Emilie Schindler

Emilie Schindler, like her husband, was committed to the rescue of as many Jews from the Nazis as possible. After Oskar moved his factory to Brinnlitz in 1944, Emilie joined him and took a hand in running the factory. She oversaw preparation of meals for the workers. Finding food for the thousand-plus residents of the factory was no easy job, and this was Emilie's responsibility. Some food was supplied by the German authorities, but Emilie had to beg flour from a nearby mill to supplement this inadequate source.

This passage tells the story of the final years of the Holocaust, from Emilie's point of view. She is vague, and even mistaken about events that she reports secondhand, but her firsthand memories are vivid and contain details not known to others.

The situation had deteriorated to such an extent that Oskar was compelled to give out ever-more-costly presents, as well as large sums of money, in order to be able to keep his Jewish workers. These "gifts" consisted of diamonds, caviar, cigarettes, cognac, and other treasures that could be obtained only on the black market at great expense.

One evening Oskar came home to our apartment in Cracow in a very depressed state of mind. With almost no word of greeting, he went straight for the cabinet in which we kept his cognac, now his constant companion.

He poured himself a goodly quantity and, without taking off his overcoat, emptied the glass in one shot, as if wanting quickly to drown a great sorrow. Being so familiar with Oskar's ways, I left him alone for a while and a little later asked him whether he was going to have any dinner. I had prepared his favorite dish, I said, cabbage and chives sautéed in butter—with the little bit of meat allowed in 1944 rations,

Excerpted from *Where Light and Shadow Meet: A Memoir* by Emilie Schindler with Erika Rosenberg, translated by Dolores M. Koch. Copyright © 1996 by Emilie Schindler and Erika Rosenberg. Copyright © 1996 by Editorial Planeta Argentina. Copyright © 1996 by Grupo Editorial Planeta. English translation copyright © 1997 by Dolores M. Koch. Used by permission of W.W. Norton & Company, Inc.

one hundred grams [about three ounces] a day, if you were lucky. Since I never cared that much about food, I mostly left my share to him. But of course, two hundred grams of meat are greatly reduced after cooking. These portions never entirely satisfied Oskar, who was a good eater.

With an almost imperceptible gesture, he agreed to come to the table with me.

We sat down, and I served the wine and the water in a state of nervous expectation while we waited for the cook to bring the food to the table. I asked myself whether I should wait until after dinner to try to find out what was wrong. Perhaps the best thing to do, I thought, was just to bide my time, but then Oskar would most likely get up and leave the table without a word. So I took my chances.

"What is the matter, Oskar? Are we in serious trouble? What's going on?"

I assumed that his unusual grief had to do with the course the war was taking. I was not wrong.

"Look, Emilie," he answered sadly, "the situation is becoming more and more unbearable. Goeth has decided to close the Plaschow camp and send all the prisoners, including our workers, to Auschwitz. I've talked to him several times, but I haven't been able to change his mind, no matter how hard I tried. The important thing is finding a way to move our people to some other place in order to go on working. I've been offered a munitions factory in Brünnlitz, which seems to be an ideal place. But I don't know what else to do to persuade him to authorize the transfer. I have offered him diamonds, jewelry, money, vodka, cigarettes, caviar. . . . I just can't think of anything else. Maybe I'll get him a couple of beautiful women to cheer him up, since the relationship with his latest mistress doesn't seem to be working. She is a good woman, but she keeps trying to get him off his bouts of sadism, and Goeth is getting tired of her. . . . Perhaps this will work. Another problem that worries me is the list of people we are to submit to him. I don't really know the men, their families; I barely know the names of a few who come to our office when something is needed. But I have no idea about the others. . . . I've spoken to the people who sold me the factory. One of the Jews will arrange to draw up a list of the workers we shall take to Brünnlitz. All this really worries and depresses me. I'm not used to not being in charge of things."

SCHINDLER'S LIST

I listened in silence to his long and painful monologue, and for the first time he seemed to me really worried. I felt that I should help him, but did not know how, as I seldom visited the Cracow factory. Still, by the end of our conversation he seemed more relaxed, relieved. He had found someone with whom to share his worries. Even if his behavior as a husband left much to be desired, I was still his wife.

This was how the list came about. I never knew the exact name of the person who drew it up, but I think it was Goldman [she means Marcel Goldberg]. A certain Dr. Schwarz from Cracow told me that he had visited this man and paid him a huge sum of money to put his wife's name on the list. When the move took place and the factory was transferred to Czechoslovakia, however, she was sent to another concentration camp, where she could have died. As fate would have it, they were reunited after the war. His wife had managed to survive almost miraculously.

Dr. Schwarz's statement, as well as stories by some others on the list, mentioning large sums of money invested to save lives, irritated both Oskar and me. My husband had not been aware of all these manipulations and frauds. It is also not true that Oskar tried to take advantage of unpaid Jewish labor. There were other similar cases, like the man who owned an army clothing factory [Julius Madritsch], with three thousand Jewish workers. But one day he fled, abandoning all of his workers. The SS herded them onto an old ship and scuttled it, drowning them all.

While the war took its course and the German army was suffering setbacks at Stalingrad, Jews were being murdered in the gas chambers of extermination camps. Yet there were people who did benefit or profit from this state of affairs.

What is one person to do when every day there are dead bodies lying around everywhere, and even unidentifiable body parts of unknown victims? What should one do in the face of all those deaths, which even today haunt me in my nightmares?

That is why when someone asks me if I am pleased that the lives of so many Jewish people were saved, I answer yes, that it makes me very happy that at least there were some people who did not die in the extermination camps. It is also true, however, that at times it was very difficult to be aware of what was happening around us. Events followed one another so fast that every morning when we woke up, life seemed accidental and miraculous. It is hard to convey that feeling to those who have never experienced war.

The list included the names of the approximately three hundred Jews who worked at the enamelware factory, making cooking pots, plus those of seven hundred and fifty from the Plaschow concentration camp. As far as I could determine, the rest, to make up the thirteen hundred on the list, were those recommended by prominent people, among whom the name Goldman was later often mentioned.

Besides the approval of the list, we had to obtain a permit from the Brünnlitz quartermaster general in order to establish ourselves there. This was no easy matter, because the quartermaster general reflected the feelings of the local population, who under no circumstances wanted any Jews around. Moreover, since a munitions factory was involved, the city could become a target for Allied bombing raids, with inherent dangers to the civilian population. But it was Brünnlitz or Brünnlitz; there was no other alternative. If the permit was not granted, Oskar would be sent to the front and the Jews would be murdered, every one of them. The Plaschow camp was going to be emptied one way or the other.

I then asked Oskar to let me handle the negotiations alone. Very determined, I went to see the quartermaster general. Imagine my surprise when I was confronted by someone whose face looked more and more familiar! Little by little I realized that he was my old swimming teacher. We talked about old times, remembered old stories together, talked about his family and mine, all of which helped me with my request. I asked him for a permit, sealed and signed by him, to set up the munitions factory in Brünnlitz.

I left the quartermaster general's premises, permit in hand.

The workers arrived at Brünnlitz in the spring of 1944, but the train carrying the women did not come. We all feared for their lives, even though my husband had paid Goeth a huge amount of money so that he would let the thirteen hundred people named in the famous list leave without any problems. After a couple of communications with the German command at Cracow, Oskar was able to find out that the transport with the women had been diverted to Auschwitz. Oskar was confused and nervous but, in spite of the difficulty of the situation, he decided not to be cowed and to try to do something, whatever that might be. As ever, I was ready to help him.

Oskar and I were at the office. On the table, the inevitable bottle of cognac. My husband picked up the telephone and called in Schöneborn, head engineer of the factory and part of the civilian personnel. When he came in, Oskar looked sternly into his eyes, took a small bag out of his pocket, the contents of which were very familiar to me, and addressed him in a tone of voice that did not admit any objections:

"I must entrust you with an important mission. Without the women we cannot go on with the factory. We need their labor, and besides, the men are getting very restless asking why their wives have not come yet. They fear something has gone seriously wrong. You are to go to Auschwitz immedi-

---

THE TRAIN FROM GOLESCHAU

Oskar Schindler was not present when the train from the Goleschau forced labor camp arrived at Brinnlitz, and Emilie Schindler remembers having to manage the matter herself. However, this passage suggests that Schindler sent the train to Brinnlitz in the first place.

On January 29 the German Catholic, Oscar Schindler, who had earlier rescued several hundred Jews from Plaszow camp, was told of a locked goods wagon at the station nearest to his armament factory at Brünnlitz. The wagon was marked 'Property of the SS', and had been travelling on the railways for ten days, covered in ice. Inside were more than a hundred Jews, starving and freezing: Jews from Birkenau who had been at the labour camp at Goleschau, Jews who had once lived in Poland, Czechoslovakia, France, Holland and Hungary.

Schindler had no authority to take the wagon. But he asked a railway official to show him the bill of lading, and when the official was momentarily distracted, wrote on it: 'Final destination, Brünnlitz.' Schindler then pointed out to the official that the wagon was intended for his factory. Schindler ordered the railway authorities to transfer the wagon to his factory siding. There he broke open the locks. Sixteen of the Jews had frozen to death. The survivors, not one of whom weighed more than thirty-five kilogrammes, he fed and guarded. Schindler was helped by his wife Emilie, who provided beds on which they could be nursed back to life.

Martin Gilbert, *The Holocaust: A History of the Jews of Europe During the Second World War*. New York: Holt, Rinehart, and Winston, 1985.

ately, speak to whomever you have to, pay whatever the price may be, but I want you to get those women here. I have full confidence in you; I know you are an honorable gentleman who can be trusted and will make good on your word."

"It will be done as you say, *Herr Direktor,*" Schöneborn answered, taking the bag with the diamonds and pressing it to his chest.

He immediately asked for permission to leave, turned on his heels, and walked out. I don't doubt that Schöneborn did give the precious stones to the SS in an effort to get the women released. Time went by, and we were still without news of the Jewish female workers. Work at the factory had already started several days before, and the anxiously awaited train from Auschwitz still did not show up. We could only speculate regarding the fate of the women, and each new conjecture seemed worse than the others. . . .

Still despairing about the fate of the female workers, and not knowing whom else to appeal to, Oskar drove to Zwittau, where he contacted an old childhood friend, Hilde, and asked her to go to Auschwitz and personally take care of the release of the women. I do not know what contacts Hilde had with the upper echelons of the Nazi bureaucracy, but the fact is that, one way or another, she succeeded. A few days later, the train with the three hundred female prisoners arrived at the esplanade.

Hilde was the daughter of a wealthy German industrialist who one day had left for Mexico, without any luggage, and never returned. She was strikingly beautiful, slender and graceful, and her pretty blond hair drew the attention of both men and women. She followed the impulses of her independent personality and loved freedom more than anything. She never wanted to tell me why she did it, nor how she managed to attain the release of the women from the concentration camp, but I suspect her great beauty played a decisive part. . . .

The arrival at Brünnlitz of the train with the female workers caused a great commotion. In the celebration there were tears and laughter, while the German soldiers watched in silence, their sidelong glances still threatening.

The women arrived from the concentration camp in disastrous condition—fragile, emaciated, weak. I took care myself of hand-feeding them semolina porridge and making them take their medications. They improved almost instantly, feeling protected and taken care of, safe at least as long as they stayed at Brünnlitz.

Oskar and I knew, however, that we were only a stage of the plan. One day, almost at the edge of desperation, I asked Oskar, who was then writing a letter, "How long is all this going to last? Will this agony of war go on forever?"

"My dear Emilie," he answered with a heavy heart, looking at me with sadness in his eyes, "we have jumped into an abyss. There is no turning back."

The day we arrived at Brünnlitz, we unpacked our belongings and then took a look at the condition of the factory. The plant, formerly a spinning mill, had belonged to a Jewish businessman. It had been abandoned for some time, and everything was in disarray. There were boxes full of wool scattered in every corner, broken windows, and reminders everywhere of what once must have been a place of intense activity.

"And is it here that we're going to set up a munitions factory?" I asked my husband, desolate at the sight of the plant.

Oskar seemed calm as usual, but he answered in a voice that evidenced his concern.

"We're like the phoenix, Emilie; we'll always rise from the ashes. You'll see how quickly everything is going to change and how soon I'll have this place running."

I wanted to believe him but somehow felt that this time his words of hope had no basis whatsoever. It was like one of those other premonitions I have had from time to time.

A few days later, the blast furnace for the manufacture of ammunition was installed. It had been brought specially from Cracow. Schöneborn, who had already been the head engineer in the enamelware factory, was in charge of all these activities; he was indeed a tireless man, capable of organizing the work, repairing the machinery, and being in control of the entire production process.

THE JEWS OF GOLESCHAU

One night while a terrible storm was raging outside, with the temperature dropping to twenty degrees below zero Fahrenheit and the room being frequently lit up by lightning, I heard some heavy pounding at the door. Still half asleep, I threw something over my nightgown and ran downstairs. Oskar had not returned yet from one of his trips to Cracow, and I was alone.

At the door I asked who it was, and a masculine voice answered: "Please open up, Frau Schindler. I have to talk with you. It's important."

It was the man in charge of transporting Jewish workers from Goleschau, a Polish mine in which subhuman conditions prevailed. He was asking me to accept the two hundred and fifty Jews, crowded into four wagons, whom he had brought in. Some plant had placed a request and then rejected them when it became known that the Russian troops were approaching. If I also rejected them, they were going to be shot.

Quick action was required if I wanted to do something for them. I ran to the phone to call Oskar, explained the situation to him, and asked for permission to accept those Jews in our factory. He agreed. I hung up, got dressed, and went out to get the engineer Schöneborn. I woke him up and asked him to come with me to the huge platform serving as the train station.

It was close to daybreak and snowing heavily. We found the railroad car bolts frozen solid and tried, unsuccessfully, to pry them open with long, heavy iron bars. Schöneborn then brought a soldering iron and, with a lot of patience, finally succeeded in forcing the compartments open.

The German commander, flanked by two dogs, was watching our every move and then called me aside.

"Stay away, Frau Schindler, it's a terrible sight. You'll never be able to erase it from your mind."

I paid no attention to him and, despite his warning, walked up to the railroad cars. The spectacle I saw was a nightmare almost beyond imagination. It was impossible to distinguish the men from the women: they were all so emaciated, . . . weighing under seventy pounds most of them, they looked like skeletons. Their eyes were shining like glowing coals in the dark.

That image of horror and human misery comes back to me every now and then, and a feeling of helplessness grips my bones, as if I were again back at the station. Twelve of them had not survived the trip. The position of their bodies seemed to say they had spent the last moments of their lives begging for answers: hands folded and eyes wide open, as if pleading to God.

The ones who had survived needed the greatest of care. We transferred them to a sort of interim emergency hospital that was set up immediately, where they would stay for over two months. At first, they required extremely special attention and even had to be spoon-fed to prevent their choking to death. After not eating for so long, they had forgotten how.

As their health improved, they started joining the work force at the plant, where they were safe and could live on the food obtained from Frau von Daubek's mill and from our black-market dealings. In the meantime, they, as well as the rest of the workers, were waiting in vain for the factory to start operating. As I mentioned before, not a single bullet ever left the plant. That factory was simply a refuge for those who had managed to evade the horrors of the concentration camps.

SCHINDLER'S FAREWELL

By then it had become evident that the end of the war was drawing near. The Russians were not far away, and rumors that they were on the brink of entering Poland were intensifying. Waiting for either salvation or death, the men spent their days tightening nuts and bolts and walking around the huge factory. The women occupied themselves knitting coats, using the wool left over from the time when the plant was a spinning mill. The atmosphere changed Friday evenings when the Kabalat Shabbat began. The anguished prayers then alternated with songs of hope. . . .

On the day the armistice was signed, Oskar ordered loudspeakers to be installed at the factory, and then he assembled all the workers, Jews and non-Jews, in the large central courtyard. After listening to Churchill's words announcing the unconditional surrender of the Wehrmacht, signed by Admiral von Friedeburg and General Jodl at General Eisenhower's headquarters, my husband announced, standing on a high iron staircase, that in view of the new situation the factory would close and that all of them were free to go wherever they pleased. He also spoke about the futility of wars and the suffering they brought to different countries. He referred to the persecutions suffered by the Jews, to the deaths of so many innocent people and of so many children. He made an appeal for us all to part without rancor in our hearts and thanked the workers for their cooperation. He advised them to find ways to rebuild their lives as best they could, and regretted that there was nothing more he could do for them.

Those were his words, the ones that had to be said at a moment like this. I felt very proud to be there, at his side.

CHAPTER 3

THE SURVIVORS

PEOPLE
WHO MADE
HISTORY

OSKAR SCHINDLER

The Rosner Family

Elinor J. Brecher

Schindler managed to save not just individuals, but sometimes whole families. The Rosner brothers, Henry, Leopold, and Wilhelm, were musicians. Henry and Leopold frequently played at parties thrown by Amon Goeth. This earned the entire family a place on Schindler's list.

Despite the special status enjoyed by the Rosners, they had to endure a number of frightening separations. Manci and Helena Rosner, the wives of Henry and Leopold, were among the women on the train that was sent to Auschwitz by mistake. Henry and his son Alexander were later sent to Auschwitz, where they managed to survive until the camp was liberated. After the war the family immigrated to New York, where the Rosner brothers continued to work as musicians. Several members of the family were interviewed by Elinor J. Brecher, for inclusion in her book.

"Come! Come! I want to show you my museum."

Long, delicate fingers tremble lightly on a visitor's arm, as Henry Rosner steers a course around the quadruple-locked front door toward a room stocked with memories.

Here is his violin—the one made in 1918 that returned to him after the war like a faithful old dog. Here, on a high shelf, rests the pearly red accordion an SS guard gave his son, Alexander, at Auschwitz. Here he keeps the LPs he and his brothers made and his violin collectibles—ashtrays, miniatures, and the like. And the photographs: Henry in his dashing prime, often mistaken for Danny Kaye; his wife Manci with Oskar Schindler, smiling and free, after the war; Alexander in his U.S. Navy officer's uniform.

In the wretched mass of thirty thousand Plaszow *Haftlinge* [prisoners], where nearly everyone looked the same, smelled the same, hungered, shivered, despaired, and feared the same, the Rosners kept their identity: They were the musi-

Excerpted from *Schindler's Legacy: True Stories of the List Survivors*, by Elinor J. Brecher. Copyright © 1994, Elinor J. Brecher. Reprinted by permission of Dutton, a division of Penguin Putnam, Inc.

cians. They weren't just numbers.

Henry played the fiddle; his brother Leopold, called Poldek, the accordion. They entertained *Hauptsturmführer* [captain] Amon Goeth's party guests with musical pleasantries and obsequious smiles. And sometimes, when Amon Goeth grew sleepy after a long, hard day torturing and murdering Jews, they played lullabyes at his bedside, consigning him to his dreams. "He liked German songs," says Henry. "He had such a good ear, he could tell when I changed violins." Often, the brothers would be called to play after a killing spree, "to ease his conscience," Henry has said.

Prisoners would see them trekking to the commandant's residence under guard, wearing tuxedos, instruments in hand. Incredibly, given Amon Goeth's volatile nature, they always returned. Oskar Schindler dined there often, as did the other Kraków-area *Treuhänders,* local and visiting SS brass, Gestapo bigshots, and a revolving harem of agreeable young women.

Wilhelm Rosner, the youngest brother, played the bugle. Promptly at seven each morning, he roused the camp from its uneasy slumber, blowing a reveille of his own composition. Fifty years later, some Plaszow veterans still can hum it. In the frigid winter, his lips froze to the mouthpiece, but he never missed a day. "Twelve, I played for lunch, and twelve-thirty, go back to work," he remembers. He alone was permitted a wristwatch, so he would always be on time. *Exactly* on time.

A sensitive and emotional boy, Bill Rosner was, to some extent, the camp's psychological barometer. "One night, my father's friend, who was a heavy smoker, was smoking in a place he shouldn't, and a Nazi came and shot him right away. I was so upset that I couldn't sleep one minute, and in the morning when I started to play, all the people said, 'Something is wrong. This is not the right sound.'"

Manci Rosner was well known too, not just as Henry-the-violinist's wife, but as a Plaszow *Blochalteste,* a housemother of sorts to three hundred women. Some still speak of how she offered hope simply by maintaining her dignity and humanity. Her snooty Viennese breeding served her well in these dire times.

Then there was Alexander. In *Schindler's List,* he is called "Olek," a diminutive his parents still use. He was four when the war began, and like the other unauthorized children at

Plaszow, materialized and vanished as the occasion demanded. Arranging and monitoring his whereabouts consumed vast stores of his parents' energy, and allied them forever with those who helped safeguard his life.

Alex Rosner says that many years after the camps, his father told him about his deal with the Nazis: "As long as you
keep my son alive, I will play for you. The minute he dies or
is taken away, it doesn't matter anymore what you do to me."
Henry understood that the Nazis' passion for music rivaled
their loathing of the Jews. . . .

The Rosners were pillars of the Krakovian inner circle
that dominated Jewish prisoner life at Plaszow, at Emalia,
and later at Oskar Schindler's Brinnlitz factory. Their connections to, and alliances with, the camp's most influential
Jews stretched back years. Henry and Poldek's frequent contacts with Schindler, chez Goeth, offered Oskar's protection
to the entire extended Rosner family, which included Regina
Rosner Horowitz—the brothers' sister—her husband, Dolek,
their son, Ryszard, and daughter Niusia.

The power of their name and status can't be overesti-
mated. Bill says it once kept him from getting shot. He had a
flashlight in Plaszow. "I was maybe fourteen. I was walking
with it: tick, tick, tick"—he mimes, swinging a flashlight by
his side, clicking it on and off—"and a Nazi comes in a private car: 'To whom did you make this signal?' He opened up
the gun, put it in my neck. I saw a guy—a Jewish guy, who
was always taking care of Amon Goeth's horses—he was going on a horse so fast. He stopped. He said, 'Officer, who are
you killing? This is Rosner! He plays for Amon Goeth!' He
said, 'Oh, I'm sorry.' This saved my life." . . .

KILLING A NAZI WITH MUSIC

Amon Goeth, who took command of the Kraków-Plaszow
camp in February 1943, occupied two less grandiose resi-
dences before he moved into the posh hillside villa shown in
Schindler's List. One of Henry Rosner's clearest and fondest
memories from his days of musical servitude involves an incident at the villa. He never tires of telling it.

Amon was entertaining the usual crowd of fun-loving
Nazis, all heavily lubricated by black-market alcoholic bev-
erages. Late in the evening, the Rosner brothers struck up a
sentimental and melancholy Hungarian tune called "Gloomy
Sunday," at the request of a *Waffen* SS officer. They played it

once, then again and then again. Henry noticed that the guest was growing increasingly morose. They played on, a fourth time, a fifth, amazed that Goeth hadn't signaled them on to something more cheerful. ("Gloomy Sunday" is the tale of a young man who decides to die for love.)

Henry fixated on the forlorn officer. He actually convinced himself that he could fiddle the man to death. Six, seven, eight. The officer couldn't stand it anymore. Nine, ten times in a row! He lurched toward the balcony door, yanked it open, and, says Henry, *"Bink!"* He shot himself in the head. *"Bink!"*

"I felt so happy that I hurt a German," says Henry, his eyes crinkling to little more than slits as he grins. He accompanies the tale with a tape he and Poldek once made of the song. He knows precisely which crescendo lured the German officer over the brink, and it never fails to delight him. . . .

For Oskar's thirty-sixth birthday, on April 28, 1944, Henry asked Goeth for permission to entertain *Herr Direktor* at Emalia. Goeth consented. Henry enlisted "Ivan the Russian," a normally bestial camp guard who happened to have a wonderful singing voice, and the two of them went to Lipowa Street. Ivan "got plastered," Henry recalls, and left the room. Henry and Oskar were alone. Oskar knew how badly the war was going for Germany, and how at any time he might be forced to shut down his subcamp.

"He wanted to take his chair and throw it on a picture of Hitler," Henry remembers. "But it fell apart in his hand."

In the late summer of 1944, when Goeth got the order to fold Kraków-Plaszow and its affiliates, Schindler devised the move to Czechoslovakia. He assured Henry and Poldek that wherever he went, he'd take the Rosner clan. And he kept his word. Everyone except the girl who would become Bill Rosner's wife, Erna Zuckerman, made the list.

On October 15, 1944, Henry, Poldek, Bill, and Olek Rosner, along with Dolek and Ryszard Horowitz, joined the cattle-car transport of Schindler men bound for Brinnlitz, through Gröss-Rosen, a transit camp. Manci, Regina, and Poldek's wife, Helena, would soon follow, with the Schindler women.

The men couldn't believe what they saw, heard, and breathed at Gröss-Rosen. Plaszow had been horrendous, granted, especially near the end, with the frantic exhumation and incineration of 10,000 decaying corpses from the Chujowa Górka. But this place was surreal. Snarling, bellowing, flailing psychopaths in uniforms ran the camp. Glazed-eyed, skeletal inmates wandered around like rag-draped scarecrows. The filth and stench could make a person swoon.

They were stripped, inspected, shaved, deloused, and divested of the few possessions to which they clung. Someone snatched Henry's cherished violin—a Guadagnini crafted in 1890 in Turin. Poldek lost his accordion. Somehow, Henry had the presence of mind to compose a brilliant lie. "I said, 'How can you take it away from me? It belongs to Oskar Schindler!'"

When the Rosners arrived at Brinnlitz without their instruments, Schindler asked Henry what had happened. "I said, 'My violin, they took away from me.' He said, 'Why didn't you tell them it belonged to me?' I told him I did tell them that." Within days, Oskar had retrieved the instruments from Gröss-Rosen. The Rosners never learned how much that particular transaction cost.

TAKEN TO AUSCHWITZ

In the meantime, Schindler's three hundred women were in cattle cars on their way to Auschwitz. "That time in Auschwitz was like a lifetime for us," says Manci Rosner, number 220 on the women's list. "I am so thankful to Oskar Schindler. I never would have survived it. At least in Plaszow, no ovens, no gas. You knew when you went to the shower, you got a shower. There is no comparison. I can remember only the smell: a terrible stench."

During the short time the women were at Auschwitz and the men were at Brinnlitz, something went seriously awry. Schindler was away from the factory for a few days (which wasn't unusual). Apparently, the Brinnlitz commandant, *Untersturmführer* Josef Liepold, decided that an ammunition factory was no place for small children. Perhaps his colleague Dr. Josef Mengele could make better use of them at Auschwitz for his medical "experiments."

Guards came and rounded up the youngest boys and their fathers. The number of boys varies: nine or eleven, depending on the account. They were sent to Auschwitz on a regular passenger train. The guard was a decent sort. He bought sandwiches for the group and actually conversed with them in a civilized manner. He mentioned to Dolek Horowitz that he had an order to bring three hundred women from Auschwitz back to the Schindler installation at Brinnlitz.

Dolek and Henry were elated. They knew their wives would be in that group. They implored the guard to find their women and deliver a note.

As Henry Rosner tells it, young Olek was convinced they were about to die. "I don't want you to talk about it," Manci admonishes her husband, to no avail. "You will start to cry." "My son, he told me: 'Daddy, it's too bad you have to go to Auschwitz because of me.' Even this guard, his eyes were crying."

Manci Rosner, Regina Horowitz, and her daughter, Niusia, already had been loaded into cattle cars on a siding when Niusia happened to glimpse Olek and Ryszard through the slats. Manci and Regina convinced the guard to let them out, and, true to his word, he delivered the notes. The women crawled under the train to urinate and were able to exchange a few words. The boys pulled up their sleeves and showed their mothers their brand-new arm tattoos. It was the last time they'd see one another for about a year.

Apprehensive but hopeful, Manci and Regina arrived at Brinnlitz to find Bill and Poldek Rosner waiting. They were numbers 414 and 365 on the men's list. One day some months later, Oskar Schindler approached Manci Rosner on the factory floor. He had something to give her: Henry's violin. She remembers that he said, "It is the same instrument, only a different tune." She wept.

By the time Henry, Olek, and the rest of the father-son entourage got to Auschwitz, all the camp's musicians were dead. But someone—Henry thinks it was a female guard—found a small accordion for Olek, who obligingly entertained his captors.

There was to be a further separation of the group. A selection was announced. The fathers and sons lined up. Alex Rosner recalls what happened next. "The commandant winked at my father, and immediately after he did, he said, 'All children back,' at which point everybody went back except me. My father held my hand and said, 'He doesn't mean you.' That's how he interpreted that wink. We kept walking. My cousin, Ryszard, was separated from his father at that point. My father said I was the only child ever to walk out of Auschwitz alive. All the other children who survived were liberated by the army, or hid, or were tortured by Mengele. That was strictly because we played for him the night before. He told me the story recently."

Henry, Dolek, and Alexander were sent to Dachau, leaving Ryszard, then five years old, alone at the Auschwitz-Birkenau death camp.

The trip in the dead of winter was nightmarish. There were no passenger coaches this time; they were back in cattle cars. The trip took days. The men starved and suffocated. Someone got the idea to hang the stinking corpses in blanket hammocks from the ceiling to get them off the floor where everyone else had to sleep. It gave Henry an idea.

"I put Olek inside a blanket like that, so he could reach the window and get air. He got icicles from the train, and I was all bloody, because everyone was trying to take the icicles from him. We didn't eat for seven days and nights. The wagon where the bread was was the last car. We didn't get any."

Alex Rosner says that Dachau, a few miles northwest of Munich, was "kind of nice, compared to Auschwitz." He remembers a Polish prisoner of war in charge of the camp infirmary took care of him when he came down with typhus. "He kept me after I got well. He said, 'If you leave, they will kill you.'"

Alex claims he had a premonition in Dachau that liberation was imminent. When he said so, he was smacked by another Jew who thought it a sin to mention such things. But he was right: On April 29, 1945, the inmates heard heavy artillery. Soon after, one of the Nazi guards in a tall tower peeled off his white undershirt and hung it on his machine gun. "There was a big commotion," Alex Rosner says, and then came the Americans. "They took the Germans, and threw supplies over the fence for us to have."

It was over . . . at least for them. Soviet troops liberated the *Schindlerjuden* of Brinnlitz eleven days later.

Abraham Zuckerman: A Voice in the Chorus

Abraham Zuckerman

As a teenager, Abraham Zuckerman was imprisoned at the Plaszow concentration camp near Krakow, Poland, where he was chosen to work at Schindler's enamelware factory. He was later transferred to Mauthausen concentration camp, and then to the Gusen II extermination camp, from which he was liberated on May 5, 1945, by American soldiers. Zuckerman, now a U.S. citizen, is active in numerous organizations dedicated to Holocaust history, including the American Gathering of Holocaust Survivors, the Simon Wiesenthal Center for Holocaust Studies, the New York Holocaust Heritage Museum, and the Holocaust Memorial Museum in Washington, D.C.

A NEW WORK ASSIGNMENT

One morning, while I was in the concentration camp at Plaszuw (Plaszow), a number of us were called out from the barracks to the *Appellplatz*—the assembly square. I was scared when this happened. I didn't know why we had been called out or why I had been included, but I was very tired from my work in the coalyard. I figured, whatever happens to me will happen, because I could no longer bear the coalyard work. I thought that whatever happened to me might or might not be an improvement in my working conditions. I did not know what to expect. Once we were assembled, the O.D. man—the Jewish policeman in charge—told us that we were going to Oskar Schindler's Emalia factory. Everyone else was excited about this, but at that time I did not know what it meant. I did not know who this Oskar Schindler was or where I was going. I was about eighteen years old at this time.

I mentioned earlier that the Nazis took over the Jewish-owned businesses when they moved into the cities of

Poland. They would install a *Volksdeutscher,* a Pole with German roots, as *Treuhänder,* or custodian. That person would siphon off the assets of the business as he was learning how to operate it. Once he understood the business, the Nazis would liquidate the owner and give the business over to the *Treuhänder.*

I learned later that Herr Schindler had been installed as the custodian of a large pots and pans company at Plaszuw by the name of Emalia. Emalia had been owned by a Jewish man named Banker (Bankier). Herr Schindler wanted to enlarge the company, so he requested additional people to work in the factory. I was among those fortunate enough to be chosen. Herr Schindler was no ordinary *Treuhänder,* though. To our minds, he was something of a living saint. He was a wealthy businessman but he was absolutely disgusted with the Nazi regime and with what they were doing to the Jews. He took very special care of the Jews who were brought to work for him. Thanks to him, thousands of Jews, myself among them, survived the rest of the ordeal of the camps. He gave us food, he gave us protection, and he gave us hope. I cannot say enough about what a great man he was.

As I said, I did not know anything about Herr Schindler before I got there. I somehow had the feeling that it would be much better for me when they lined us up to go there. My friends told me that it was going to be good. By the time I arrived at Emalia, I knew of his reputation. When I arrived, though, I couldn't believe what I saw. You could roam around the camp. This was unheard of anywhere else. You could walk around, and nobody bothered you. There were no Nazi or Ukrainian soldiers roaming around the camp. I was surprised to see that the atmosphere was so unrestricted.

A PORTRAIT OF SCHINDLER

I saw Herr Schindler almost every day when he was on the camp premises. I saw him while I was at work. He would check with the kitchen. I guess he checked to make sure there was enough food for all the people there. He greeted me when he saw me. He nodded his head. I greeted him in return. This was unimaginable in any other concentration camp. I was not so close that I would go over to him, but nobody, myself included, ran away when they saw him. Nobody was afraid of him. It seemed that he respected every one of us. He gave us a protective, fatherly feeling. He was always immaculately dressed. He was a very handsome person, like a statesman. I remember that in wintertime, he wore a fur coat. The fur was on the outside, which was a very rare sight for me. In Europe at that time, only men from noble ranks wore coats with fur on the outside. It symbolized great wealth and grandeur, both of which he possessed. He had horses and expensive cars. When I saw him, I felt good. I saw a man who was really taking care of us. With him, I felt, I might survive.

Many years later, after the war ended, I heard him describe his feelings about the war this way: "I hated the brutality, the sadism and the insanity of Nazism. I just couldn't stand by and see people destroyed. I did what I could, what I had to do, what my conscience told me I must do. That's all there is to it. Really. Nothing more." As you can imagine, this was an extraordinary way for a person to feel. He had known Jewish people when he was growing up and he felt compassion for us when the war began and the Nazis began their brutality and killing. Herr Schindler built decent barracks for his Jewish workers. He even smuggled his workers' wives, parents, and children into the camp he ran. He would hide them until the Jewish underground made it possible for them to escape Nazi-occupied territory. On the High Holidays, he saw to it that challah bread was distributed. When a Jewish worker died of illness at the camp, Herr Schindler even arranged for a Jewish burial service.

I later learned that in 1945, when the war was about to end, Herr Schindler gave a party for his workers in the camp and told them that "it was all over." He even gave guns and rifles to a small group of prisoners so they could protect the others in case the retreating Nazi army came through the camp to kill everyone. In my life, I have never come face-to-face with a more courageous, decent, and brilliant man. It goes without saying that I owe my life to him, but I am getting ahead of my story.

THE EMALIA FACTORY

At Emalia, Herr Schindler's factory, as far as I knew, there were three divisions. In one part of the factory, the workers manufactured enamel pots and pans. In the second part of the factory, they were making shells for bullets. The third division was construction. The Simmons company had contracted to do the job of extending Herr Schindler's factory. I was assigned to work on the addition to the factory. I just took whatever job they assigned me. It was hard work, but I felt different about it because nobody stood with the whip above me to make sure I did the work.

To be honest, I don't know why I was assigned to Herr Schindler's Emalia factory. I guess he needed some more workers. It might have been because of my skills as an electrician. When I was assigned to him, though, my life changed. It was as though I was no longer under the same sort of Nazi administration. I was treated differently. They gave me enough food. I had decent sleeping quarters. In Poland, winters were very harsh. Even in Herr Schindler's camp, I did not get enough warm clothes. I still had my uniform from Julag camp, and it was not a very warm uniform. In order to keep warm, I had to wrap empty cement bags in three or four layers around my body, underneath my jacket. This would not have been permissible at any other camp. The camp barracks were located on the same premises as the factory, so I did not have to travel to work. No trucks, no railroad cars, which had been an everyday torture at the other camps. It was completely different from the other camps. Even the schedule for the work was completely different, because Herr Schindler had ordered it that way.

Here is a typical day at the construction site. We got up early. We got our food. As soon as we finished eating, we went to work. We worked at least ten hours. We did a lot. I tried to conserve my strength. I kept my eyes on the watchmen. When they were not looking, we did not have to work as hard. The work didn't go away; it was always there. The project did not seem to have a time schedule—we did not have to finish by a particular time. As a matter of fact, when I left Herr Schindler, the factory addition still wasn't finished. Herr Schindler did not insist that the addition had to be done by any certain time; he just bided the time together with us. He wanted to stretch out the work for as long as possible, to keep his workers—his people—with him. This was a sign to the Nazis that he needed us. It was his way of keeping us from deportation to the death camps.

THE IMPORTANCE OF BEING FED

While I was working in Herr Schindler's camp, it was possible for me to talk to the other workers. There were ways to talk. I couldn't complain about conditions because that did me no good. I had to accept what I got, but compared to the other camps, it wasn't too bad. I did not have to work as hard for Herr Schindler as I did in Julag or the other camps. Most important, I was never hungry. When you're not hungry, somehow life is bearable. Sometimes I worked until ten at night. For instance, when railroad cars arrived with cement, we had to unload it. The next day we didn't get up as early to work again, because we had worked so many hours the night before. This would never have happened in any other camp I had been in. This is the way Herr Schindler treated his people. I was very surprised to find decent, humane treatment in a concentration camp.

At Herr Schindler's factory, there were mountains of potatoes. This was due to Herr Schindler's thinking of his people. I was told that he used to take truckloads of pots and pans and he would trade them with the Polish farmers for potatoes and other kinds of food. This way, he would have enough food for his people. You have to remember that he risked his life in order to protect the lives of the people working for him. This is why I call him a living saint.

I could always take some potatoes from the factory yard, bring them inside the factory, peel them, and put them in water. I could cook them because the kilns for the glazing of the pots and pans had rims on the outside, and those rims were always red-hot. If I put the pot with the potatoes there, in ten minutes I had cooked potatoes. That really kept me alive and not hungry. Nobody ever accused me of stealing when I took the potatoes. It must have been Herr Schindler's orders.

I don't know whether it made sense for an employer to treat workers in a forced labor camp so well. Again, it was Oskar Schindler who did it and nobody else but Oskar Schindler. To me, as I said before, he was a living saint. Because of him I was treated like a human being. And because of him, I was physically able to survive my other ordeals when I was shipped to Mauthausen, the next stop for me after Emalia/Plaszuw. I was a person when I came to Mauthausen, I wasn't what they called a *Muselmann,* an extremely thin person. A *Muselmann* was what they called people who were skinny, dehydrated, dried out—ready for the crematorium.

Oskar Schindler managed somehow to outsmart the Nazi administration, to keep them happy, and to keep them from investigating conditions inside the camp. We did not know how he kept the Nazis from finding out that he was taking such good care of us. For example, the Nazi higher-ups often conducted inspections of the camp. Herr Schindler always gave us advance notice of these inspections. When the day arrived, I could see the high Nazi officers at the gate. But Herr Schindler managed somehow to keep the Nazi officers from entering the camp. He would take them to his quarters, where, I heard, he would wine them and dine them. Somehow, they would not enter the camp itself to see what was going on. When they would leave, then we could relax again. This is how much effort he put into protecting his people.

I don't think that Herr Schindler could have done more than he did. He took care of his workers. Everybody was fed well. There was a real infirmary. If anyone was sick, Herr Schindler saw to it that he was given good medical care, as much as was possible. In the other camps where I had been interned, this did not exist. If you went to the infirmary, you were a dead person. If you were not well enough to work, the Nazis would kill you. My friend Yekel Fuhrer became very sick at Plaszuw. If it weren't for his being in Herr Schindler's Emalia camp, I don't know whether he would have survived.

Celina Karp

Elinor J. Brecher

Celina Karp Biniaz and her parents, Irwin and Phyllis Karp, worked at Julius Madritsch's textile factory inside the Plaszow concentration camp. They were among the people put on Schindler's list by Raimond Titsch, Madritsch's manager who helped Schindler compile the original list.

In addition to depicting Amon Goeth and life in Plaszow, this passage reflects the crisis of faith, and conversion to atheism, that many Holocaust Jews underwent. Celina Karp Biniaz was interviewed by Elinor J. Brecher for inclusion in her book.

THE GIRL IN THE MIRROR

For her fourteenth birthday, May 28, 1945, Celina Karp wanted just one gift: a movie ticket. She didn't really care what she saw, as long as she could put on real clothes and go to the theater.

As it happened, a 1938 Deanna Durbin film was playing in Kraków. In English it was called *Mad About Music,* in Polish *Pensionarka.* It was a silly bit of Hollywood fluff about girls at a Swiss boarding school. All those sparkly American actresses with their long, wavy hair and their cute little outfits—it was just perfect.

Celina borrowed a skirt and blouse and headed alone to the theater, where full-length mirrors lined the lobby. She can't recall whether she glanced toward the glass while entering or leaving, but she'll never forget what she saw.

"I was absolutely shocked," says the woman who is now retired teacher Celina Biniaz of Camarillo, California. "I couldn't believe that was me. It made such an impression to see myself looking so gawky and scrawny, like a scarecrow."

Celina and her parents had been free of Nazi captivity for all of three weeks. Her hair, sheared at Auschwitz the previous autumn, hadn't grown out much, and she weighed only

Excerpted from *Schindler's Legacy: True Stories of the List Survivors,* by Elinor J. Brecher. Copyright © 1994, Elinor J. Brecher. Reprinted by permission of Dutton, a division of Penguin Putnam, Inc.

seventy pounds. The borrowed skirt was wrapped nearly twice around her waist. She was beside herself by the time she got back home. "I can't remember if I cried," she says, "but I do know I felt so ugly."

Celina Karp hadn't seen her own head-to-toe reflection in four or five years, and what stared back at her bore scant resemblance to the person she remembered. Could this be the refined little girl whose mother made her wear white gloves to play in the park? This Celina was a teenager who'd talked her way out of an Auschwitz crematorium, who'd witnessed so much mayhem and depravity that she no longer believed in God.

"I became a total, total atheist at the age of twelve," she explains. "I remember asking my mother and other people how God could let certain things happen, and getting the answer that in Judaism, the sins of the forefathers are visited upon the children. I just couldn't accept that. I said, 'There is no God, because no God would allow children to be smashed against walls and killed.'"

Today Celina Karp Biniaz lives in a place with few Jews—outside the local Leisure Village retirement community—and no synagogues. Camarillo is high and dry, about fifty miles northwest of Los Angeles. The chamber of commerce calls it "the bougainvillea capital" of California. Celina Biniaz calls it "very WASP." She and her Iranian-born husband, Amir, moved there from Long Island in 1993. Home is an airy, hilltop ranch house on more than an acre, with a courtyard pool, hummingbird feeders, kumquat and other citrus trees, white-on-white decor, and Middle Eastern *objets.*

POLAND BEFORE THE WAR

Celina is the only child of Izak and Feiga Wittenberg Karp—now Irvin and Phyllis—of Des Moines, Iowa. Her father, born in January 1903, may be the oldest of the *Schindlerjuden* in the United States. Her mother, born two years later, isn't far behind. Irvin spends much of his time in a wheelchair, his command of English gradually slipping away. Phyllis is in good health, though increasingly frail.

The elder Karps were accountants before, during, and after the war. They came from Radomsko, a Polish city of thirty-five thousand—ten percent Jewish—known for its steel and furniture industries. They married in 1929 and moved to Kraków, about one hundred miles to the southeast.

Irvin Karp's main account there was the Hogo shirt company, a concern he would later compare in stature to the American firm Arrow. Feiga did the books for a cafe where the Rosners played.

Poland at the time had a "professional middle class, with certain trappings that went with it and a certain kind of lifestyle," says Celina. The Karps lived it and enjoyed it. Their apartment at 22 Krupnicza Street—in a "mixed" Krakow neighborhood—had beautiful furniture. "The dining room table extended to seat eighteen, and there was service for twenty-four: china, crystal, and sterling. My parents' bedroom set was light African buried wood, very elegant. I remember all that because they sold all of it to a neighbor, and my mother felt bad about it because it was her trousseau."

Phyllis and Irvin kept a Telefunken shortwave radio in their bedroom. As the summer of 1939 wound down, they spent more and more time listening to the increasingly ominous news. Men gathered to talk politics in the building's courtyard, aware of what the Germans were up to, disbelieving that it would affect them and their families.

"When it did come," Celina says of the September 1 invasion, "we discovered that the people we were talking to were Fifth Columnists, supporters of the Anschluss. The next day, they appeared with [swastika] armbands."

According to Celina Biniaz, one of the first bombs that fell on Poland destroyed her maternal grandparents' house in Radomsko. She remembers clearly the day her mother got the news. "Mother was not feeling well and was lying on a divan. The maid came in with a letter for Mother. She started reading and crying, and I couldn't figure out why. It was a letter from a former maid from Radomsko, saying how sorry she was. I still have that picture before my eyes."

It was very painful at the time to have lost loved ones that way, says Celina, "but at the end of the war, in retrospect, we realized that at least they were lost in their own home, together."

The bomb killed Phyllis's parents, who ran a general store; a sister; a brother; and many other relatives. Another sister lived with the Karps in Kraków, but died during the war in a particularly sadistic massacre. Another brother also perished in France.

Celina's father ultimately lost two sisters. One brother

was living in the United States, another in Palestine. A third, who had been in the Polish Army, survived the war as a Soviet POW.

JULIUS MADRITSCH

Life changed dramatically for Celina after the invasion. Her father joined the flight of men to eastern Poland. She was sent, briefly, to the small village of a family maid. But what hurt the most was giving up her puppy, a Spitz named Leda. "That was very painful for me, and I could not quite understand why my parents were making me do this. But they felt we couldn't take care of a dog."

A Viennese gentleman named Julius Madritsch took over the shirt company, Hogo. He converted it to a uniform factory bearing his name. "My father ran the factory," says Celina. "What [the accountant Itzhak] Stern did for Schindler [in the film], my father did for Madritsch. That's one reason we got on the list."

In the early spring of 1941, the Karps had to leave their home and move into the Kraków Ghetto. They shared one room and a kitchen with Phyllis's sister, Gucia, and Gucia's husband. He survived the war. Gucia was transported to Auschwitz, then shipped out to the North Sea, where hundreds of Jews were told that they must walk out on the ice to eventually reach Sweden. "All of them were shot." Celina says.

She and her parents could have been among them, but at the last minute her father managed to extract them from the Auschwitz transport. He couldn't do as much for Gucia, who had traded places with someone to remain with her family.

Everyone in the Kraków Ghetto had to work or risk transport. While her parents went every day to Madritsch's factory, Celina spent her days at an envelope cooperative, then at a brush factory. But neither granted her the coveted *Blauschein*, the "blue card" that designated its bearer an "essential" worker. In a 1983 videotaped lecture, Phyllis Karp explained how Celina finally got a card.

"One Friday, someone came out [to Madritsch] and told us they [had] killed everyone who wasn't working, in the ghetto. On the street you could see corpses. [Celina] was sick in bed. Thank God she was home. I vowed she would be with me all the time, and what happened would happen to both of us. We had a [Polish] neighbor who worked in the place where they made the ID cards, and we asked if she would do us the favor to make [Celina] two years older, twelve." It helped that Celina was tall for her age.

Celina went to work as a seamstress at Madritsch, igniting a lifelong avocation. For years, she made all of her children's clothes and her own—this despite poor circulation in her hands, a painful reminder of the frostbite she suffered clearing the Kraków streets of snow, barehanded.

DIFFERING PORTRAITS OF AMON GOETH

Many Plaszow residents have vivid (and unpleasant) memories of the camp's commandant, Amon Goeth. However, the details of those memories can be surprisingly different. Emilie Schindler is Oskar Schindler's wife. Ana Novac was a prisoner at Plaszow. She was not on Schindler's list.

EMILIE SCHINDLER: Goeth was the most despicable man I have ever met in my whole life. He had a double personality: on the one hand he seemed to be a refined gentleman, like a true Viennese, and on the other he seemed to relish submitting the Jews under his jurisdiction to constant terror.

To my amazement, Oskar had won his friendship and one evening brought him home for dinner. I shall never forget his physical appearance: he was more than six feet tall, had rounded, feminine hips and dark hair, and a huge mouth with fleshy lips that laughed nonstop opening as if to swallow up everything. I remember Goeth as rather slender, not as depicted in the Spielberg film, where much is made of his corpulence and weight problems.

ANA NOVAC: The man on the white horse was there where Liese had been standing shortly before. A panting whale, with an enormous belly and fat, pendulous breasts. Numerous medals trembled on his chest. So this was the famous cannibal aesthete! His head reminded me of a smooth, naked ass. How could those swollen paws hold a revolver? How could decisions emerge from above that triple chin? How could cruelty, perversity, or any other "trait" penetrate that obscene layer of fat? Was it believable that this shapeless mass could be anything more than a lazy metabolism, that it could want anything other than to digest, to catch its breath, to preserve its huge organism from apoplexy? No matter how long I looked at it, it expressed nothing but obesity.

Emilie Schindler, *Where Light and Shadow Meet: A Memoir.* New York: W.W. Norton, 1996.

Ana Novac, *The Beautiful Days of My Youth: My Six Months in Auschwitz and Plaszow.* New York: Henry Holt, 1997.

For a time, Madritsch's workers marched from the ghetto to his factory in another part of the Podgorze section of Kraków. Then they moved to Plaszow continuing the daily trek. It took about ninety minutes each way, no matter the weather, but Celina says no one minded. "We were so glad to get out of Plaszow. Just like Schindler people felt safe [at Emalia], we felt safe at Madritsch. Then they brought all the factories inside the camp."

Madritsch—"more elegant and classy than Schindler," says Celina—set up his operation in several barracks: one for offices and storage, one for cutting, one for sewing. He and his manager, Raimund Titsch, treated their workers kindly.

"He was a very capable man, very organized," says Phyllis Karp. "He was a good human being with a heart." She says that when word reached him that Amon Goeth had slaughtered eight hundred Jewish children in the ghetto— after giving their Plaszow-bound parents his "word of honor" that the children would follow—Julius Madritsch wept uncontrollably.

Celina says Raimund Titsch was "out of his element" among the Nazis, "a wonderful man who got caught in the wrong place at the wrong time." He and his boss saw to it that their workers got extra food and, when possible, medication. "Because [Madritsch] was on good terms with Goeth, that's how he protected us."

The protection, however, went only so far. "We would come out on the *Appellplatz* [parade ground], be counted and dispatched to work areas. But as soon as we walked back through the gates, we were no longer protected."

Unlike Schindler, Julius Madritsch did not establish a camp-within-a-camp at his Plaszow factory. His workers lived in the barracks, exposed to every caprice of Amon Goeth's reign. Neither Celina nor her parents ever were beaten, "but there was always the fear that we could be, and we were forced to watch it happening to other people. It was horrible."

Celina Karp witnessed the assassinations of the Chilowiczes, the camp's ruling Jewish family, on a day Julius Madritsch wasn't around. "Chilowicz's brother-in-law was working at Madritsch. Goeth shot him. His wife ran out to see what was happening and he shot her too. There were the bales of fabric stacked up in a barrack. Rumor was that Goeth was coming, and I climbed up and hid in the bales.

The little ones used to do this often, so we wouldn't be so obvious. When he came, if you didn't need to be around, you weren't around."

Celina Biniaz says that fear was "the ruling passion" at Plaszow. "I was petrified all the time, incredibly tense. I had horrible migraine headaches all the time, for which Madritsch got medication. You just didn't live any other way but afraid, and that has stayed with me the rest of my life. I'm very fearful of authority. It was a problem even with the principal at school."

In spite of the fear, and of Goeth, and of their lives' stultifying baseness, the Jewish slaves of Plaszow determined to preserve their culture. Adults taught. Children learned. The community clung to its values.

"I remember reading a great deal," says Celina Biniaz. "They brought in books for burning, and the crew assigned to bring in the books, under penalty of death, would smuggle them into the barracks. You would read at night and pass it on. At the end of the war, I knew how to read but couldn't write. I hadn't held a pencil in my hand for six years. Women would sing and tell stories. That's where I learned all my Shalom Aleichem [the Jewish short-story writer whose stories were adapted into the musical *Fiddler on the Roof*]."

ON THE LIST

It is said that Oskar Schindler tried to talk Julius Madritsch into moving with him to Czechoslovakia when Plaszow shut down, but that Madritsch declined. He and Raimund Titsch did, however, make sure that sixty of their workers, including the Karps, got on Schindler's list.

"I was doing very well until the train pulled into Auschwitz," Celina recalls of the transition to Brinnlitz. "My mother kept saying that she would always be with me. I asked her at Auschwitz if I was sent to the crematorium would she go with me? She said yes. I fully realized what was happening there. I could see life around me. It was bitter cold, rainy, miserable, filthy, mud up to your ankles. The latrines were overflowing. And they made us stand to be counted for long periods of time. We stood in fives, so we took turns being in the middle. They had fur coats on, and we were naked. And hungry! All we got was water with a few vegetables in it."

Phyllis Karp had promised her daughter that they would

never be separated, but at Auschwitz she made an exception to her own rule. Celina says, "One day they came into the barracks and said they needed twenty-five, thirty women to go and peel potatoes, and Mother volunteered because she thought she could get me something to eat. While she was gone, they took the rest of the barrack for another selection."

Dr. Josef Mengele was in charge, sending some to the left, some to the right. With his own hand, the murderous physician—"he was a handsome devil"—pushed Celina Karp into the line headed for the ovens. Then, for no apparent reason, he decided to winnow the doomed left line again.

"He made us go through a second time, and when we went through, I looked at him and said three words in German: *'Lassen Sie mich.'* 'Let me go.' He pushed me to the right, and I ran out. I wouldn't be this brave now. My mother came back, running around hysterical, stark raving mad."

The women arrived at Brinnlitz "haggard and shaved," says Celina. "My mother was very sick with pneumonia; they were not ready for us—there were no bunks—and we slept on the floor. But it was warm, on top of the factory, and there was such an overwhelming feeling of relief that we were reunited. That was the thing about Schindler; he saved families."

Celina was among a handful of teenagers at Schindler's Brinnlitz factory, including Niusia Horowitz, Leon Leyson, and Janka Feigenbaum. She spent part of the seven-month stay in the camp's infirmary, in a bunk above Janka, who was thought to have bone cancer. Janka died at nineteen, shortly before liberation.

"I had picked up scarlet fever; then, because of poor sanitation, that left me with jaundice and an impaired liver," Celina says. She remembers that Janka was in great pain and suffered terrible bedsores. "But I got to know her very well. It was so sad that she didn't make it."

Celina and Niusia Horowitz had make-work jobs cleaning the big machines. But at least once, she picked up some lucrative work on the side. "My father made needles, and there was a woman in the kitchen who got some white thread from someplace. I knitted a pair of underpants and a camisole for her, and she gave me *two* loaves of bread! We shared that with my father. I was very pleased I was able to do that."

She also remembers Raimund Titsch visiting Schindler at the factory. "He was walking through with him, and he asked if there was anything I wanted. I had a pair of wooden clogs, and I said I would really like other kinds of shoes. After that, a load of shoes with wooden soles but leather uppers came in. I don't know if that was Titsch or Schindler."

On May 9, 1945, first one Soviet soldier, then others, liberated the slave laborers of Brinnlitz. "One of the hardest things to get used to was to be able to walk by yourself or with one other person, because we always had to be in fives," Celina says, chuckling. "It was so strange. I kept thinking, 'Where is my five?' My parents and I walked into the village. It was so strange to be able to walk out of the camp to begin with."

The Karps lost no time heading for Kraków. Like the other *Schindlerjuden,* they carried several yards of cloth and other trade items left to them by Schindler. Celina got five pairs of scissors. Four she traded, but she still uses the fifth in her sewing room. (Phyllis still has her red enamel Brinnlitz soup bowl.)

The Karps stayed in Kraków until the end of September. During the summer, Irvin and Phyllis went to Vienna where they testified on behalf of Madritsch and Titsch. Celina studied with a tutor, took high school entrance exams, and prepared to enroll in classes for the first time since the second grade.

"Then there was a pogrom that had to do with Rosh Hashana, and my parents decided not to stay. We were smuggled over the border in a Russian truck, stayed in Prague a few days, then crossed the border to Germany."

The family spent the next two years in Mindelheim, Bavaria, supported by Jewish relief agencies and relatives in the United States. They lived near the Landsberg Displaced Persons' camp, in a room requisitioned from the widow of a Nazi.

"Those two years among normal German families were my salvation," says Celina. "I would have hated Germans for the rest of my life, but what I saw there was that not all Germans were bad, that people are people."

Sam Birenzweig: Number 233 on the List

Lisa Petrillo

Sam Birenzweig was put on Schindler's list only because, as one of the workers ordered to disassemble the Plaszow concentration camp and destroy evidence of the mass killings performed there, he was one of the last to leave Plaszow. The following selection is an interview he did with Lisa Petrillo, a reporter with the *San Diego Union-Tribune.*

Sam Birenzweig is number 233 on the list of life.

He survived those first crushing years of the Holocaust because, he figures, he had enough youth, smarts and skill.

But in the Nazis' last desperate slaughter of 1944, Birenzweig barely escaped ending like his parents and sisters, lost in the mass of 6 million murdered Jews.

Instead, luck landed him on Oskar Schindler's list.

A LITTLE SAFE

He is number 233 on the list of 1,150 souls saved by the amazing Schindler, the war profiteer who hustled his way to heroism.

"How I come to Schindler is a good story. Everybody who survived has enough story for a whole book," says Birenzweig, who lived to have a "happily ever after."

He retired a success from the wholesale cosmetics business in New York and settled in a posh, pink retirement center here overlooking the Pacific, far from his miserable days in Polish concentration camps. At 78, he has only just started telling strangers about his life as a leaf in Hitler's cyclone. Despite the acclaim for the movie, "Schindler's List," Birenzweig, believed to be the only "List" survivor living in San Diego County, only recently agreed to share his own story. "Thank God, I remember everything that's happened, the names, the dates, why it happened. There were people who got confused right away, when it started to get bad. You ask a lot of people and they don't remember." This is what marks a survivor, even more than the concentration camp tattoo on his forearm. He is a man who considers it a blessing to forever remember some of the worst horrors known to humanity. . . .

"IT'S TOO MUCH"

Still, there remain unspeakable parts of his story, for to give voice to such evil is to resurrect nightmares so powerful they possess him for months and hurt his heart, literally.

"When I talk, I don't talk about the special things," he said, his growling accent and rolling Rs all that is left of his lost home, Poland. "I skip a lot because it's too much."

His sharp eyes stare through his rimless spectacles. "You know what I'm saying?"

He never watches World War II movies because he wants no more Nazis in his life. He won't see "Schindler's List," the acclaimed Hollywood drama of the Jewish principle that he who saves one man saves the world. Schindler used Jews to help him make his fortune manufacturing pots for Nazi soldiers, then used that fortune to "buy" protection so his workers were saved [from] the death camps.

Birenzweig did watch the Academy Awards to see seven honors bestowed on the film considered director Steven Spielberg's masterpiece.

"That big shot, what's his name? What he said was nice, that we should teach this in the schools and explain what happened to make the world so bad," he says.

When Europe went to war in September 1939 to stop Hitler from taking over the world, Simka Birenzweig was living in a Jewish ghetto in the southern Poland city of Ostrovitc, about 60 miles outside Krakow, where Schindler came to make his fortune.

Birenzweig was the middle child of seven born to parents who ran a wholesale window-glass business. So, he began the cyclone as a healthy, educated male in his early 20s armed with cash and a trade. In the Nazis' insanely meticulous killing system, his was the kind of Jew who usually survived the first cut.

"In the beginning, it is not so bad," he says. "Something happens, you can buy your way out for a few dollars."

In that corner of hell he met a rich and prominent German who, although technically the enemy, seemed to possess that same spark of goodness that would eventually lead Schindler to devote his considerable fortune and cunning to rescuing Jews.

CAUGHT BY SS

"Two Germans got a place that was a warehouse as big as a city and loaded with goods. One say, 'Tell all the Jewish people if they are hungry they have some goods to sell, come to me, don't be afraid.' Something was a little too good to be true."

The German big shot who called himself Jung even took Birenzweig scavenging with him to a nearby city. After buying a truckload of goods and paying the Jewish population any price they asked, as his German patron had insisted, Birenzweig was caught in an SS raid and sent to a concentration camp. He escaped that night, got back to the city and was transported home by his German benefactor the next day. He had survived another cut, but the good German did not. The SS discovered he was really Jewish and shot him and his partner.

"If he didn't do like this too often maybe he would be alive today," says Birenzweig. "Yes, he help a lot, a lot. But if you want to help, you should help in a quiet way. You understand what I say?"

Maybe more like Schindler's way.

For Schindler was a Nazi Party member and war profiteer with one wife and two mistresses. He was a towering man who lived on Hennessy brandy yet never suffered hangovers. A man who greased the SS at night with black-market liquor and prostitutes and came back clear-eyed the next morning to hustle them. His "heroic liver" is how writer Thomas Keneally describes Schindler's internal battle with morality in the best-selling book that inspired the hit movie.

Yet Schindler was a man who risked his own life to deal with the devil for the sake of good.

Schindler was already rich from war profits and black marketeering by 1941, when, miles away, Birenzweig was sent into a factory as a slave laborer, one of 7,000 Jews making war planes in exchange for soup and bread. "It was to push away the days. We are counting day to day. The situation is bad, very bad," he says. "With the Germans, temporarily you are a little safe."

But only a little safe, considering the random terrorism of

the SS guards. Birenzweig worked quietly making wind-shield glass and doing books in the front office, he says, and so through competency survived the Nazis' killing process.

"When I got bread, I would divide it into pieces," he says. "In the morning I take a little bit, in the afternoon I take a lit-tle bit. Somebody else would take his bread and eat it and right away he was hungry again. This was the reason I can control myself. The body was more stabilized." But then the cyclone blew harder as Germany started destroying its fac-tories across Eastern Europe—and most of the workers in them—so nothing would be left for the advancing Russians.

Birenzweig survived that next cut and was sent to a salt mine outside Krakow where the Nazis believed they could build a factory that would be safe from bombardment. But that factory, too, was abandoned and the workers pushed one step closer to death.

This time the survivors were slated for Auschwitz, where mass murder had been by now perfected.

The Jewish manager for this concentration camp group was another rare man. It fell to him to compile what was surely a death list.

"He was a marvelous guy," Birenzweig says. "He knows he has to send away 1,400 Jewish people to a bad place. He say, 'How I can pick out: This guy should be alive, and this guy should be dead?'

"Then he said to the people, 'Who feels he is old, who feels sick, who can't work? Here will be hard work, plain la-bor, but really hard. If you can work you should stay here. The rest should go away.' Then he put himself on the list."

NOT FOR AUSCHWITZ

Birenzweig again made the cut, one of the 300 who missed the train to Auschwitz, 300 left out of 7,000 workers. This time be-fore luck ran out, he was sent into Oskar Schindler's sphere.

He was ordered to dig trenches outside the barbed wire of Plaszow, Krakow's concentration-camp factory site. To his astonishment, the Polish civilians boldly came up to the Jewish workers to cut some black-market deals, and their SS guard wanted in on the deal.

"The SS guy comes right up to me. He say, 'Tell them to bring a kilogram of butter.' Butter at this time was like dia-monds. He told me, 'You bring me this and you can do the business.'"

In Plaszow, he saw SS Commandant Amon Goethe, who dealt and drank with Schindler. Goethe was so cruel—he liked to perform target practice on people from his balcony—that even the Nazis sought to punish him during the war. In the end he was hanged for war crimes.

By the time Birenzweig arrived, however, Goeth had liquidated most of his camp, save the cleanup crew and the Schindler workers whose names were being put on a list to make their destiny official.

Birenzweig got himself on that list but, instead of being shipped to Schindler's new factory over the Czech border in Brinnlitz, the 800 male Schindlerjuden, as they were called, were sent to the Gross-Rosen concentration camp.

"This was a bad murder camp," Birenzweig says. "They cut stones in the quarry and they throw people from the stones. A bad place. Not just special Jews. All people. I saw people hanging from beams, hanging from their wrists 'til they died. These were Polish people who try to make a revolt." Birenzweig spent five days on the edge of hell, until, suddenly, the Schindlerjuden found themselves being treated differently.

Luckily Schindler's connections got them out of that concentration camp, but paperwork problems kept the 350 women on the list trapped in Auschwitz for weeks. . . .

BRINNLITZ SHAM

To get his people back, Schindler himself had to do some supreme wheeling and dealing. But he got them to Brinnlitz, where he ostensibly set out to convert a textile factory into one producing bombs. "They never got one shell from him," Birenzweig says, a point of pride in the Schindler legend.

"In Brinnlitz, Schindler give us bunks and baths. He tried to feed us good. On Sunday he tried to give us white bread," he recalls.

"He was working very slowly. The Germans don't have too many modern machines anymore. Nobody push us to work hard. He tell the SS that if anybody does something wrong, they don't have the right to hit him or shoot him. He would take care of it. This was marvelous."

Birenzweig remembers Schindler coming to talk to the workers at lunchtime often, sometimes with his wife, Emilie.

"He used to say, 'If I will be alive, so will you.'"

Schindler used to watch the train station to appropriate

stray supplies, food, goods, whatever, and on one such trip he found a carload of Jews nearly frozen to death and on their way to a death camp. He persuaded the SS guards he could use them as workers. Twenty-five were dead. "The other 75 he bring to us. He make a special place for them to get well. He buy medicine on the black market. He bring 65 back to life. I know. Myself, I feed them farina milk. By this time in the war, to get farina was like gold."

COMING TO AMERICA

And so the cyclone raged on as the war ended and Birenzweig bounced around in the chaotic ruins of Europe, attending trade school in Germany, saving for America, learning to ride the intimidating New York subway in a day, getting himself a job in a rubber factory, then moving on to mirrormaking. In the mirror business he saved enough to go out on his own, though his boss didn't understand why he would give up a good, steady job.

"I tell him, 'Right now, I'm young and healthy, but when I get a little bit older, maybe you don't need me, you send me away. What am I going to do then? If I go into business, maybe I save a few dollars." The lessons learned in wartime never leave, good and bad. "The war makes you feel more, more . . . more confident in yourself," he says. "Because you're passed by so much. I was not so smart, just I was a little lucky." Birenzweig married a Holocaust survivor. They had no children, and, after she died, he moved west to be near family.

Ironically he fared better after the war than Schindler, who died almost broke in 1974, 20 years before Spielberg made him a superstar.

CHAPTER 4

DISCUSSIONS OF SCHINDLER'S MORAL CHARACTER AND MOTIVATIONS

OSKAR SCHINDLER

Oskar Schindler's Moral Development

Luitgard N. Wundheiler

Luitgard N. Wundheiler is a psychotherapist at the Brooklyn Institute for Psychotherapy. The paper from which this selection was taken was based on interviews with twenty-four of Schindler's Jewish workers, and on interviews with several friends and relatives who knew Schindler both before and after the war. The paper also draws on a report that Schindler himself wrote for Yad Vashim, the Holocaust museum in Israel. Wundheiler takes the view that before the war Schindler was an insecure person, but his experiences caused him to undergo a process of moral growth and personal self-definition.

SCHINDLER'S PERSONALITY

The question I want to explore in the following pages is how Schindler developed from the person he was in 1939—kind and compassionate, but also on the look-out for his own interests and eager for his advancement—into the person he was during the last two to three years of the war—a man whose energies were focused on one goal: to help and rescue as many Jews as possible, a man who put his vices as well as his virtues and talents into the service of this one goal. The problem becomes even more interesting, if we look at Schindler's own explanations of his actions. Like many of those he saved, he considered himself impulsive. The German word he used to describe himself was "maß-los." Literally, "maßlos" means without moderation or restraint, but it has the additional connotation of the presence of an irresistable inner force that drives a person beyond what is considered acceptable behavior.

Two (true) anecdotes will serve to illustrate Schindler's impulsivity and his self-perception as an impulsive person.

Excerpted from "Oskar Schindler's Moral Development During the Holocaust," by Luitgard N. Wundheiler, *Humboldt Journal of Social Relations*, vol. 13, nos. 1 & 2, pp. 333–56. Used with permission.

[Israeli Supreme Court justice Moshe] Bejski asked Schindler the same question many others had asked themselves and him: "Why did you do what you did, why did you risk your life for us?" He asked this question approximately 15 years after the war, and this is the answer Schindler gave: "If you would cross the street, and there were a dog in danger of being run over by a car, wouldn't you try to help?" This reply is revealing. Schindler apparently thought of his rescue actions as direct and simple human responses to the sight of suffering; he thought them so normal that it did not occur to him that they needed an explanation; hence the challenging question at the end: "wouldn't you try to help?" One almost senses a certain impatience at being asked something so obvious. There is also an endearing innocence in this reply, as if, even after the Holocaust, he still did not realize that most people do not try to help another creature in danger, if by doing so they endanger themselves.

It is unlikely that this reply reveals anything about Schindler's real motives, rather, it says something about his personality. One purpose of this paper is to show that Schindler did not act from impulse alone, but learned to train and rein his impulses in order to put them to use on behalf of the many he saved. His words reveal something about his personality; he was a man of action, not of introspection—the question of motives probably did not seem important to him. He was an unselfconscious person, and for that reason, it *seemed* to him that his early impulsive behavior did not change and was a sufficient explanation of his later behavior.

The other incident was reported to me by a woman who knew Schindler well for many years after the war. One day, she and her family and Schindler wanted to take a boat ride together. As the ferry approached which was to take them across the river to the bank where the boats were anchored, an accident happened. The ferry rammed into a motorcyclist, and the impact was enough to throw him and his motorcycle into the river. Hardly a moment passed before Schindler jumped into the river to rescue the motorcyclist. A totally spontaneous action. This incident is like an illustration of Schindler's words: when there is a dog in danger of being run over, it is the most natural thing in the world to try to help. When there is a human being in danger of drowning, he felt it the most natural thing in the world to try to help.

Although he learned to control his impulses in situations

that required thoughtfulness, he never lost his impulse to help nor his readiness to follow that impulse. His impulse may have been the same when he saw large numbers of human beings threatened by the most vicious death machinery ever invented. And there were times when he followed that impulse at great risk to himself. There is a moving account in Keneally's book of Schindler, coincidentally coming upon a long train of cattle cars which stood in the blazing heat on a summer day in 1944, being readied to transport thousands of Jews to Mauthausen for "special treatment." When Schindler saw the suffering of those in the train, he distributed food and drink and persuaded the officer in charge to open the doors and refill the water buckets, when the train stopped near stations.

The question: How did Schindler develop from the kind of person he was in 1939 to the person he was during the last two or three years of the war forced me to look very closely at his actions and changes in his actions during the war years with the result that I arrived at the following two-pronged hypothesis: Schindler underwent two closely related developments, 1) from an impulsive and sometimes opportunistic helper to a compassionate, more thoughtful helper, and finally to a principled altruist, and 2) from a man whose concern was limited to people he knew personally to someone whose concern included many human beings he did not know at all. Logically, there is as direct a connection between these two developments as any psychologist, in search of manifest behavior to demonstrate the existence of latent personality trends, could wish for. The connection is this: to help only those one knows can often, not always, be explained in terms of the wish to eliminate one's own anguish at the sight of suffering; that anguish is greatest when it involves people we know. There does not seem to be a comparable urge that drives us to be concerned for strangers whose suffering we do not see. That kind of concern, when it manifests itself, would be an expression of principled helpfulness which I call altruism. I do not mean to imply with this definition that altruism is affectless; on the contrary, feeling for and with others is compassion and a necessary ingredient of altruism. Rather, I want to stress that altruism is more than compassion in that it is based on a set of moral principles while also embracing the feelings of compassion.

In order to show the gradual change in Schindler which

was outlined above, it is useful to divide the war years into three periods and present illustrative evidence for each. . . .

THE FIRST PERIOD: 1939–1941

During the first period, Schindler devoted much energy to setting himself up as an industrialist who contributed to the German war effort. He thereby built the Nazi façade behind which he would later operate for the benefit of the Jews and Poles in his care. It may be doubtful that he erected this façade with the conscious motive of using it later to hide his subversive, humane activities from his Nazi superiors; but only his motives, not the facts can be in doubt. During this first period, Schindler was consistently kind and helpful to Jews and Poles, but there were as yet few signs of a concerted effort to provide succor and rescue. During this time, his factory was not yet a part of a forced-labor camp or any other kind of concentration camp. He was master in his own house although it was already risky to be kind to Jews. But if he was clever and careful, he could still be kind without endangering himself. The limits of kindness, however, were laid down and enforced when rebellious nonconformists were caught. It was forbidden to have any kind of social intercourse with Jews, or to add to their food rations, or to greet them or show other signs of courtesy—to mention only a few of the numerous, official pronouncements that regulated Jewish-German relations during those years. During the first year of that period, Schindler increased the number of Jewish workers. A Jew who was doing "useful" work for the Germans, was still somewhat safer than a Jew who was not. Stern knew that and asked Schindler repeatedly to shelter Jews who were too old or debilitated to work elsewhere or work at all.

Schindler took good care of them. He bought extra food for them on the black market, although that was strictly forbidden, and treated them with a degree of sensitivity that was rare, almost non-existent, during those days. Not only was he kind and polite to them, but he gave them many reassurances concerning the future and in that way maintained their hope and will to live. Such reassurances may seem grandiose in retrospect because we know now that no person could be sure how or that he would survive the war and certainly could not give others reassurances to that effect. But these statements did not seem grandiose at the time, nor did Schindler mean them to be grandiose. Such reassurances were of the utmost importance to his workers' survival, for man does not live on bread alone—hope is equally important. As one woman, who testified for Schindler after the war, put it: "nobody helped us, Schindler was our father, our mother, and he never let us down." There is no question that Schindler himself also benefited from his actions as he was expanding his factory and therefore needed satisfied workers. But does that diminish what he did for the many helpless Jews in his care?

As stated before, it is one of my purposes to show that Schindler underwent a development from a person whose concerns were limited to people he knew to someone whose concerns included many human beings he did not know at all. Obviously, one might argue that many of the workers he employed during those first 15 months were also strangers to him. But firstly, one needs to consider that he employed many at Stern's request. He not only knew Stern, but a very special relationship between him and Stern had already begun to develop. From early on, Schindler seemed eager to please Stern. In addition, he had a great talent to get to know people quickly, so that when a person had been with him for as short a time as a day or two, Schindler knew him and felt responsible for him. It would be more accurate to say that many of the persons on whose behalf he was helpful toward the *end* of his moral development during the war, not only were unknown to him to begin with, but remained strangers to him, while all those he helped *early* in the war were people he had reason to think would remain workers in his factory throughout the war.

THE SECOND PERIOD: 1941–1944

The second period of Schindler's war-time development lasted from March 1941 until the summer of 1944. In March 1941, the ghetto of Cracow was set up, and in March 1943, it was liquidated. Stern's requests that Schindler employ Jews became more frequent during that period. The Jews of Cracow had compiled a list of "good Germans," of Germans sympathetic to the Jews who could therefore be approached with requests for help. Schindler was on that list. Stern hoped that the larger the number of Jews who were employed, the safer the economic base of the ghetto, and that a sound economic base would give the ghetto a certain degree of independence and stability. Schindler complied with Stern's request and, in addition, employed many others who came on their own initiative. From 1941 to 1942, the number of Jews employed in Schindler's factory rose from 190 to 550, by 1943, Schindler employed 900 Jews; and by 1944, one year after the liquidation of the ghetto, that number had risen to 1,000.

One extraordinary action of Schindler's falls into this second period of his development during the war. It is an action which prognosticates much of his later development into an altruist. He saved some children (the number is not known) by smuggling them out of the ghetto with the help of a man named Bosco, a German of kindred spirit, and delivering them into the hands of Polish nuns. I am corresponding with Josef Ströder, a German, who was the pediatrician at the hospital where some of these admirable nuns worked. Ströder believes that, until he had to go into hiding for being a friend to Poles, some children he treated in his hospital were Jewish, and that most of them came to his hospital with the help of Schindler.

This was an act of compassion, deepened and enhanced by Schindler's identification with the children as well as their parents. These parents surrendered their children to strangers in the anxious and uncertain hope of saving them. Schindler recognized that the greatest need of these parents was to have their children saved, that the pain of temporary loss accompanied by the hope, however slim, of seeing them again is more bearable than certain loss through death. It is noteworthy that his was an action not suggested by his friend and mentor, Stern. Not all of Schindler's actions were motivated by his wish to please Stern. Sometimes, that was his motive, but it is unlikely that it ever was the only motive.

March 14, 1943, was the last day of the liquidation of the ghetto of Cracow. Schindler witnessed a few hours of the bestiality with which the liquidation was executed. The horror of what he saw undoubtedly played a role in his indignation and his unfailing and consistent compassion with the persecuted. Months, even years later, he still had difficulty believing what he had seen. As he put it, he *knew* that he saw what he saw, but it remained beyond belief. The liquidation of the ghetto signaled, as in other Polish cities, the end of the last shreds of hope for the Jews. Thousands were massacred, thousands were deported to labor camps, and thousands to the death camps where the "final solution" was in full swing. In Cracow, miraculously, one half of the Jewish population survived the liquidation of the ghetto.

After the liquidation of the ghetto, Schindler's workers were imprisoned in forced labor camp Plaszow. When, as was briefly described earlier, Göth, the commandant of the camp, detained the camp population for hours at roll call in order to harass and torture them, Schindler had barracks built for his workers near his factory and outside forced-labor camp Plaszow. To be sure, he got permission to do that because the barracks remained officially a subcamp of Plaszow. But it is equally certain that he insisted—for the most part successfully—on running his subcamp as he wished. It cannot be repeated too often that his factory became a haven for Jews and Poles, and that Schindler sheltered many who were old and weak, and therefore inefficient workers. It is important to keep this in mind when one hears the charge that Schindler had his self-interest in mind when he built his subcamp. Without a doubt, there is some truth in this. By saving his workers from daily harrassment and torture he increased their efficiency and thereby the output of his factory and his profits. But it is equally evident that his compassion outweighed his profit motive whenever there was a conflict between them.

In order to appreciate Schindler's talent, one must know how he got permission to build separate barracks for his workers. First, he contacted an army engineer from the German Armaments Inspectorate and asked him to write a letter supporting his plan. Then he bought the land he needed from a Polish couple. When he had both the land and the letter, he approached the appropriate officials of the Government General. He turned out to be in luck: the officials of the Government General liked the idea of additional barracks in view of the fact that the Jews in the ghetto of Tarnow, 45 miles east of Plaszow, as well as thousands of Jews who still lived in the *shtetls* of southern Poland, had to be absorbed into Plaszow. Schindler's barracks would make that easier. Schindler knew how to approach the engineer from the Armaments Inspectorate. He told him production in his factory would increase. He took advantage of the rivalries between the Armaments Inspectorate, the Gestapo, and the SS, since he knew that the Armaments Inspectorate was likely to support any scheme that would add to the difficulties of the SS.

It is not difficult to imagine the pleasure and sense of power he got from playing various Nazi institutions and officials against each other. Schindler made good use of his contacts with the Armaments Inspectorate throughout the war, thereby acquiring the reputation of an industrialist interested in producing weapons required by the army. The result of this reputation was that he was able to increase the leeway he needed to pursue other purposes, and the more invulnerable his reputation made him, the more help and protection he could offer his workers and other Jews outside his camp as well.

In accordance with requirements, his subcamp had guard towers and an electrified fence, like any forced-labor camp, and a small SS garrison was assigned to it. But Schindler's talent to fool the official world by displaying a Nazi façade when his purpose required it made it possible for him to forbid the SS to enter his factory and barracks. When he had his subcamp, it was, of course, easier for him to perform acts of kindness for his workers. He took to visiting the factory daily and always left cigarettes and sandwiches in inconspicuous places, and, most important, he spoke to small groups of workers, reassuring them and giving them hope. How important his reassuring words were was brought to my attention by many of my informants.

The following is an example of the personal, individual concern he felt and expressed for his workers. Among them, there was a 14-year old girl, an orphan; Schindler gave her a weekly allowance so that she, too, would be able to buy a few necessities for herself on the black market. He never gave her the allowance personally, but asked someone else to deliver it to her. The girl, now of course an elderly woman, never doubted the reason. "He did not want to embarrass me—he always was very considerate of other people's feelings."

Another major event whose beginning falls into this second period of Schindler's development during the Holocaust was his association with the Zionist group in Budapest. In the summer of 1943, he was approached by a man named Sedlacek, a messenger for this Zionist rescue organization. Sedlacek asked Schindler to report to himself as well as Springmann and Kastner, the heads of the Budapest chapter of the Zionist organization, all he knew of the extermination of Europe's Jews. This necessitated an uncomfortable and risky trip to Budapest. Once there, Schindler reported not only what he had witnessed of the cruelty with which the Jews of Poland were murdered, but he gave his listeners hard numbers: 80% of the Jews of Warsaw had already been murdered, 66% of the Jews of the ghetto of Lódź, and 50% of the population of the Cracow ghetto. Those who were still alive after the ghetto liquidations rapidly disappeared in forced-labor camps and in those camps where the new "scientific" method of killing was used. After this report, the Zionists in Budapest trusted Schindler enough to ask him to transmit rescue money to Zionists in Cracow and to enlist his long-term cooperation in regard to rescue acts.

His long-range cooperation with the Zionists is possibly the most important evidence for the development I am trying to sketch. Certainly, this cooperation was risky, and one might argue that Schindler did what he did because he enjoyed taking risks. Perhaps, but so what? Is an action less high-minded and admirable because the actor enjoys it? Besides, one should keep in mind that the typical adventurer usually takes risks because any victory in a life full of risks adds to the risk-taker's glory in his eyes as well as the eyes of others. It would be difficult, to say the least, to construe what Schindler did in this way. Since his activities had to be entirely clandestine, there was not even the reward of temporary glory. There was no monetary reward either since, unlike some others who transmitted money to Zionists in various eastern European cities, Schindler never kept a percentage of the money for himself.

Whether his cooperation with the Zionists appealed to the gambler in him, may be doubtful. It certainly drew on his compassion and altruism in that it required selfless actions on behalf of people who were strangers to him. Indeed, he knew nothing about them, except that they were in terrible danger. In summary, then, he continued during this second period of his moral development to shelter Jews he knew and, in addition, he took many under his wing whom he did not know, but who needed protection.

THE THIRD PERIOD: 1944–1945

The third period, from the summer of 1944 until the end of the war, began with Schindler's decision to transfer his camp to some place safer than Plaszow and, in addition, it is marked by numerous rescue acts initiated as well as carried out by Schindler himself. As a result of the rapid advance of the Russian front, he lost contact with the Zionists he worked for and, therefore, had to act on his own, if he wanted to act at all.

Schindler decided to transfer his camp to Brünnlitz in Czechoslovakia. The following events led up to this decision: in the summer of 1944, orders came from Berlin that Plaszow, including Schindler's subcamp, was to be disbanded. Prisoners from Schindler's camp were to await "relocation." In the distorted and distorting language of the SS, "relocation" meant transport to the killing centers. According to his own report, Schindler could have moved the machines of his factory to any place in Germany he chose, but he would never have been allowed to let his Jewish workers, who had become dear to him, go west with him.

He had to make good use of his acting talent and his talent to persuade and bribe once again in order to get all the permission slips he needed. This time it was easier than he expected because he got support from his friend Erich Lange in the Army High Command who was one of many passive dissidents in the German army and from engineer Sussmuth of the Armaments Inspectorate who shared not only Schindler's convictions, but also his wish for action. Goldberg was asked to make up a list of individuals to be transferred to Brünnlitz. When I read Schindler's file in the archives of Yad Vashem, I saw the list of names. We all have our moments of shock when we think of the Holocaust. My most terrifying moment of shock was the moment when I saw the list and read on the first page: *Bill of Lading. Merchandise: Jews.* Despite all my frighteningly detailed knowledge of the Holocaust, the *dehumanization* expressed in those words appalled me more than anything else had terrified me.

That Schindler's decision to transfer his camp was motivated by his attachment to his people is clear from his own report. There he speaks of his workers as "meine Schützlinge." The best translation of "Schützling" is charge or ward. A nursemaid might refer to the children in her charge as "Schützlinge." It refers to someone in real need of protection, and not to someone one chooses to protect although that person might be able to make it on his own, the latter seems to me a definition of "protégé" rather than of "Schützling."

As stated above, the most distinguishing characteristic of this third period of Schindler's development was that he engaged in rescue actions which were not suggested by some other individual or organization, but conceived and initiated by himself. To mention just a few more: he made a deal with the police of the Brünnlitz area to the effect that they would send Jewish escapees to him rather than return them to their persecutors. During the last months of the war, there were, of course, an increasing number of Jewish escapees because Jewish prisoners became more desperate and daring and because the disorganization of the giant Nazi state became rapidly evident. Another action, initiated by Schindler, was his request for 30 additional metal workers (whom he did not need) from one of the worst quarries of Auschwitz. A third one—about whose outcome no exact data was obtainable—was his request for the transfer of small groups of women from Auschwitz to small factories in the Brünnlitz area on the pretext that these small factories manufactured products that were essential to Schindler's munitions factory. All these were actions that required initiative and careful planning. Thus, they are additional evidence for the third stage of development I sketched. Careful planning is not the mark of a person who acts from emotion and impulse alone, however compassionate that impulse may be. Rather, it is the mark of a person who has learned to rein his impulses and emotions so that they can serve a purpose. To find ways to persuade one's opponents—the police, even the Gestapo and SS—to cooperate with a factory owner, rather than foil his plans and denounce him, takes the special kind of intelligence which Gardner (1983) calls "interpersonal intelligence" and without which Schindler would have been just as impotent as many others. People become passive because they feel helpless, and often they feel helpless because they lack the imagination and intelligence as well as the courage to act in accordance with their convictions. . . .

SELF-DEFINITION

Before closing this paper, I want to present a few thoughts which I consider crucial for a deeper understanding of Schindler. One thought deals with the way in which he was defined by others and with his self-definition. When he came to Cracow as a young man of 31, he did not seem to have a clear sense of who he was. He seems to have felt competent in a general way, but he also felt insecure, and this manifested itself, above all, in his wish to please and his need for approval. It seems likely that this contributed to his

kindness. Individuals who are insecure are often highly
sensitive to the opinions others have of them. Among the
first people he came in contact with in Cracow were the
Jews. Schindler recognized that the Jews were treated as
outlaws and needed protection. He provided it and thereby
endangered himself. That he was protective in his attitude
to Jews had another result: his reputation as a compassionate, kind person grew, and this led to the beginning of his
self-definition as a kind and compassionate person. Self-
definitions have motivating power. A developmental spiral
was set in motion: The definition by others as compassionate
and kind made him see himself that way. As a result, he acted
more in line with that definition; and that, in turn, enhanced
the view others had of him, as well as his self-definition. It is
well known that even persons with negative and demeaning
self-definitions tend to act in line with them. It is even more
likely that persons with positive self-definitions act in accordance with them. That Schindler liked the view the Jews had
of him as a compassionate person is apparent from much
that he said. It seems clear that he accepted their view of
him as a good person and a good German whole-heartedly
and that it helped him to form a clearer sense of identity.

Psychoanalyzing Schindler

Robert Jay Lifton

Psychiatrist Robert Jay Lifton teaches at John Jay College and at City University of New York. He is the author of *The Nazi Doctors*, a book on the doctors who worked at concentration camps, sometimes performing medical experiments on Jewish prisoners. In this viewpoint, Lifton portrays Schindler's character less in terms of moral development as in terms of "doubling," i.e., an ability to maintain two distinct, and even contradictory, selves.

Oskar Schindler seems an insoluble puzzle. We know him to have been an amoral, exploitative Nazi businessman, and also the savior of 1,100 Jews. What confuses us is the idea of a less-than-good man performing, with considerable courage, a more-than-good deed.

Steven Spielberg's film *Schindler's List* and the Thomas Keneally book on which it was based depict Schindler's transformation over time. But the nature of this psychological change is never made entirely clear. In a thoughtful essay in *The New York Review of Books*, literary critic John Gross speaks of the unanswerable riddle: "Why did he do it?" He then suggests, "Perhaps we should stop fretting about his motives, and simply accept him with gratitude, for what he was." Similar things have been said by "Schindler Jews," people he enabled to survive.

But the Schindler puzzle remains insoluble only if we hold on to certain assumptions about the nature of the individual self. We're in the habit of thinking of it as relatively fixed in its structure, so that we tend to see people as consistent and predictable: One is a lively or dull person, a good or bad person, and one is expected to behave accordingly.

But the self isn't that simple, especially over the course of

Reprinted, with permission, from "Schindler's Puzzle," by Robert Jay Lifton, *American Health*, June 1994.

the chaotic 20th century. Novelist Don DeLillo speaks of "the back and forthness" of experience, of "ambiguities, contradictions, whispers, hints." These are characteristics of what I call the "protean self"; named after Proteus, the Greek sea god who took many forms. The protean self is many-sided and fluid, capable of constant change and even transformation. It can be made up of odd combinations, or images and inclinations that seem incompatible.

From that vantage point, the Schindler puzzle looks a little different—by no means fully solved but no longer insoluble. Schindler began by seeking to exploit Jews more thoroughly than anyone else—to obtain capital from them for his factory, to use not only their cheap labor but also their organizational and accounting skills in his business. To do so he had no choice but to work closely with them and to experience them as human beings. In that way his callous greed could be joined by an emerging sense of compassion toward

---

SCHINDLER'S OWN ACCOUNT OF HIMSELF

On several occasions people asked Schindler why he did what he did. Plater Robinson has compiled Schindler's replies as part of a study guide for students reading Keneally's Schindler's List.

Twenty years after the war, Mosche Bejski, a *Schindlerjude* and later a Supreme Court justice in Israel, asked Schindler why he did it. Schindler replied, "I knew the people who worked for me. When you know people, you have to behave towards them like human beings."

The same question was asked by Poldek Pfefferberg, another *Schindlerjude*. Schindler answered, "There was no choice. If you saw a dog going to be crushed under a car, wouldn't you help him?"

In a 1964 interview, standing in front of his dingy Frankfurt apartment. Schindler said, "The persecution of Jews in occupied Poland meant that we could see horror emerging gradually in many ways. In 1939, they were forced to wear Jewish stars, and people were herded and shut up into ghettos. Then, in the years '41 and '42 there was plenty of public evidence of pure sadism. With people behaving like pigs, I felt the Jews were being destroyed. I had to help them. There was no choice."

Plater Robinson, *Schindler's List Teaching Guide.* New Orleans, LA: Southern Institute for Education and Research at Tulane University, 1995.

those upon whom he had to depend so thoroughly.

I encountered a similar psychological process in the research I did for my book on Nazi doctors. For some Auschwitz physicians, sustained contact with imprisoned Jewish doctors, whom they needed for actual medical work, brought about relationships that improved the lot of the imprisoned doctors. These prisoner-doctors in turn were able to help many others survive.

Schindler's dual life as Nazi and rescuer can also be looked at from this perspective. Throughout the war he continued to be a high-living, heavy-drinking Nazi businessman who sought constant and varied sexual pleasure. He bribed and cajoled his Nazi contacts for his business purposes, but at the same time he was expressing a true aspect of himself. He especially manipulated Amon Goeth, the sadistic commandant of a nearby concentration camp, but we have no reason to believe that he didn't also continue to derive enjoyment from Goeth's lavish and wild dinner parties. In so doing, Schindler underwent a pattern I've called "doubling," the formation of what is functionally a second self, which can behave more or less autonomously from the prior self. Doubling is a form of dissociation, a severance of one part of the mind from another. But it can also be a means of staving off more severe fragmentation of the self as occurs, for instance, in multiple personality disorder.

SCHINDLER'S TWO SELVES

I first observed doubling in Nazi doctors who drew upon an *Auschwitz self* for the dirty work they did in that camp and then called forth their prior selves as ordinary fathers and husbands during periods of leave back in Germany. Likewise, in certain circumstances Schindler could call forth his *Nazi businessmen self* and on other occasions his *rescuer self*. As with the Nazi doctors, Schindler's doubling was a way of dealing with moral conflict caused by the pressures and temptations of an extreme environment. The difference was that the Nazi doctors used their doubling for the purpose of killing, while Schindler used his for the purpose of saving lives.

One reason Schindler could be so malleable was that he was bound to no ideology. While he was originally drawn to the Nazi party, and might well have been attracted by its promise of economic renewal, his approach was essentially pragmatic and, at least at the beginning, self-aggrandizing. His manipulative talents—skillful bribery and conviviality— were particularly well suited to the corrupt atmosphere of Nazi-occupied Krakow, Poland. Those same talents, moreover, could be put to equally effective use in protecting Jews.

Schindler's compassion toward Jews was shared by a few other Nazis who, like him, recoiled from the excesses of the SS. Schindler ultimately acted more boldly than these men, but being able to share feelings with them, however cautiously, enabled him to connect his Nazi self with his emerging rescuer self.

As the rescuer self took shape, it was nurtured by the meaning Schindler took from protecting the Jews—of being, as one woman put it, "our father . . . our mother . . . our only faith." I observed a similar pattern in a Nazi doctor I interviewed whose life-sustaining kindnesses to prisoners made him revered at Auschwitz; he too found support for his behavior from like-minded Nazi doctors, even as he remained on good terms with their crueler colleagues, including the notorious Josef Mengele.

Schindler's rescuer self was also strongly supported by his relationship with Itzhak Stern, the Jewish leader who worked closely with him and who quickly recognized his potential for decency, for being a "just Gentile." Stern undoubtedly conveyed this recognition to Schindler in a variety of ways. Whether or not Stern was, as Keneally writes, "the only father confessor Oskar ever had," he was surely a significant influence in bringing about Schindler's changing sense of himself.

While we can't be certain that Schindler's witnessing the cruel annihilation of the Krakow ghetto by the SS in June of 1942 brought about the epiphany suggested in both the book and the film, it undoubtedly made a powerful impression on him. For by that time Schindler's rescuer self, sensitive to Jewish suffering, was able to respond with sympathy, with anger and, most important, with constructive action. Indeed, by the end of the war, Schindler had given his emerging rescuer self such full expression that he was devoting virtually all his energies to saving lives.

But the Nazis' defeat eliminated the place for that rescuer self to operate, and Schindler suddenly found his life bereft of meaning. Although he did partially revert to his earlier self, he couldn't go back to being simply an amoral manipulator. With few psychological resources for an alternative way of life, he wandered from Germany to South America to Israel. His marriage failed, as did his postwar business ventures. In a reversal of roles, he became the "survivor" and the Schindler Jews his "protectors." Their moral and financial support undoubtedly helped him survive as long as he did—he died in 1974 at the age of 66—without ever finding a successful way to live in the post-Holocaust world.

Oskar Schindler never became a saint—or even a man who consistently behaved well. But his remarkable life illustrates the many possibilities of the individual self, the way in which latent elements can emerge and new combinations take shape. It demonstrates the human possibility for change—change that may be woefully incomplete and yet, under certain conditions, decisive.

The Economic Puzzle of Oskar Schindler

Ray Jones

Ray Jones is a Ph.D. candidate at the Katz School of
Business at the University of Pittsburgh. In this selection, he tries to explain Schindler's behavior by
referring to the economic concept of "amenity potential." Amenity potential explains behavior not
just in terms of greatest financial advantage, but in
terms of any desired outcome, including such altruistic outcomes as preserving the environment, en-
hancing the happiness of workers, or even saving
lives. However, the *desire* to achieve these goals
must be balanced against the *ability* (or potential) to
achieve these goals.

This selection explains Schindler's behavior, not as a
moral development from greedy industrialist to altruist,
nor as the result of a two-sided personality, but as a coin
with two sides: he was *able* to save his Jewish workers—a
goal that he believed to be desirable—precisely because exploiting their labor had given him the resources he needed
to do so.

In economics, choice is typically explained using the utility
maximization approach, which holds that an individual's
utility motivated self interest is the guiding motivation for
choice, as well as the driving motivation for efficient economic outcomes. Simply stated, utility maximization is the
idea that individuals are motivated by their personal
preferences (or utility) when making choices and when as-
sessing the results of these choices. Since the economies of
most modern societies are based on some variation of a
competitive market, utility maximization is typically applied
to describe actors who are making choices and evaluating
outcomes in a competitive market, based on a desire to

achieve the highest possible financial gain.

While the utility maximization approach is useful for explaining the choices of actors who are pursuing the highest possible financial gain, choice is a vast phenomenon which involves much more than the pursuit of the highest possible profit. In fact, the theoretical foundation of the utility maximization approach, rational choice, which dates back to the work of Thomas Hobbes and Adam Smith in the eighteenth century, is an expansive view of choice which does not assume that economic actors will pursue the highest possible financial gain in all situations. Rather, the theory is based on three distinct assumptions:

1. Individuals act in order to attain preferred ends.
2. An individual's likelihood of attaining his or her preferred ends is affected by constraints and opportunities, in the form of resources under an individual's control and social institutions to which the individual is subject.
3. Subject to their constraints, individuals choose the course-of-action, among those available to them, that realizes their preferred end to the greatest extent.

Thus, in order to understand how and why choices are made, one must consider the various preferred ends of an actor, profit maximization or otherwise, in the context of the constraints and opportunities available to that actor in particular situations. . . .

The factual account of Schindler's behavior reveals an intriguing mix of rescue and war profiteering activities. Schindler arrived in Krakow at the beginning of World War II hoping to make a fortune. As he became familiar with his Jewish workers and witnessed the Nazis' escalating anti-Jewish policies, however, he began taking steps to protect his workers from this persecution. Finally, when his workers were most at risk of being harmed, he devoted his efforts to the pursuit of saving as many Jews as possible. Schindler's various choices along the way reveal his progression from fortune-seeking, to protective business activities, to actions to save as many Jews as possible. The solution to the economic puzzle of Oskar Schindler lies in the explanation of these choices, a thorough depiction of his preferences, the resources that were available to him and the constraints that were imposed on him in the course of the choices he made. Applying the economic concept of amenity potential to Schindler's choices will provide this thorough depiction by examining the following attributes of Schindler's choices:

1. The various preferences that influenced his choices.
2. The resources he utilized in making these choices.
3. The legal, societal and market constraints that affected his choices.

SCHINDLER AS OPPORTUNIST

When Schindler first arrived in Krakow, he acted as a war profiteer, looking to take advantage of the business opportunities that would arise in the seat of the Generalgouvernement. One could even argue that, at that time, Schindler was an opportunist, a person "without strong political convictions, who decided that the best way to get ahead in a world dominated by the Third Reich was by collaborating with the winners.

Schindler's opportunistic behavior during the establishment of the Emalia factory suggest that Schindler was influenced by a strong preference to generate the highest possible profits for himself. He was even able to overlook the dehumanizing condition of the Jewish person whose factory he took over and the Jewish workers who earned meager wages in his factory, because he was using the resources available to him as Emalia's owner-manager to generate the highest possible profits for himself. He used such tangible resources as capital and labor, as well as intangible resources, such as his connections to the Armaments Inspectorate, to generate supply contracts in hopes of making a profit. These profit-making choices were supported by laws encouraging Aryanization and the exploitation of Jewish labor. The fact that Schindler did not face any legal or market constraints in the pursuit of his desired ends shows that his opportunistic behavior did not involve the exercise of amenity potential. He simply used his firm's resources to pursue lucrative war contracts, in a manner consistent with the laws of Nazi-occupied Poland.

While Schindler made several opportunistic choices after his arrival in Krakow, a few of his choices involved the exercise of amenity potential. Even though he was willing to take advantage of the Jews when he Aryanized Emalia, he quickly became dependent on his Jewish workers both for their labor and for their expertise in managing the factory. As a result of his regular interactions with his workers, he soon developed an interest in their personal welfare. As he stated after the war, "I knew the people who worked for me. When you know people, you have to behave towards them as human beings."

Schindler's actions in alerting his workers of an upcoming SS Aktion, as well as his complaints to the SS about the mistreatment of the workers, show the beginnings of a preference for protecting his Jewish workers. As owner-manager of Emalia, he had access to intangible resources in the form of his contacts in the SS. Schindler realized the constraint of the law, which mandated that helping Jews in any way was a crime punishable by death. Thus, when he complained to his SS associates, he did not portray himself as a person who was worried about how the Jews were being mistreated, but instead as a businessman, who was concerned over how the mistreatment of his workers would affect his factory's performance.

By June of 1942, Schindler had witnessed the Nazis' brutal anti-Jewish policies and the effects these policies had on his workers. Schindler now believed that "A Jew who had an economic value in a precocious empire hungry for skilled workers was safe from worse things." From the time when Schindler rescued his workers from the deportation train to Belzec to the end of the Emalia sub-camp, Schindler's behavior exhibits the development of a desire to protect his Jewish workers from the Nazis' persecution, combined with his pursuit of profit from his business.

As these behaviors show, Schindler exercised his preference for protecting his workers while at the same time following his desire to maintain a profitable factory. One could even argue that Schindler saved his workers from daily harassment and torture to increase their efficiency and thereby the output of the factory and its profits. But this is too simplistic an explanation, as is evident in his taking it upon himself to build the subcamp, paying black market prices so that his workers would have extra food, and acquiring children, and the sick and the elderly as "essential" workers for the factory. Thus, his preference for saving as many Jews as possible was beginning to emerge.

BALANCING PROFIT AND PROTECTION

Schindler utilized the resources available to him as owner-manager of Emalia to pursue his preference for blending the protection of his workers into his profit-making activities. As Keneally stated, "It was Oskar's nature to believe that you could drink with the devil and adjust the balance of evil over a snifter of cognac. . . . He'd always been a man of transactions." Psychologists Samuel and Pearl Oliner discussed the significance of such transactions in their study of the rescuers, those who saved Jews during the Holocaust:

> Without resources . . . rescuers could not have undertaken their tasks. They needed money, appropriate shelters, and help from others. . . . Money, in particular, was essential to the entire enterprise of rescue. It was needed to purchase food, shelter, forged papers, transportation, and all other basic needs; it was also needed for bribing. . . .

In Schindler's case, his workers were relatively safe from the Nazis' persecution because of his creative use of his firm's cash and trade goods. Because he was willing and able to use these resources, the forced labor camp was allowed at Emalia, and thus, a thousand Jewish workers were safe from seizure and random execution.

While Schindler's use of tangible resources, such as money, goods and shelter, was necessary in protecting his workers, it was his use of intangible resources, such as his connections with Nazi officials, which ultimately enabled him to blend the protection of his workers into the pursuit of profit. This can be seen in Schindler's development of his contacts with the Armaments Inspectorate. Schindler's dealings with the Inspectorate as owner-manager of the Emalia factory gave him the reputation of being a serious industrialist, interested in producing supplies that were needed by the army. This reputation made it possible for him to pursue other purposes. Thus, if a zealous SS guard tried to enter the Emalia subcamp, he would contact General Scherner at the Inspectorate and have the guard transferred. The workers were protected from the guards, and the factory's progress was unimpeded by unnecessary disruptions in production.

The fact that Schindler blended protection into his business activities is essential in understanding how Schindler was able to legitimately make Emalia a safe haven. When Schindler decided that his workers were not safe at Emalia, he did not simply storm into Plaszow and take his workers away. He recognized that bold and brazen actions on his part were not necessary since he could accomplish the same results by simply acting within the limits of his position and its resources and constraints. He realized that the appearance of a legitimate business was the essential point and that he could literally do anything he wanted, including building a barracks that would protect his workers from the brutal murderer Goeth, with the permission and encouragement of Goeth himself. Schindler was careful not to "openly spit in the system's eye," and took care to ensure that these protection activities appeared to be part of the Nazi's exploitation of Jewish slave labor. He protected his workers through the opportunities afforded to him by being able to legitimately request such a barracks from Goeth, since he acted as a businessman making a business decision and obtained Goeth's permission as part of a business transaction to more fully exploit his labor source. Instead of open defiance of the Nazis' anti-Jewish laws and beliefs, "Oskar put on his big Party pin and went to deliver high class liquor to Amon Goeth in Plaszow."

SAVING AS MANY AS POSSIBLE

At Emalia, Schindler was able to maintain a comfortable balance between protecting his workers and operating a profitable factory. By the end of the summer of 1944, however, the main SS office in Oranienberg closed the Emalia factory, placing Schindler's workers in grave danger. While Schindler may have been able to creatively incorporate his rescue activities into his business dealings at Emalia, the situation had now become desperate for his workers. Schindler had witnessed 14,000 Krakow Jews being deported to Belzec, never to return. Unless Schindler could find a way to save the workers, they would be sent to Gross Rosen or Auschwitz-Birkenau, which guaranteed a similar fate. Schindler began undertaking numerous actions with the primary purpose of saving as many Jews as possible. . . .

Profit was no longer a consideration for him, as his desire to save as many Jews as possible had become the driving force behind his behavior. Even though he paid a great deal in the course of establishing and maintaining the factory, he had no serious industrial intentions. He was, in the words of psychologist Luitgard Wundheiler, "A man who put his vices as well as his virtues and talents into the service of this one goal."

Schindler used the money he had made at Emalia as a resource for the service of his main goal. He used money to pay bribes to acquire permission for the factory, to convert the factory into an armaments factory and subcamp, to transport his workers to the factory, to pay the SS for the prisoners' labor, to purchase food for them on the black market, to acquire additional laborers, and to pay the necessary bribes to keep the Brunnlitz factory open. By the end of the war, he had literally spent all of the money that he had made at Emalia, his entire personal fortune. This sequence of choices marks the first time in Schindler's wartime dealings when the market was a constraint on his activities. While he had paid above-market prices for food, paid bribes, and had devoted a great deal of money to purchase the barracks at Emalia, none of his previous protection efforts required him to take such a tremendous financial loss.

Even though making a profit was clearly not a priority, Schindler still contrived to keep up the appearance of obeying the law and maintaining a legitimate business. Even his dramatic rescue, the list of 1,161 Jewish workers, which inspired the title of the novel and the movie, and his incredible rescue of his 300 female prisoners from the Auschwitz-Birkenau death camp, appeared to follow the letter of the law, with Schindler arguing that "these are skilled munitions workers. I have trained them myself over a period of years. They possess skills I cannot quickly replace."

As was the case in Emalia, however, having money was a necessary, but not sufficient resource for accomplishing his objectives. He again relied on the various contacts he had developed as a wartime industrialist, the intangible resources of his position as owner-manager. He was able to acquire the Brunnlitz factory because he was able to obtain the support of individuals such as Erich Lange and Sussmuth in the Armaments Inspectorate. Rasch, the SS police chief of Moravia, was also essential because an SS police chief's support could shield the Brunnlitz factory from a barrage of protests from the Moravians. There would have never been a Brunnlitz factory without the assistance of these officials.

This is the ultimate irony of Oskar Schindler, that Nazis were responsible for giving him permission to engage in activities which violated the spirit of the laws and beliefs they valued. Individuals who had committed terrible atrocities against Jews, an SS colonel and even an SS police chief, literally helped Schindler obtain permission to take 1,100 Jews to a safe haven in the middle of Nazi-occupied Europe, simply because Schindler came to them as a businessman, appearing to follow the letter of the law. Schindler was given permission to engage in activities which violated the spirit of Nazi law, because his proposed factory appeared to be in compliance with the Nazis' industrial exploitation of the Jewish population. Schindler was literally able to save his workers from the Holocaust because he undertook his rescue activities under the guise of being a war profiteer who wanted to extract labor from Jewish workers while exploiting them to the fullest extent. One of the workers Schindler saved said the following of him: "One cannot fight evil with saintliness. In order to fight the Nazis, one had to outwit them, one had to be inventive, and not fall in with conventional ways of thinking." The 1,161 people who survived one of the darkest periods in history did so because this single individual did not fall into conventional ways of thinking. . . .

Schindler's constant devotion to maintaining the facade of being a "good Nazi" bears a striking resemblance to the myriad of U.S. firms who make a conscious effort to establish and maintain their socially responsible image. Oskar Schindler's methods and mindset are very similar to those found in today's socially responsible business movement, where executives in firms such as Ben & Jerry's and the Body Shop operate their businesses on the premise that they are responsible to society. As the concept of amenity potential shows, concerning one's self solely with the identification of an actor's intentions will not fully explain the choices the actor makes. To more fully understand the choices economic actors make, we must generate a reasoned explanation of such choices, and avoid the tautology of believing that one can fully understand another's behavior by knowing that person's intention. Amenity potential offers a more sophisticated analysis, a depiction of an actor's choices through the consideration of an actor's preferences, the resources that were available to the actor and the constraints which were imposed on the actor.

Schindler's Challenge to Moral Theory

M.W. Jackson

M.W. Jackson is a professor in the Department of Government and Public Administration at the University of Sydney in Australia. In this selection he argues that, according to the principles of "contemporary moral theory," Schindler's actions must be judged to be immoral, since they were not based on adequate rational reflection. Jackson does not believe that Schindler acted immorally. Instead, he argues that contemporary moral theory is mistaken. A better approach to moral theory, Jackson suggests, is the older tradition known as "virtue theory," which holds that people develop habits of virtue, and then act accordingly without having to reflect rationally.

AN EXAMPLE FROM HISTORY

Oskar Schindler was a minor industrialist in the 1930s, a member of the neo-Nazi Sudeten German Party. He was a colourful man, famed for drinking and whoring. Throughout the war he manufactured enamelware and, toward the end, shell casings for the German army. His works were in Poland, but as the war drew to a close he succeeded in moving his factory to Czechoslovakia. His enamelware business was successful even after the war began, but his effort at munitions manufacturing was a failure. He made little, if any profit from it, and his products were inferior. On top of this failure he also squandered the firm's assets from the enamelware on wine, women, and endless bribes and gifts to officials. All in all Schindler's Deutsche Emailwaren Fabrik was not a success story destined for the immortality of the *Harvard Business Review* or *Fortune*.

What the accountant's ledger does not show is that from the fall of 1943 to the bitter end of the war, Schindler devoted

Excerpted from "Oskar Schindler and Moral Theory," by M.W. Jackson, *Journal of Applied Philosophy*, vol. 5, no. 2 (1998), pp. 175–82. Copyright © 1998 Society for Applied Philosophy. Used by permission of Blackwell Publishers.

his firm and himself to recruiting and protecting Jews. Combining bravado in equal measure with bribery, Schindler managed to draw into his firm about 1000 Jews who were otherwise destined for the Final Solution. Once on his payroll each of them was classified by Berlin as a valuable war worker, thanks to Schindler's inventive chicanery. Schindler's adventure into the manufacture of munitions was not the search for profits in a war economy but the search for a good cover story for the protection of his workforce and himself for even the S.S. was chary about disrupting arms works. As Thomas Keneally makes clear in his novel based upon Oskar Schindler's exploits, *Schindler's Ark*, [published in the United States under the title *Schindler's List*], Schindler collected Jews quite literally as he came across them. It is also quite clear that but for Schindler these thousand would have been swallowed up in the maw of the Holocaust. The personal risk that Schindler took and the financial losses that he suffered were real. . . .

The millions of readers of Thomas Keneally's novel may be surprised to know that despite the good that Oskar did in saving that 1000 Jews, according to a strict interpretation of the dominant strain of contemporary moral theory, he cannot be said to have acted morally. Contemporary moral theory posits certain criteria of moral reasoning and behaviour. Schindler's intentions and actions do not meet these criteria. Consequently, his virtue cannot be recognised. That moral theory in its dominant contemporary form cannot recognise Schindler's virtue is not because Schindler had no virtue but because contemporary moral theory has little if any, place for virtue. Readers of Hegel may recall his aphorism that "no man is a hero to his valet; not because the man is not a hero, but because a valet—is a valet. . . ." Contemporary moral theory, like Hegel's valet, has insufficient perspective to understand moral practice in the case of someone like Oskar Schindler. Schindler's case is of interest in its own right as the record of a virtuous man *and* also as a limiting case for the dominant version of contemporary moral theory. . . .

CONTEMPORARY MORAL THEORY

The aim [of contemporary moral theory] has been to make moral theory relevant to the kinds of problems we face. One celebrated moral theorist is Stephen Toulmin who put it this way:

> Ethics is everybody's concern. . . . Everyone is faced with
> *moral problems*—problems about which, after more or less
> reflection, a decision must be reached.

In the effort to ensure that moral theory is not taken to be the history of what moral theorists have written, R.M. Hare began his book *Freedom and Reason* by asking "the reader to start by supposing that someone (himself perhaps) is faced with a serious moral *problem.* . . ." Contemporary "ethical theory must be about the *solution* to such [moral] problems" as we all have, R.M. Brandt has written.

Focusing on problems is the first, not the last, step in the analysis of contemporary moral theory. The purpose of focusing on problems is not to revel in them, but to solve them. Marcus Singer has written that his,

> ultimate aim is to determine . . . how moral judgements can
> *rationally* be supported, how moral perplexities can be *re-
> solved*, and how moral disputes can rationally be settled.

The key words in this passage from Singer are 'solution' (resolved) and 'rational' (rationally). The programme of contemporary moral theory is nothing less than the *rational so- lution* of *moral problems.* This then is the dominant consensus that underlies the superficial disputes that mainly occupy contemporary moral theorists. It is, as Edmund Pincoffs has written, a consensus so pervasive that it would be tedious to document it. From its foundation this consensus has expanded and become institutionalised, notably with the creation and prosperity of *Philosophy & Pub- lic Affairs,* a learned journal devoted to the rational resolution of moral problems like abortion and war crimes.

If moral problems are the focus of moral theory, then Oskar Schindler would seem to come within the ambit of moral theory. He certainly had problems. But to win the palm from moral theory the criteria of rationality and solution must also be met. It is on these grounds that moral theory rules Oskar Schindler beyond the pale. Seen from the heights of moral theory Oskar's fault is not that he tried and failed to find a rational solution, but that he did not even try to be rational or to find a solution. Had he tried to follow the North Star of rationality, I suspect, he would not have been able to save many Jews. There will be more on this point presently. Admittedly, there are many who accept the dominant consensus of contemporary moral theory and yet recognise Schindler's virtue. Their human sympathy prevails over the gleaming logic of contemporary moral theory. A less sympathetic subscriber to the dominant strain of contemporary moral theory cannot even say of Schindler that he did what a moral person would do but that he did not do it as a moral person would do it. This Aristotelian concession does not apply, as I shall show, because Schindler did not act morally according to the criteria of contemporary moral theory.

If there is an Olympus in contemporary moral theory it is *A Theory of Justice,* published in 1971 by John Rawls. In *A Theory of Justice* the kind of morality that would rationally solve our problems was spelled out. It was one based on what James Fishkin has since, appositely, termed 'transcultural criteria'. It is a morality of rules and principles that are free of the "contamination of sex, age, race, class, socialisation" and the other impurities that putatively determine our moral judgment, according to Fishkin. Rules and principles free of such contaminations are, like Rawls's principles of justice, meant to apply anywhere and at any time. In short, they are universal. This is the received character of moral theory. . . .

In a morality composed of universal rules and principles, the solution to problems lies in deciding which rules or principles apply to a particular case. This adjudication of application can be a difficult and complex procedure. It was the kind of decision that Immanuel Kant called a 'determinative judgement'. One determines which rule or principle applies. Once that is decided the rule is applied.

SCHINDLER'S IRRATIONAL BEHAVIOR

Oskar Schindler would not recognise himself in this description. He certainly had no solutions. If he had been asked—by an all-seeing angel—whether he was doing the right thing, I doubt that he could or would have had an answer. Though I am sure he would have offered his heavenly interlocuter a cognac while they discussed the matter. A persistent acolyte of contemporary moral theory might insist that Oskar's actions were consistent with the principle of the human right to life, but the case cannot be sustained. First Schindler did not think, speak, or act in terms of rights. He simply responded to life, to the lives that came within his purview. Ergo, he did not try in any way to aid Jews or other victims of Naziism beyond his ken. Yet he was all too well aware of what was happening to the millions of Jews outside the twilight zone of Deutsch Emailwaren Fabrik. This knowledge did not make him guilty or make him feel guilty. He simply pressed on.

Nor did Oskar act in a way so as to be a maxim for all others *pace* Immanuel Kant. Not everyone else was placed to deal with, or experienced at dealing with, the German, Nazi, S.S. and Gestapo authorities that Schindler dealt with daily. For most, to try would have led to failure if not fatality, as it almost did for him. Indeed, Oskar did not even seem ever to ask himself if he had done the right thing. He never ignored the opportunity to recruit yet another Jew. It never occurred to him that the boat was full. He did not rationally calculate. When some of his Jewish workers were mistakenly transported to Auschwitz while his factory was being re-located, . . . he moved the earth to get them back, drawing the attention of numerous little Eichmanns to himself in the process. He did not hesitate in trying to rescue his workers from Auschwitz as a utilitarian would surely have hesitated, calculating the lives of *Schindlerjuden* in Auschwitz against the remainder who might be lost if his efforts aroused the notice of the S.S. Nor did he, as a deontologist would require, strive to save every Jew in Europe. Still less did he ask himself if he had done as much as he could. . . .

If it is right for me to save a drowning swimmer by tossing in a life preserver, involving absolutely no risk and very little effort to myself, it would be right for anyone else so situated to do so. If I am a strong swimmer lolling on the beach, I cannot pick and choose whom I will save, assuming that the act of saving involves no risk or loss to myself. I cannot save one drowning swimmer, but later neglect another because the soccer match on the radio has reached its climax. To discriminate is to violate the universal rule, acting in a way that it would not be right for everyone to emulate. Where there are costs or risks to be borne by the saviour, as they were by Oskar, it is more complicated. It would not be wrong for me to refuse to risk my life to save another person. On the other hand to risk my life once to save another and to refuse to do it again is less obviously acceptable, though it is easy to imagine the explanation that could be given for the failure to act for the second time:

> I did it once, but never again!
> I was almost killed!

However, these cases of supererogation do not fit Oskar's case. He was constantly at risk as soon as he sheltered the

first Jew. Taking one refugee after another may have contributed to the probability of exposure in the calculus of a
reasonable person, but it did not increase the penalty that
would befall Oskar and his employees if they were found
out. According to Keneally's account, Schindler never turned
away a Jew. Obviously he was not a reasonable person who
calculated the probability of exposure against the lives at
risk. But then again he was not a deontologist who martyred
himself the first time he saw something terrible or heard
something worse. If it exists, he waived John Stuart Mill's
right to a quiet life.

The most astonishing thing shout Schindler is that he became neither a martyr nor a paralytic. Frustration and confusion did not drive him to end it all in a death wish, say by
provoking the S.S.'s suspicions or by suicide. Not did he
paralyse himself with doubts, as the characters of an early
Woody Allen film would have done. Cast as Schindler, one of
these Allen personae would have intellectualised the problem in the search for a rational solution exactly as contemporary moral theory requires. A solution would have to be a
universal rule. "How can I save, for who knows how long,
this one when there are thousands and thousands more suffering and dying while I'm drowning in cognac?" such a self-
doubting character would say. I should think that this Woody
Allen/Schindler would not be able to answer this question
rationally. The answer, of course, is that he saved those that
he could, but that is not a rational justification. After all, he
could have tried harder or gone to one place rather than another where he might have recruited different people. The
people he recruited were usually those who were lucky
enough to cross his path, nothing more, nothing less. They
came to him. For his part he never systematically searched
for Jews. Nor was there any reason to end up with 1000. Why
not 1200? The futility of saving one, but not all others is a
common tenet in our intellectual life when self-styled revo-
lutionaries decry the limited—in their view, pathetic—en-
deavours of reformers, as for example allegorically in Luis
Bunuel's film *La Viridiana.*

The truth on Keneally's showing is that Schindler avoided
Woody Allen's intellectual paralysis by not thinking too
much. He operated on feelings, failing to respect the Enlightenment divide between thinking and feeling. When he
saw someone in need he responded. He did not think about

all of those he was not helping. He concentrated on those he was helping.

If Schindler's instinctive reactions do not obtain the crown from contemporary moral philosophy, it may be just as well, as far as those whom he saved are concerned. It seems all too likely that many people throughout Europe before, during, and after the war were paralysed by the test of universality as much as by the fear of the risks. They could not help nor save all under threat; so they said to themselves, 'There is no point in helping even one'. It was all, or none. It is certainly a defence of inaction that many people have since given. One of the merits of Keneally's novel is that he makes clear that Schindler was not alone in his human sympathy for the suffering of others. He documents many instances of bystanders, officials, German soldiers, and others in small ways aiding individual Jews. These *kleinen* Schindlers did what they could. Schindler could do more, and he did it. Nowhere in Schindler's story is there a problem, a solution, or rationality defined as universality. Consequently, what he did fails to meet the criteria of contemporary moral theory.

SCHINDLER AS AN EXEMPLAR OF VIRTUE

I have made a number of related claims about Schindler. Before going on it is time to take stock. First, I have claimed that Schindler acted on feeling. He did not calculate or ratiocinate, as the dominant criteria of contemporary moral theory require. Secondly, I have noted in passing that Schindler was absolutely loyal to the Jews he chanced to recruit. This is a minor point. Thirdly, I emphasised that Schindler saved some, but not others. The dominant version of contemporary moral theory equates rationality with universality as defining characteristics of morality. Particular and partial acts do not meet the criteria of moral theory. This is my main point.

Against my third point immediately above, a defender of the consensus in contemporary moral theory might argue from the tenet that 'ought implies can'. Such a defender would see the rationality in Oskar's actions to be that he did what he could, as I have said earlier in this article. The defender would then conclude that contemporary moral theory can interpret the moral reality of Schindler and so is vindicated.

What the defender fails to appreciate is the force of my first point. Schindler acted as opportunities presented themselves. As I have stressed he did not set out to save Jews, search for Jews to save, or decide to save one kind of Jew rather than another (a young woman rather than an old woman). The punch line is that Schindler probably did not do all he could have done. Had he tried harder, been more systematic he might well have saved more Jews.

There is a second, more general weakness in the defender's argument that cannot pass in silence. Ought may imply can but the realm of the possible marked by the word 'can' is not determinant. Schindler had no foreknowledge of what he could do (i.e. succeed in doing) until 1945 (nor did he know the war would end in that year). He discovered what he could do by doing it, as do most of us.

If we realise Schindler's virtues today it is despite, not because of the dominant character of moral theory. It is because we hear the voice still of an older tradition kept alive by a distinct minority of contemporary contributors to moral theory like Iris Murdoch, Peter Winch, Alasdair MacIntyre and Bernard Williams. Recently Stanley G. Clarke has attempted to synthesize the older tradition into the newer tradition that I have described as dominant. He does so by characterising the newer consensus as theoretical and the older as anti-theoretical. Predictably, he then argues that the anti-theory school has a theory and consequently is a part of the newer, dominant consensus. Clarke is to be congratulated on his ingenuity.

However, lost in the glare of this ingenuity is that the older, minority tradition recognises a different kind of morality. This other tradition concerns moral enlightenment, moral education, moral character, and, above all, virtue. It does not address problems, search for solutions, or aspire to universal rationality. This other tradition includes Socrates (with a foot in both camps), Aristotle, the Stoics, Augustine, Aquinas, Hume, and Hegel among others. A thinker like Aristotle does not proceed by the study of problems. He is not interested in rationally resolving problems, but in how we should live. On the few occasions when he produces an example, the purpose is to warn his auditors against falling into traps that will have undesirable effects on their character in the long run.

Morality for Aristotle was what a person did, not the rules, principles, and procedures flourished. The measure of morality for him was what a person does, not what the person demands of others in the way of uncontaminated rules and principles. One's actions are based on one's character. In turn, character is not formed by learning rules and principles, nor is it equipped for action by the possession of a set of rules, principles, and procedures. Character is formed throughout a lifetime. It starts as habit. We learn to do good deeds by doing good at the instruction of an adult, and gradually we learn to do this autonomously and gradually we learn why it is good, though we may never be able to articulate and define its goodness by universal criteria on a philosophy examination paper. . . .

The limit of universality is easily shown in the case of Schindler. According to a precept of universality like Kant's categorical imperative an act is right if and only if it would be right for everyone so situated to do it. The standard example in textbooks, and one used by Kant himself, is lying. It would not be right for everyone to lie, so it is never right for anyone to lie. Hence, it is always right to tell the truth. But would it have been right for Oskar to have told the truth to the Gestapo officials who occasionally questioned him? Certainly not. Was it wrong for him to lie to them? Certainly not.

Lest it be supposed that the criterion of universality is not a general feature of contemporary moral theory, but only of Kantian deontological theory, the same limitation is to be found in the prime alternative, namely utilitarianism. Utilitarianism demands a universal point of view before which all pleasures, pains, and lives are equal. Schindler did not adopt this point of view. For all he knew the faulty munitions that Deutsch Emailwaren Fabrik despatched to the Wehrmacht may have contributed to more than a thousand deaths. Even if that were the case we could hardly convict him of immorality, though a strict utilitarian would have to do so. Oskar was not a rational person in the prescribed fashion of contemporary moral theory.

Oskar Schindler acted instinctively in the face of direct experience. At the moment of truth he discovered the kind of character he had. It probably surprised him as much as everyone who knew him. His wife, Emilie, whom he had treated badly, said in 1973 that before the war there was nothing special about Oskar, nor was there after. Like Hector, he was fortunate that in a few short years of his life he had met a challenge that had found the angel within himself. The first soul that Oskar Schindler saved when he began to help Jews was his own. So, too, for all the little Schindlers who do some good.

Schindler's Compulsion

Dwight Furrow

Dwight Furrow is a professor of philosophy at Mesa College in San Diego, California. In this selection he offers an account of the forces that cause a person to feel morally compelled to act in a certain way. This sense of moral compulsion, Furrow says, was perhaps best expressed by Martin Luther when he wrote, "God help me, I can do no other." Furrow thinks that Schindler found himself in a position in which his conception of himself simply would not allow him to do other than he did.

WHEN WE CANNOT DO OTHERWISE

From 1939–1945 the German industrialist Oskar Schindler, despite enormous obstacles and at great cost and risk to himself, preserved the well-being and saved the lives of roughly 1300 of his Jewish workers who were threatened by Nazi genocide. His actions are those of a moral hero despite the fact that by most conventional moral standards he was not a particularly good person, devoted as he was to profiteering and pleasure-seeking. Thus, Schindler is a puzzle. Why did such a person sacrifice so much? We stand to learn much about moral motivation and character by answering this question.

In this essay, I want to view Schindler's actions as a particularly powerful example of an apparently common moral phenomenon—practical necessity. We sometimes say of a moral prescription that enjoins us to perform or not perform a particular action that one *must* do it, or *must not* do it. Apparently, some moral prescriptions powerfully engage the will. They "bind" us; we find them inescapable. Schindler's extraordinary moral resolve suggests that he feels so bound by an imperative to rescue his Jewish workers. If we can provide an adequate account of practical necessity, we should go some distance toward explaining Schindler's actions. . . .

Excerpted from "Schindler's Compulsion: An Essay on Practical Necessity," by Dwight Furrow, *American Philosophical Quarterly*, vol. 35, no. 3 (July 1998), pp. 209–29. Copyright © 1998, North American Philosophical Publications, Inc. Used with permission.

I rely on the intuition that for an action to be practically necessary, there must be some sense in which the agent could not have done otherwise. This intuition is supported by the logic of the word "must." To say that "I should (x)" or "I ought to (x)" is at best to imply that I have most reason to (x). The appropriate use of "should" or "ought" does not require that other courses of action are unavailable to me. However, the term "must" does imply that alternative courses of action are unavailable. . . .

In fact it would seem that "must" is most at home in contexts in which agents require great resolve to carry out what they perceive to be their moral commitments. The single-mindedness that allows substantial obstacles (internal and external) to be overcome encourages the idea that some sort of genuine necessity is involved, since such agents seem immune to the temptation of alternative courses of action, as if alternatives are unavailable.

SCHINDLER'S CHOICES

The particular account of practical necessity I will defend best explains the case of Oskar Schindler. Any explanation of this case must take into account a number of peculiar features of Schindler's life and this episode. Schindler's life shows no pattern of consistent moral reasoning. He is motivated primarily by self-interest and the pursuit of pleasure. He exploits cheap Jewish labor, acts shamelessly toward his wife, and his initial assessment of Nazi atrocities does not dissuade him from identifying with and assisting the regime. He only acts against the regime when personally affected, when threatened with the loss of cheap labor. After the war his life is unremarkable. His transformation into a moral hero involves very little specifically moral deliberation. He doesn't deliberate about what his obligations are or what sort of life he should lead. His thoughts are focused on understanding the behavior of the Nazis. Once he has the description right, once it is clear that extermination and humiliation is the aim of the Nazis, he is clear regarding what he must do.

These peculiar features are insurmountable obstacles to attempts to use traditional accounts of practical reason to explain Schindler's actions. Schindler is no universal legislator of values. Consistency, the salient element of practical reason, is not one of his virtues. Moreover, appeals to extraordinary qualities of moral character explain little in Schindler's case. He exhibits no inclination toward beneficence or agape love, only an exaggerated *bonhomie* [good will] and courage. He is sometimes caring and decent, but only within conventional parameters—an unlikely moral hero, yet a moral hero nevertheless.

One could argue that Schindler is simply acting on his strongest desire. Prior to the events described above he has one package of dominant desires—to make money and chase women. After those events he acquires a different package dominated by a desire to rescue the helpless. But such a transformation seems inexplicable. If his desires are so susceptible to fluctuation, why did they not shift under the considerable pressure of the enormous responsibility he undertakes?

Clearly witnessing the roundup of Jews in the Cracow ghetto had everything to do with his change in conduct. Some account of how these perceptions connect to Schindler's psychology is required to make sense of his subsequent actions, but appeals to consistent reasons or shifting desires won't do the work. His actions, in fact, border on the compulsive. His rescue of the helpless is pursued as relentlessly as he pursued his pleasures. But if some form of compulsion explains his conduct, we are in the vicinity of necessity.

What then is the sense of practical necessity that best explains Schindler's conduct? In broad outline my argument will be as follows. After witnessing the events in the Cracow ghetto, Schindler has three general options to consider with regard to the status of his workers. He can:

(A) resist genocidal policies by protecting his workers,
(B) remain neutral, acquiescing to the regime's demands when necessary but refraining from intentional cruelty, or
(C) continue to actively cooperate with the regime.

I argue that with regard to (B) and (C) Schindler was unable to form the intention to carry out either course of action. If Schindler could not form the intention to (B) or (C), then (A), the intention to resist, was the only course psychologically available to him. Thus, (A) is practically necessary. Schindler *must* undermine the regime because he is unable to form or sustain the intention to acquiesce or cooperate. (A), (B), and (C) are general, future-directed intentions. As far as I can tell, they exhaust the options that Schindler might have. Of course, he could have accidently or unknowingly acquiesced or cooperated; and there are innumerable ways of carrying out each long range intention, but these will not be at issue here. What will matter is establishing that (B) and (C) are intentions that Schindler could not form.

If this is the case, the notion of decision will not apply, since Schindler could not have done otherwise, and (A), (B), and (C) exhaust the alternatives. Cooperation and acquiescence are logically and physically possible. No factors external to Schindler's psychology provide insurmountable obstacles to him acquiescing or cooperating. In what sense could Schindler have lacked the capacity to form the intention to (B) or (C)?

My strategy in answering this question is to explain how moral incapacities are generated in an agent's psychology. That is, I want to describe the structural elements that are involved. . . .

MORAL INCAPACITIES AND EMOTIONS

Moral incapacities differ from non-moral psychological incapacities in that the moral type rest on moral emotions—emotions that contain judgments of moral worth such as admiration, contempt, shame, dignity, remorse, moral indignation, compassion, respect, and self-respect. These emotions function as a filter precluding agents from forming certain intentions to act and requiring others. If an agent feels contempt for a person or a way of life, she will strive to avoid contact or emulation. The prospect of experiencing shame typically precludes an agent from engaging in the shameful act. Moral indignation requires a commitment to seeking redress, rendering inadmissible attitudes of neutrality or endorsement.

These are commonplace observations, but cast light on what we would say if the filter were not functioning well. If a person expresses contempt for religious practice but prays when under duress, or expresses moral indignation by the sincere proffering of gifts, we would be forced to withdraw the claim that the agent was genuinely experiencing the emotion. In typical cases, emotions impose constraints on the kinds of intentions to act an agent must or cannot form. Notice, however, that the admissibility conditions of intentions to act in emotions function differently than those of ordinary practical reason. In practical reason the inability to form an intention is typically a contingent matter—circumstances make it impossible to intend to meet someone for lunch at noon if I plan to be in class at noon. With regard to emotions such as moral indignation, the inability to express it by sincerely proffering gifts is necessary. It is not the circumstances that make it impossible; the conceptual requirements, expressed through feelings, of the emotion itself render such intentions impossible.

The fact that emotions embody conceptual requirements is an important component of moral incapacity because it confers a genuine sense of necessity on the inability to form certain intentions. But I have yet to explain how emotional dispositions persist in an agent's psychology in ways that make them resistant to modification. Although, as dispositions, emotions can be strongly resistant to reconsideration, they are not necessarily so. Often emotions are short-term responses to unusual situations, their strength waning over time thereby eviscerating the incapacity. Moreover, the stability of emotional response is highly variable between persons. What accounts for the stability of emotional response?

As evaluations, emotions are expressions of what we take to have value. It is through emotions that our values engage our disposition to form or not form intentions to act. When we feel sadness, love, respect, etc. we are bringing what we value to bear on a situation. Emotions express consistent judgments when agents are able to persist in their sense of what is important and significant.

The persistence of our emotional lives can therefore be explained by the persistence of what we value. The notion of a constitutive good will help here. Some things we value become constitutive of who we are in a way that contributes significantly to psychological stability. The process through which particular attachments and commitments begin to congeal into a center and a periphery, into a sense of what is important unconditionally, on the one hand, and what is important but can be discarded in the face of competing considerations, on the other, is in part a natural, dispositional process. As I described above, to the extent we form intentions to act, either practical or emotional, we implicitly rule out alternatives. The goods expressed in stable future-directed intentions become constitutive of the self, and the motivational base for such goods becomes more extensive than ordinary desires because constitutive goods occupy a center that gives structure and coherence to a life. Thus, psychological capacities and the emotions that support them are deeply entangled with entire ways of life, commitments and attachments that are constitutive of the self in that they occupy the center around which the activities of one's life revolves. . . .

With regard to the problem of moral necessity, I want to emphasize that some of these commitments are unconditional in that they cannot be disengaged from one's life without massive conceptual and emotional transformation. To deny the importance of some pursuits would be to deny the importance of one's life *simpliciter.* Thus, they define what one can or cannot attach importance to and help to determine our psychological dispositions and capacities, emotions, and the range of intentions we can or cannot form. When we express sadness, grief, love, contempt, admiration, moral indignation, etc. we express the importance of these commitments and attachments, and do so with the necessity that I argued above was constitutive of these emotions. In well-functioning psychologies these dispositions constrain ordinary practical reason, supporting the formation of future-directed intentions by allowing only those intentions to act that are compatible with the agent's underlying dispositions.

It is important to emphasize the resilience of these dispositions. They are not particularly responsive to preference shifts, divergences between our expectations of how the world is and discoveries about how it is in fact, or modifications at the level of intentions to act. Our emotions conspire to keep these structures in place, for the psychological costs of change at this level are substantial. Their loss would be the occasion for grief, sadness, *ennui,* self-contempt, etc.

THE IMPORTANCE OF SELF-RESPECT

I have been arguing that intentions to act that an agent is able to form or not form are products of a certain kind of psychological stability. As I have characterized it thus far, psychological stability is a natural process, a property of normal human psychologies, which explain commonplace dispositions. This may go some distance toward explaining cases of moral incapacity that arise in ordinary contexts. Some intentions to act are ruled out by the attachments and commitments that occupy the center of our concern. Barring a *force majeure* that disrupts this stability, they are psychological incapacities of a sort. Thus, an agent who finds she cannot lie to a friend, harm a child, or ignore someone's suffering cannot do so because of the place that friends, children, and other persons occupy in the realm of her concern. The sense of "cannot" here is that there is no inducement that would get her to do it. There is a genuine sense of impossibility here because the agent need not attach conditions to "cannot." Given who she is, there is no other course of action she can permit herself to pursue under the circumstances.

There is still some question, however, regarding the reach of such an incapacity. Some agents will be incapable of forming particular intentions in normal contexts but their resolve weakens under pressure, especially threats. Some of the cases of practical necessity we want to explain are of agents who hold on to their moral resolve in spite of significant threats. Moreover, in some cases, the beneficiaries of the action do not seem intimately connected to an agent's realm of concern, for instance, when perfect strangers are rescued at considerable risk. These worries return us to Schindler's case. Schindler acted in the face of substantial threat under extraordinary circumstances. Moreover, it is not obvious why Schindler would have acquired the protection of his workers as his constitutive good. The final piece of the puzzle will be supplied by the role that self-respect plays in the psychologies of some persons.

Commitments and attachments impose expectations on us. It is impossible to have certain commitments without also having some view of what is expected or required to sustain the commitment. This does not have to be very articulate and may be formulated only when confronted by certain types of action or certain forms of treatment. The nature of these expectations depends on what the agent takes to be important given the life she wants to live. To fail to live up to an expectation generated by a constitutive good is to fail to be oneself. To have such a conception of expectations is therefore to have a conception of what sorts of conduct will protect or endanger the self since these attachments are constitutive of the self. Put differently, to have a sense of what one's constitutive attachments and commitments require is to have a conception of self-respect, and to be disposed to act in accordance with that conception is an essential element in having self-respect.

Self-respect is an emotion that takes as its object the self as worthy—worthy of meeting those standards entailed by one's core commitments. As an emotion with its own strategy, self-respect demands that the expectations be met; a failure to do so is both an injury to self-respect and a threat to the self. This suggests that self-respect is a protective emotion in which the strategy is to reduce the agent's vulnerability both to the loss of a sense of what is important and significant, and the consequent threat of being a mere conduit for the designs of others, forces of nature, etc. For agents with strong attachments to constitutive goods, the loss of core commitments entails an inability to judge others or oneself, and ultimately the inability to act effectively in the world.

As an emotion that consists in part of intentions to act, self-respect imposes a filter of admissibility on options. We might call self-respect a hyper-regulative emotion, because it takes as its object the evaluative content of the other emotions. It is a disposition to hold on to our admirations and contempt, our moral indignation, our loves and hatreds. For an agent who has self-respect, and whose self is formed by strong attachments to constitutive goods, there are intentions she cannot form if she is to maintain self-respect. The force and scope of "cannot" depends on the degree to which the proposed act threatens an agent's self-conception. However, if self-respect is to explain why some agents under duress are incapable of forming intentions that violate their self-expectations, some account must be provided of the pressures that keep self-respect in place as the dominant regulative element in an agent's psychology. Most of us, after all, would give up a lot of self-respect for a little survival.

SELF-RESPECT IS MORE THAN A SENSE OF SHAME

It is tempting to argue that the prospect of shame supports the constancy of self-respect and, as a result, the persistence of moral incapacity. When we fail to meet the expectations others have for us, expectations that we have internalized, we experience shame. In shame we suffer a loss of self-respect, because we see ourselves as judged by others and diminished according to standards that we share with others. On this view, we strive to avoid the painful experience of shame by never failing to act in accordance with expectations.

Prospective shame may in some cases support moral incapacities. However, there are three problems with treating shame as the operative emotion in cases of practical necessity such as Schindler's. It will not explain the incapacity to form an intention to act—only the incapacity to act on an intention. I might form an intention to steal a large sum of money from the bank but find that I am unable to do it. I ought to suffer a loss of self-respect, since I have discovered I am the sort of person who can form the intention to rob a bank. However, presuming I did not make my intention to rob the bank known, I would not experience shame since one necessary component of shame—an actual or potential audience—is absent.

Furthermore, loss of self-respect is not always or even typically occasioned by shame because, unlike shame, self-respect is not closely connected to the expectations of others. Self-respect, in part, involves the judgment that common expectations do no work, for self-respect demands that we not view the approval of others as its sole criterion. To have self-respect is to accept oneself—foibles and flaws included—as the basis for one's actions, despite the judgments of others. Thus, the prospect of losing the approval of others will not explain why an agent would hold on to self-respect come what may.

More importantly, shame will not apply to many cases of practical necessity, particularly Schindler's. It is a necessary condition of shame that the agent view her actions as deficient in light of the expectations of others. Supererogatory acts are not in accordance with the expectations of others. They by definition exceed those expectations. Thus, agents will not incur the disapproval of others if they should fail to live up to those higher standards and will not experience shame. However, they will suffer a loss of self-respect in failing to live up to their own expectations. Suppose that when the Nazis closed down Schindler's factory in Cracow, where he had been harboring Jews for most of the war, Schindler had decided there was nothing he could do any longer to carry out his intention to protect his workers and allowed the Nazis to take them. He would not have felt shame since no one, not even the *Schindlerjuden,* expected him to overcome the obstacles and incur the risk involved in relocating such an illegal operation in Nazi territory. Yet, I imagine he would have felt a substantial loss of self-respect (and remorse) for he would have failed to satisfy an intention to which he had been committed. Prospective shame will not explain why Schindler could not have acquiesced in Nazi brutality.

In fact, loss of self-respect is a much more pervasive and

threatening experience than shame. Agents who wholly lack self-respect lack basic affect through which life sustains meaning, for without self-respect every action is a potential failure, every relationship a deception, and everything one values, by *a priori* judgment, unworthy. Complete loss of self-respect is thus the loss of basic psychological security, an experience vastly more painful than the terror or disgust which support non-moral psychological incapacities. Although we can suffer some loss of self-respect without psychological debilitation, there is a threshold below which we cannot fall while sustaining our basic orientation toward the world.

SCHINDLER'S CONCEPTION OF HIMSELF

In order to find that threshold, in order to be precise about the role that self-respect plays in an individual's psychology, we have to appeal to the idiosyncracies of individual agents rather than widely distributed capacities. Agents, like Schindler, who engage in these extraordinary actions will not accept much compromise. Why that is the case may only be learned, if at all, through intimate knowledge of an individual's distinctive outlook, knowledge we do not have with regard to Schindler. However, we do know quite a bit about the situation that Schindler confronts. The circumstances he confronts contribute to the emergence of self-respect as a dominant element in Schindler's psychology.

Schindler was in the position of having been chosen for an extraordinary task. He simply found himself responsible for the lives of people who were utterly dependent on him. Most of us know what it is like to feel the burden of responsibility for our children who are utterly dependent on us. Schindler's burden was similar but multiplied exponentially. A palpable responsibility of such magnitude is not merely a burden that presses upon an agent from outside. It is individualizing in that only that agent and none other can respond. There is no recourse to others, no place to turn to alleviate the responsibility. One feels the burden, not of others, but of oneself; one's own substance is put to the test. To be in a situation such as Schindler's is to elevate self-respect as a dominant, regulative norm, for all choices will either enhance or diminish it. The thought is not "Should I accept this burden or not?" for the burden has already been imposed. The thought is rather "Am I up to the task?" What makes Schindler extraordinary is that he is not crushed by this question.

Schindler is not crushed by the question because of the characteristics we know him to possess. He is a charming, persuasive, opportunistic, manipulator with the self-confidence to pull off a massive charade under the noses of brutal and suspicious guards. These peculiar talents make Schindler what he is. These are Schindler's constitutive goods, and they are precisely the qualities called for under the circumstances. Only a person who had built his life around these sorts of abilities could have seen promise in these circumstances. This is not to underestimate common decency and the natural sociability that enables agents to invite and sustain relationships. Schindler possessed both, but, aside from these, we need not attribute any special "other-directed" moral qualities to Schindler. Schindler's unique abilities and the importance of these abilities to his self-conception explain his moral incapacity to acquiesce in Nazi genocide.

Thus, for Schindler and agents like him whose sense of self is bound up with constitutive goods and self-respect in the way I have described, moral incapacities are irresistible. They are irresistible because loss of self produces unique forms of suffering as aversive as those produced by non-moral psychological incapacities. These are not the intense physiological responses of fear and disgust, but the more pervasive feelings that accompany meaninglessness, impotence, and helplessness. A tacit presentiment of the self's vulnerability gives rise to self-respect as the dominant, regulative emotion.

CHAPTER 5

REFLECTIONS ON THE MOVIE *SCHINDLER'S LIST*

OSKAR SCHINDLER

Herr Direktor

Clifford J. Marks and Robert Torry

Clifford J. Marks and Robert Torry teach in the
English department at the University of Wyoming.
Among their various areas of study, Marks special-
izes in Holocaust studies, while Torry teaches film.
In this selection they analyze the movie *Schindler's
List*, not as a historically accurate representation of
Oskar Schindler's life, but as a metaphorical representation of Steven Spielberg's life. Aside from the insights this provides on the meaning of the film, this
selection serves the useful purpose of pointing out
some of the film's numerous historical inaccuracies.
Despite their view that the film is not particularly accurate historically, Marks and Torry claim to admire the film,
and give it a generally favorable review.

A POPULAR MOVIE ON AN UNPOPULAR SUBJECT

Schindler's List, Steven Spielberg's first attempt to narrate a
topic as historically unwieldy as the Holocaust, tells the now
famous story of a German entrepreneur, Oskar Schindler,
who through a series of events transforms himself from a
practical capitalist into a savior. In the film, Schindler trades
in his wealth to protect his Jewish workers from the gas
chambers at Auschwitz, in the end bankrupting himself and
his business. Often construed as the most significant cinematic statement on the Holocaust, *Schindler's List* has already made the leap from popular culture to historical and
educational material. A major television network has broadcast the film with little or no commercial interruption, and
it is often shown in high schools to teach students about the
Holocaust. Receiving an Oscar for the Best Film of 1993,
Schindler's List was a remarkable commercial and aesthetic
success. Most mainstream critics lauded Spielberg's story-
telling abilities, and his Hollywood brethren held up the film
as an unparalleled achievement. Though a few writers, jour-

Excerpted from "'Herr Direktor': Biography and Autobiography in *Schindler's List*," by
Clifford J. Marks and Robert Torry, *Biography*, vol. 23, no. 1 (Winter 2000), pp. 49–70.
Copyright © 2000, University of Hawaii Press. Used with permission. This reprint rep-
resents less than half the original article.

nals, and newspapers checked in with some critical commentary, none of it has relegated the film to anything less
than its epic rank in American culture.

But why a German hero, and a Nazi one at that? This essay explores the role of biography and autobiography in
Schindler's List. By autobiography, we mean how the film
not only tells the story of Oskar Schindler, but in a meta-
phoric way tells the story of Steven Spielberg as well. . . .

It is significant that rather than attempting the dramatiza-
tion of a survivor's narrative, or an overarching fictional
treatment like NBC's *Holocaust* (1978), or a vast historical
depiction like Alain Resnais's *Night and Fog* (1955), or an
in-depth factual documentary like Claude Lanzmann's
Shoah (1985), Spielberg chooses to narrate this Holocaust
story—which Keneally describes as "the pragmatic triumph
of good over evil, a triumph in eminently measurable, sta-
tistical, unsubtle terms"—through the medium of fictional-
ized biography. Although familiar with other cinematic versions of the Holocaust, and even borrowing certain styles of
filming and narration, by choosing to make a good German
his focal point, Spielberg rejects any previous mass culture
vehicle. Instead, he enlists the genre of biography in the service of a crucial purpose. If a real person—Oskar Schindler
in this case—could succeed under such severe conditions,
then the potential for good acts resides in everyone. Or as Eley
and Grossman point out, "As Spielberg tells it, Schindler's
story is a humanist parable of self recognition, in which this
amoral beneficiary of wartime accumulation finds the good
in himself."

But to depict Schindler's transformation, Spielberg left out
some important facts. Foremost once more is the motivation
for Schindler's actions. Although he experiences an apparent
conversion at the sight of the little girl in a red coat seeking
cover amidst the horrors of the liquidation of the Krakow
ghetto, Schindler's transformation does not appear to have
any other major causes. As a result, he seems to be an amorphous, postmodern everyman who, when confronted with
evil, apparently employs the means to stop it simply to see
good triumph. But in actuality, Schindler had more pointed
reasons for saving the Jews. He grew up with them. He ad-
mired them, as those who have studied the historical
Schindler have remarked. "I am struck with, from some of my
documentation," writes Herbert Steinhouse, "the anomaly of

a man who was long fascinated by Jewishness, by all the fabulous material of the nineteenth century, of the eighteenth, who had nothing but basic respect for Jews, it seemed, even when he agreed with his party on all but its racism."

There is no question that the historical Schindler, and the figure represented by Keneally, also had a concern for his personal advantage. He could, and did, profit off Jewish slave labor, in part because his lack of antiSemitism allowed him to accept that Jewish workers would build a quality product, and because Jewish management would allow his company to thrive. But this Schindler did not view the Jews solely as a way to maximize his business. He took their needs into account in a compassionate way. In keeping with his everyman narrative, however, Spielberg downplays Schindler's existing sympathy for the Jews. During the scene when Schindler haggles with unnamed Jewish investors and Stern about the Jews investing in the factory, Schindler comes across as a cold and calculating capitalist, with limited compassion for the plight of these people, and a strong determination to profit off the disempowered group's harsh realities. The film Schindler at best knows that while money was of no use to the Jews, he could offer something back for their investment. What Spielberg does not choose to display, however, is Schindler's complete disagreement with the Nazi's racial agenda.

In this instance, biography conflicts with history and autobiography, and cannot tell the story the director wants to tell. Motivation seems to be a main concern of Spielberg's, but he often seems more interested in his own motivation than in Schindler's. The question "Why did you make this film?" has been posed to Spielberg in numerous forms. In an interview, he discusses how he had the project on hold for ten years, and how he tried to persuade other directors—most notably Roman Polanski and Martin Scorcese—to take it on, because he had not gained the requisite maturity to embark on such a movie. As Spielberg gained fame and commercial success by making *Jaws* (1975), *Close Encounters of the Third Kind* (1977), *Raiders of the Lost Ark* (1981), and *E.T.* (1982), he became securely enshrined as a Hollywood luminary who could manufacture massive profits from his projects. But the culture received him on two levels: though his artistry in *E.T.* or *Raiders of the Lost Ark* could move an audience, through entertainment and imagination, when he chose to direct more "adult" films like *The Color Purple* (1985) or *Empire of the Sun* (1987), the critics, and the audience, usually had mixed reactions.

PARALLEL MORAL DEVELOPMENT

In the film, Schindler's maturation process parallels Spielberg's. Schindler inaugurates his persona in the initial cabaret sequence by entertaining Nazi officials—a scene the novel only hints at. Having thus developed his relationship with his Nazi colleagues, Schindler builds his business and his profits until, when his wife visits him, he says, "they won't soon forget the name Schindler here," because he has made so much money. The line is of course ironic, because both the audience and the survivors remember Schindler not for his business acumen, but for his success in outwitting the Nazi death machine and saving Jewish workers and victims. The film tells the story of his successful transformation from a Nazi industrialist, profiting from an evil system, into a doer of great deeds, even though his quest to save lives runs the risk of infuriating the Nazi hierarchy. Spielberg's own career is loosely analogous. As Joseph McBride points out, "Like Schindler, Spielberg struggled for years with the conflicting urges of commercial success and social responsibility, self interest, and the service of humanity." When Spielberg decided to narrate a Holocaust story, he was the premier Hollywood director of "entertaining" movies, a talent that made him one of the most powerful men in his industry. He had not, however, solidified his reputation as a serious filmmaker. By embarking on the Schindler project, Spielberg undertook to transform himself from a director of entertaining, highly profitable movies, to a filmmaker willing to take risks with historically challenging material. Or put another way, Spielberg had evolved to the point where a rethinking of his own notion of what it meant to make a profit could lead him to make a socially conscious film about the Holocaust.

But by structuring his film to universalize the act of doing good, Spielberg diminished some of the story's specific Jewish elements. This too has a biographical dimension. Although Spielberg recalled being frequently accosted as a senior in high school because of his Jewishness as one of the formative moments of his adult consciousness, the lack of overt antiSemitism, as he moved from Ohio to New Jersey to

Arizona to California, seems to have been Spielberg's common experience with racial hatred. In fact, the only significant tension regarding religious issues was, perhaps, young
Steven's desire to assimilate more fully into the Christian
culture that surrounded him. . . .

From all reports, early in his film career Spielberg tended
to shy away from identifying with Judaism, going so far as to
embrace Christianity's tenets of salvation, redemption, and
mercy as major themes in many of his movies, including *E.T.*
and *Indiana Jones and the Last Crusade* (1989), where he
aptly "completes" the Old Testament–inspired *Raiders of the
Lost Ark* by sending Indy on a search for the Holy Grail.
Childhood fantasies of identifying with the majority culture
thus became enmeshed with his adult successes as a director.

In some ways, *Schindler's List* traces out Spielberg's own
anxieties about his minority culture status and his struggles
to overcome them. As we have seen, unlike the historical
Schindler, who valued his Jewish friendships, the industrialist begins the film seemingly oblivious to the humanity of his
workers. His only concern is an increased profit margin. Although we witness his altruistic acts increase as the plot de-
velops—complaining about the S.S. murdering a one-armed
worker, hosing down the cattle cars stuffed full of Jewish
prisoners before they go to Auschwitz, saving and safely employing over one thousand Jews by the war's end—we get no
glimpse into his ideas about race, or into his reasons, beyond
a benevolent form of humanism, for doing any of this in the
first place. Spielberg's career follows a similar path. From
early in his youth up through his young adult success, Spielberg had one passion: to make popular, entertaining, and
imaginative films that appealed to a large cross-section of
the American public. Culminating in *Jaws,* his early achieve-
ments as a director created for him a reputation not as a sophisticated auteur, but as someone who knew how to entertain a mass audience. For this reason, when he first came
upon Keneally's book in 1983, Spielberg could not even con-
ceive of making the film. His economic success was unparalleled; he was, in fact, an industry unto himself. He was not
ready to risk sacrificing his position at the top of the pan-
theon of popular culture by making a movie about the Holocaust—to become an entrepreneur who shifted his focus
from hoarding his profits to spending them in the cause of
liberating human beings. Spielberg, in short, did not yet en-

vision Schindler's life as potentially paralleling his own.

It was ten years later when a more financially and emotionally secure Spielberg told the Holocaust story that he had long been contemplating. Like Schindler, he was ready to risk his accumulated capital on a project that differed in degree and in kind from what he had previously attempted. And yet, though Spielberg recognized in Schindler the kind of person he thought he could be, he still could not get a clear fix on Oskar's character. His method for resolving this difficulty is autobiographically significant. He prepared Liam Neeson for the role by showing him home movies of Steve Ross, the late chairman of [the recording company] MCA. It was Ross who had taught Spielberg to share his wealth. Before meeting Ross, Spielberg had saved most of his money; afterwards he became much more philanthropic, getting involved in charities and political causes. Spielberg had modeled himself after Ross, and he wanted the actor playing Schindler to have a similar model. In fact, Spielberg had "always" told Ross that "if he was fifteen years younger, I'd cast him as Schindler." . . .

That race becomes less of a factor in Schindler's motivations suggests something about how race had affected Spielberg's own actions. Though we can, for instance, dismiss the presence of Christian themes in his earlier films by suggesting that through them the director is responding to the needs of the dominant culture, Spielberg's universalizing vision had also granted all willing participants the opportunity to check their ethnic identities at the door of the theater, as they enter into an economic world that has ample opportunity for everybody. It must of course be acknowledged that Spielberg's downplaying his race and ethnicity in his earlier work, and in the character of Oskar Schindler, is not simply an investment strategy. Undeniably, Spielberg is foregrounding a plot in which the discovery of evil and the responsibility to combat that evil become components of a necessary quest in the evolution of a man's life. Further, Schindler's amorphous transformation stresses how events that take people from their comfortable, secure places and put them in the face of danger are often the motivating force for righteous and even heroic acts.

What is truly remarkable, however, is that in the making of *Schindler's List*, as in the film itself, the result of this strategy is the character's, and the director's, eventual assumption of the role of ethnic conscience. In the film, subtle hints about the atrocity of racism and the need to overcome cultural expectations become fully realized with the shift in Schindler's perceptions, which occurs only after the ghetto is liquidated, and his empty factory confronts him with the real struggle he must now face. The results are dramatic, as Schindler's ensuing actions transform him from profiteering industrialist to Germany's minority Holocaust conscience. In Spielberg's case as well, it is the transformation of the hero and the suffering of the victims that transform America's most successful director into America's Holocaust conscience. As we have suggested, Spielberg's slight rebellion against his Jewish heritage was accompanied by film after film that generated huge profits. Made after many years of evading his own minority culture background, *Schindler's List* provided Spielberg with the opportunity to shift dramatically his reputation in public and intellectual circles. In an interview granted around the time of the film's release, Spielberg remarked that "*Schindler's List* is as close to my own life as anything since *E.T.*", and certainly the film's release and publicity had written large for the first time Spielberg's Jewishness, making *Schindler's List* conceivably an act of expiation.

THE DIRECTOR AND THE DIREKTOR

Another cinematic parallel between Spielberg and Schindler is perhaps the most obvious one—that of director. Schindler's initial scenes—moments that find little elaboration in Keneally's novel—underscore Spielberg's strategy of self-representation through his title character. These sequences present Schindler as an artist, engrossed in the creation and presentation of a carefully devised spectacle. In the first scene, we watch as Schindler, his face significantly hidden in shadow, prepares himself for his appearance in a nightclub frequented by high-ranking Nazis. As he selects the appropriate suit, tie, and cufflinks to create the planned effect, Schindler carries out an act of self creation—the construction of a persona suited to his purpose of winning the friendship and confidence of the Nazis, from whom he hopes to secure his business contracts. That this shadow and camera placement obscure Schindler's face until, in a subsequent sequence, he actually enters the night club and is shown to his table only emphasizes the point. Deferring our introduction to Schindler's face until he has located himself within his meticulously planned performance scene allows the audience to witness the stages of artistic self fashioning, which lead to the face as the sign of an achieved, purposeful identity.

Having organized his identity to fulfill his entrepreneurial hopes, he proceeds to organize the night club into a stage set in which he is the primary actor. Before long, he has gathered every German officer in the club to his table, selected the appropriate food, wine, and dining companions from the club's show girls, and is leading the group in song. That his creative effort has created for him instant celebrity is confirmed by the response of the maitre d' when a newly arrived officer asks the name of the party's host: "Why, that's Oskar Schindler!" the maitre d' replies, suggesting that within minutes, Schindler has become a "well known" local bon vivant.

That Schindler's achievement of celebrity is also an artistic success is underscored through a series of photographs which, though his guests jostle to appear in the frame, are clearly being composed by the host. In this way, Spielberg introduces Schindler to us as, above all, an imagemaker. When Schindler, with no money of his own, convinces the embattled Jews of Krakow to "invest" their capital in his plan to acquire Deutsche Emailwaren Fabrik (DEF), he justifies his own role as director of DEF to Stern in promotional terms: "That's what I'm good at," he explains, "presentation," as his arms spread wide to encompass the entire movie screen. Schindler will provide the necessary Blitz and slickness to give a superficial impression to the outside world, and most significantly to his Nazi contacts, who would have the ultimate say in his ability to do business. Controlling the company from a seat overlooking the set, Herr Direktor Schindler mediates between the outer world and Stern and the other Jews, those actually running the company soundly and producing its significant profit.

Similarly, it was Spielberg's success as an imagemaker that accounted for the wunderkind's transformation from an obscure Ohio kid into one of the wealthiest and most powerful men in Hollywood. In making *Schindler's List*, Spielberg felt a responsibility to be true to history, and true to his employees. To make the film, he transported hundreds of actors and technicians to Poland, and provided for their livelihoods. Because he considered the making of the movie to be a personal quest, unlike Schindler, Spielberg invested much of his own money in the project. Like Schindler, however, though with a much greater reserve of cash, Spielberg gave away his profits from the film to help survivors and the preservation of their memories. But most importantly, Spielberg's awareness of both business and aesthetic demands made him realize that a Holocaust film whose only audience is Jews and survivors could not possibly accomplish his didactic goals. Also like Schindler, then, though Spielberg risked his well-deserved reputation as a master showman to "do the right thing" instead of the profitable thing, he also realized that success required him to produce a product that contained enough value to draw a mass audience.

This was a daunting challenge. Though there certainly had been effective treatments of the Holocaust on film and video, no feature-length film had directly used the Holocaust as the complete background. Often criticized for using black and white to depict the Holocaust past, while the American present was shown in color, *Sophie's Choice* (1982) treated the Holocaust as a past significant historical event that continued to traumatize the various characters in the present. Spielberg not only made that event his subject, but filmed the entire story in black and white—a stunning disconnect from his cinematic past of exploding colors and stories. Or to put it succinctly, *Schindler's List* followed on the heels of *Jurassic Park.*

Spielberg's use of the hand-held camera, the use of intimate cinematic methods, the chiaroscuro, and the attempt at a documentary style of filmmaking paradoxically proclaimed that the film would be not only different, but an attempt to expand its director's reputation. Abandoning many of the techniques that had made Spielberg a successful director, in making *Schindler's List* he studied many cinematic documentaries—most notably Lanzmann's *Shoah*—and tried to appropriate their style." These techniques appear in arguably the most powerful sequence in *Schindler's List,* where Schindler and one of his mistresses view the bloody search through the Krakow Ghetto. Watching from a hill above the town, Schindler is increasingly revolted by the demonic violence of the scene below. As the SS slaughters Jews attempting to escape forced evacuation, a young girl wanders from scene to terrifying scene of brutality and murder. Spielberg's inspired decision to insert into the black and white of the film a single red patch of color—the child's coat—does more than provide us with a powerful image of innocence amidst horror. It also confronts us with the cinematic expertise of the director conveying to us the totality of the scene's horror. Terror and technique merge through Spielberg's presentation—an image of cinema's potentially transformative power.

More than any other moment in the film, this scene points to the supposed source of Schindler's ultimate decision to sacrifice all he has gained to save the lives of his Jews. Observing from his privileged position as the horror spreads out before him, Schindler obviously occupies a role similar to that of the film spectator. As a result, his response to the scene is presumed to be shared by the audience, whose look he represents. As Spielberg's shot/reverse shot pattern shuttles between the scene's violence and Schindler's increasing shock, the audience's own disgust is invoked through the cinematic representation of the historical outrage. Perhaps even more subtly, Schindler's status as Direktor renders his own shocked reaction highly ironic. As Direktor of a firm manufacturing war material, a position achieved through the exploitation of Nazi racist policy and through his cultivation of Nazi officials, he is himself a contributor to the agony he witnesses. A similar irony pervades *Schindler's List* itself. Just as Schindler as Direktor oversees the production of military goods, so does Spielberg oversee the production of the film, forcing him to acknowledge the responsibilities of his own vocation and the potential for good or evil his own immense success in the manipulation of this century's most powerful medium grants him. . . .

We admire *Schindler's List* for its attempt to narrate a story that many find untenable. Steven Spielberg committed himself to a project that would forever take the emphasis off his great talent for entertaining, and shift it to his ability to tell a didactic story. Spielberg himself shifted the economic emphasis of his industry. Apparently, he did not receive one cent of profit from the film, devoting it instead to a number of charitable causes, the most significant of which was an endowment for Yale to collect survivors' stories. In this, he may be said to be following Oskar Schindler's example. Schindler too amassed a fortune, and then used that fortune first to free the workers, and then to set them up in a factory and camp where their lives would generally not be threatened. Spielberg could tell this story because he saw it as a far larger version of his own. By giving Schindler and Stern traits he would like to see in himself, he not only made the story personal, but sought to make the viewer see the story as personal too. In this way, perhaps, historical figure, Hollywood director, and biopic audience can discern the seeming impossibility of goodness within the Holocaust, yet recognize that at times it truly exists.

The *Schindler's List* Effect

Michael André Bernstein

Michael André Bernstein is a professor of English and Comparative Literature at the University of California, Berkeley. In this selection he gives the movie *Schindler's List* a bad review on several counts. Concerning the movie itself, he feels it manipulates the emotions and oversimplifies its subject in the interest of mere entertainment. Concerning the movie's effect on society, he feels it will make teaching about the Holocaust more difficult, and does little to promote racial understanding.

A DISASTER SEEN FROM THE WRONG POINT OF VIEW

There is little pleasure in being troubled by what so many have found deeply moving. For several months now, scarcely a day has gone by without a chorus of impassioned voices, recently augmented by New Jersey Senator Bill Bradley and California Governor Pete Wilson, publicly testifying to the profound impression Steven Spielberg's film *Schindler's List* made on them personally, while insisting on the movie's educational value for our society as a whole. Skepticism about the entire phenomenon of attributing such edifying power to a Hollywood movie must seem simultaneously blinkered and ungenerous: blinkered since it is bound to be condemned as elitist snobbery, and ungenerous since what it hesitates to applaud is so earnestly intended to be both individually uplifting and communally responsible. But the earnestness of the movie's ambition, far from excusing its intellectual and moral blind spots, only makes these all the more disturbing. *Schindler's List* is not just an ambitious but flawed movie; it is a work that manipulates the emotions raised by the enormity of its historical theme in order to disguise the simplistic melodrama of its actual realization. The

Reprinted from "The *Schindler's List* Effect," by Michael André Bernstein, *The American Scholar*, vol. 63, no. 3 (Summer 1994), pp. 429–32. Copyright © 1994 by Michael André Bernstein. Used with permission of *The American Scholar*.

surprising thing, surely, is not that this film should demonstrate all the sentimental facileness of its director's other
works, but that, when applied to the Holocaust, the inappro-
priateness of these same techniques should not have raised
more widespread and serious misgivings.

Perhaps the most succinct way to register the kinds of
qualms with which I left the movie theater is simply to ask
why *Schindler's List* is so complicit with the Hollywood con-
vention of showing catastrophe primarily from the point of
view of the perpetrators. For long stretches, the film's energy
derives chiefly from the battle between Oskar Schindler and
Amon Goeth, the commandant of the Plaszow labor camp.
The stakes of the contest are, of course, the lives of "their"
Jews, who are depicted as a largely anonymous mass from
whose midst an occasional figure emerges to show his in-
dividuality by the shuffling fervor of his gratitude for
Schindler's aid. Repeatedly, *Schindler's List* seems to turn
into an allegory about the nature of the German soul, with
its "good" and "evil" aspects embodied by Schindler and
Goeth, functioning as each other's symbolic double.

As though the film's commitment to high seriousness
could be expressed only through the moral conventions of
the Hollywood films of another era, throughout *Schindler's
List* evil is directly connected with sexuality and physical
pleasure. A contrast is regularly drawn between decadently
carousing Nazis and starving Jews (whose lethal hunger
Spielberg wisely omits trying to represent, no doubt because
it is technically beyond the resources of even the most adroit
makeup experts). And even Schindler's own enigmatic jour-
ney from cynical opportunist to heroic rescuer is portrayed
as joined to a gradual renunciation of any sensual interests.
As his concern for the Jews under his protection increases,
Schindler stops the rampant womanizing and extravagant
living that had marked his earlier existence and rejoins his
wife in what is represented as an essentially asexual union.
(Emilie Schindler's rather different recollection of her husband is conveniently set aside, both in the film and in
Thomas Keneally's novel from which Spielberg's screenplay
was adapted.) To underscore still further the movie's link
between virtue and asceticism, the one Jew who is particu-
larized at any length in the movie, Itzhak Stern, an accountant who becomes the agent of Schindler's moral awakening,
is completely indifferent to everything carnal.

So intent is *Schindler's List* on its didactic simplifications that it can only show morality as always absolute and homogeneous. In the rarefied universe of the movie, there is no hint of the "gray zone" about which Primo Levi wrote with such lucidity, no awareness of the agonizing choices and ethically intolerable alternatives that Jews were compelled by their tormentors to confront moment by moment as part of staying alive in the camps. Desperate with hunger and fear or not, the Jews in Spielberg's account have to continue to help one another at every turn and without exception, because, in a film whose representation of good and evil is so simplistic, only by being completely pure can they function as appropriate objects of our sympathy.

But life finds it extraordinarily hard not to be on the side of whatever pulses with energy; and the passivity of the film's Jews and the increasing sentimentalization of Schindler have the curious effect of making Amon Goeth the most compelling figure in *Schindler's List.* Ralph Fiennes plays Goeth brilliantly just as Liam Neeson plays Schindler himself, and Ben Kingsley plays Itzhak Stern), and what we might call the viewer's affective identification, the focus of his fascination and attention, is directed toward Goeth in much the same way as it fixes on Iago whenever he enters a scene in *Othello.* Moral lessons need moral density in order to move one at all, and it is the absence of that density that vitiates Spielberg's film in spite of, perhaps even as a direct result of, its zealous efforts to construct a morally unequivocal story.

EMBARRASSING MOMENTS

It would be easy to put together a detailed catalogue of the film's most embarrassing moments, including lengthy set pieces like Schindler's virtual apotheosis as a modern Christ figure in his sermon to the awestruck Jews looking up at him from the Brinnlitz factory floor (a direct crib from every Hollywood sand-and-sandals epic, from The Ten Commandments and Ben-Hur to Jesus Christ Superstar), or the clumsy literalization of George Steiner's meditations on Nazism in the scene of an SS officer sitting down to play "either Mozart or Bach" in a room "cleansed" of its Jews only moments earlier during the savage annihilation of the Krakow ghetto. But such a catalogue would be curiously beside the point, if only because many of the film's passionate advocates have already noticed—and quickly excused—each of the lapses it contains. Virtually every laudatory discussion I have come across has been careful to register some criticism of the very scenes I have just mentioned, but without permitting that acknowledgment to temper its overall praise beyond the briefest of hesitations. For me, one of the most disturbing of all the film's effects is this readiness to suspend critical judgment, with its implicit premise that any work that aims to make accessible to a large audience even a portion of so crucial a story ought to be exempt from careful evaluation because of that intention.

Part of the general reluctance to think critically about *Schindler's List* arises, I suspect, because in the face of suffering on as great a scale as the Holocaust, there is a general freezing up of normal intellectual discriminations. Yet these moments of confrontation with the monstrous require more, not less, clarity and demand a greater measure, rather than an abdication, of the ability to concentrate on fundamental distinctions. If there is an elitist position in this whole discussion, I believe it is represented by those who recognize the film's evasions and simplifications but are willing to overlook them because of their hope that it will teach people about the Holocaust who otherwise would never take an interest in it. It is this kind of condescension, the conviction that while "we" may read Primo Levi or see Claude Lanzmann's *Shoah* for our knowledge of the Holocaust, "they" could never be expected to do so, that seems to me deeply arrogant. Hence, when as intelligent a reviewer as Bryan Cheyette celebrates *Schindler's List* in the Times Literary Supplement because it is "the best film on this subject within its particular set of conventions," the hollowness of such praise is especially demoralizing. "Its particular set of conventions" is precisely what makes it impossible for *Schindler's List* to succeed in any more than the most trivial of ways, and by now the triviality of those conventions has rippled outward from the film to debase the terms within which the Holocaust itself is discussed.

For the moment at least, the most audible public discourse on the fate of European Jewry under the Nazis is being framed by the context of Spielberg's movie. The worrisome question is how long this moment will last. There is a cultural version, as well as an economic one, of "Gresham's law": "bad money drives out good," and in the ways a society takes up and defines the issues that engage its attention, the success of an appealingly facile articulation can set to the side, or even silence altogether, more complex and troubling expressions. This is also why to speak about a *"Schindler's List* Effect" is by now perhaps more useful than to concentrate exclusively on the film. Among the most vertiginous of these effects is the way the Holocaust is currently at risk of being presented, if only in people's first exposure to the subject, chiefly as the factual "basis" for Steven Spielberg's movie. The Mallarmean boast that "everything in the world exists in order to end in a book" has reached an abject incarnation in the more contemporary notion that only what has been presented on screen can continue to have significance today, that for us either "everything in the world exists in order to end up in a popular movie" or it will lose its hold on our interest altogether. Aided in this by both Democratic and Republican political leaders, as well as by an eager contingent of high school teachers, Steven Spielberg has encouraged free, and often even mandatory, showings of his movie for students in ethnically mixed school districts throughout the country, because, in the filmmaker's words, "this is a story about tolerance and remembrance, and it is for everyone. . . . [It] represents racial hatred everywhere in the world." At present, there appears to be widespread official support for the assumption that screening a film about the horrors inflicted on European Jews will improve relations between African-Americans and Jews in this country, especially in urban high schools and universities.

Spielberg has insisted repeatedly that his movie is as pertinent to the Bosnian Muslims or African-Americans as it is to Jews. In an inconsequential sense, he is right, because in spite of all its scrupulous specificity in the matter of local props, settings, and details, *Schindler's List* is so conventional and formulaic at its imaginative core that it actually engages no real historical catastrophe—and hence excludes none either. This eagerness to interpret the Holocaust as a parable of universal suffering—when its very essence was a deliberate, systematic, and, if such a word can be permitted in this context, "principled" denial of even minimal humanity to those it condemned to genocidal extermination bespeaks a characteristic American urge to find a redemptive meaning in every event. This is why, then, Spielberg decided to concentrate on a small group of Jews who survived and on the good German who aided them, rather than on all the millions who did not live and the millions of Germans and German sympathizers who did nothing to help.

COMPETING FOR WORST HISTORY

Beyond the transparent grotesqueness of trying to extract an uplifting meaning from the Holocaust, the attempt to use it as a sort of emotional and moral object lesson to foster racial tolerance has been derisively challenged by many of those to whom these lessons are specifically directed. Although Castlemont High School in Oakland received the widest coverage in the national media, it is not the only school in which a showing of *Schindler's List* clearly did not lead to any rapprochement in its student body. Instead, it helped trigger a bitter controversy, as different ethnic groups competed over whose history had been more traumatic. After more than sixty Castlemont students who had been taken for a required viewing of *Schindler's List* (on Martin Luther King Day!) were ejected from the movie theater because they continued to talk and laugh throughout some especially brutal scenes, the predictable but still disheartening accusations of black anti-Semitism versus Jewish ignorance about the suffering of African-Americans reverberated throughout both groups.

The whole notion that whatever hostility and misunderstanding exists between two ethnic groups living in the United States today could be diffused by showing that one of them had, in another time and country, suffered catastrophic persecution, appears both psychologically and historically naive, willfully so. In spite of such pious wishes, there is no reason whatsoever to assume that the sight of Jews being brutalized by the Nazis will do anything to change the ways in which American Jews are viewed today. Such a project testifies to only two things: the longing for quick and painless solutions to complicated social problems, and a radical confusion between the box-office success of a movie and its capacity to make people reevaluate their prejudices.

Predictably enough, when Spielberg himself visited Castlemont High, he enthusiastically endorsed a new program instituted as a result of the controversy that followed the initial screening of *Schindler's List.* The title of the new course is "The Human Holocaust: The African-American Experience." Clearly, in a culture as wedded as ours to the notion that victimhood endows one with special claims and rights, the scramble to attain that designation for one's own interest group is as heated as any other race for legitimacy and power. But victimhood, as this conflict over ownership of the term holocaust makes clear, is not a fixed category, and there is something depressing in the clamor of competing voices to prove whose distress has been more persistent and devastating, and whose claims to compensatory rectification are therefore more worthy. But because any sense of identity as constituted primarily by victimization is an extraordinarily problematic basis for either an individual or a group to build upon, what we need to do is question the centrality of the category itself, not simply apply it with more ecumenical generosity.

At the level of its explicit didacticism, *Schindler's List* is deeply complicit with the sentimentalization of victimhood as a guarantor of inner nobility, while at the level of the affective identification that it triggers, the film is equally complicit with the fascination exercised upon our imagination by the spectacle of absolute evil and power. Yet there is no dialectic, no inner struggle between these two contradictory impulses in the film: they coexist effortlessly because each is represented entirely within the most familiar moviemaking conventions. Spielberg's real talent has been to use the Holocaust as a plausible backdrop so that he can invoke both of these conventions simultaneously for their emotional charge while seeming to offer us something morally probing and original.

In my local video store, there is now a shelf of films about both the Holocaust in particular and World War II in general. Its label reads, simply: "Videos in the Category of *Schindler's List.*" A small manifestation, no doubt, but one that seems to me an accurate gauge of the "*Schindler's List* Effect." Spielberg's movie does not merely, in Claude Lanzmann's devastating phrase, "fabricate archives," it is already beginning to affect the way our culture understands, historically orders, and teaches how the Holocaust should be remembered—and effects like these require a sharp-eyed and unembarrassed resistance.

Not the Last Word

Geoff Eley and Atina Grossmann

Geoff Eley and Atina Grossmann are German historians who saw *Schindler's List* in 1994 while attending a conference of the American Historical Association held in San Francisco. Given Hollywood's
reputation for distorting history, they were surprised
that they liked the film.

In this selection they defend the movie, challenging
some of the negative criticisms made against it. They do
not feel the movie tells the story from an inappropriate
point of view, nor do they feel that the movie tries to be the
last word on Holocaust history. Since it focuses on a single
story, it serves as a powerful introduction to Holocaust history that will encourage a new generation to search for a
deeper understanding.

As German historians with a stake in the subject, knowing
this to be no ordinary filmgoing experience, and expecting
to be embroiled in resulting debates, we decided to use our
attendance at yet another conference, the American Historical Association in January 1994, to see the film that had just
opened to enormous public discussion and media hype. In a
mood of edgy anticipation, we watched *Schindler's List* on a
large screen with Dolby sound, in a packed full house at the
Kabuki cinema in San Francisco's Japantown. The mixing of
genres signaled by the previews played a part here: this was
no documentary playing on a campus screen, in a specialty
movie house, or in an arts theater; but it was also no ordinary Spielberg blockbuster.

Writing this essay has been inseparable from the film's
viewing and early reception, which replicated something of
the ambivalence we've described before its release. As we
talked to friends and colleagues, it seemed precisely this
mixed quality of the film (its promiscuity, its impurity, its
transgression of borders) that made many uncomfortable.

Excerpted from "Watching *Schindler's List:* Not the Last Word," by Geoff Eley and
Atina Grossmann, *New German Critique*, Spring/Summer 1997. Used with permission
of Telos Press.

Our own response was strongly positive. We emerged moved and shaken by a powerful film deeply respectful of the events. Our reaction was still undisturbed by the emerging critical anxiety, that this would become the last word in publicly influential Holocaust interpretation, or even the only film version to have impact for decades to come. That worry seemed imposed on the film by those who perhaps—ironically enough—granted Spielberg too much power. We began to feel that the strongest critics had not quite seen the film we had seen. So we began the conversation that led to this article, not with the aim of joining a polarized debate (the film is brilliant, it's awful; I love it, I hate it), but because we were curious about our own reactions and those of our friends and colleagues. We wrote from the desire to take the film and its resonances seriously without being boxed into a defense of Spielberg and of Hollywood per se (although both can certainly be done). We wanted to explore what worked so powerfully in the film at the time of its viewing. We wanted to see what we could learn: about film and about history. . . .

Whose film is *Schindler's List?* The obvious answer is Oskar Schindler's: his story remains extraordinary, and deserves to be honored. But he makes a difficult protagonist. As others have said, there are problems with making a non-Jew, a "good German," into the hero of what aspires to be an authoritative film about the Holocaust. In a cynical reading of the film's reception, the man of conscience (and better still an industrialist), who sacrificed his fortune to save the Jews, is a godsend to German conservatives, who are always on the lookout for some new alibi for Nazism, a new way to get the German nation off the hook. Given the overall record, allowing Schindler's story to become an allegory of the Holocaust has to be a distortion, it can be argued. By seeming to heroise Schindler, the film makes itself vulnerable. He's the liberal capitalist, the paternalist, the good plantation-owner, the benevolent potentate who looks after his Jews; he's the Christian who restores Judaism; he's the great white father, the protector of "his" people, who leads the Jews to safety ("Who are you," Goeth asks sarcastically, "Moses?").

But in many ways, this misses the point. In the film's logic, Schindler is hardly a very appealing character. He's an opportunist, a war profiteer, a carpet-bagger of the worst sort, capitalizing on the Jews' misfortune. Constantly on the make,

he uses people, although openly, via the cash nexus. His original arrangement with Itzhak Stern is scarcely an equal
transaction, and the Jewish investors are cynically used. He
prefers Jewish to Polish labor for its minimal costs. When
Schindler extricates Stern from a transport, there are no sentiments, only an instrumental calculus: he needs Stern in the
business, and if he'd been deported, "Then where would I
be?" Schindler is also an incurable womanizer, whose infi-
delities flagrantly demean his wife. He judges women, it
seems, purely by their bodies, although his encounter with
Goeth's enslaved servant Helen Hirsch later in the film engineers some redemptive transformation, we are led to believe.
Of course, he's a rogue. He's larger than life. His appetites for
drink and sex are voracious, and this capacity for excess becomes part of saving "his" Jews—the single-mindedness, the
risk-taking, the recklessness, the courage.

As Spielberg tells it, Schindler's story is a humanist parable of self-recognition, in which this amoral beneficiary of
wartime accumulation finds the good in himself. Schindler's
initial overture to the Jews, mediated via the accountant
Stern, is pure business pragmatics. The film is at some pains
to point this out: his deal with Jewish investors disavows the
Nazi ideology his party membership seemingly entailed, but
implies no human sympathy for the Jewish plight, merely
an eye for the main chance. Self-interest and the good life
are his only rules. Several times he's offered descriptions of
virtue ("You are a good man"; "They say you are good"), and
refuses. In fact, Schindler is presented as unintelligible and
labile, capable of moving in various ways. Dramatically, the
film shows a primary moment of change, when Schindler's
moral agency is released: namely, during the ghetto clearance, which he watches on horseback from the hillside
above, when the recognition of violence and inhumanity,
the spur to action, unfolds in direct counterpoint to the terror being wreaked below. The move into conscious agency
is marked by a conversation with Stern, where Schindler reflects on the pathologies of wartime: "And war brings out the
worst in people, never the good."

However, this isn't only Schindler's film. The film's reception has effaced the centrality of Itzhak Stern. For us he's the
prime mover of *Schindler's List*, who shuttles back and forth
between the film's two registers, the personal and the documentary, managing the interactions of the two, mediating

Schindler's relationship to history. When they meet, Stern tells Schindler he's obliged to declare himself a Jew, to which Oskar replies: "I'm a German. So there we are." This enormously pregnant exchange defines the parameters of a delicate and remarkably successful partnership, in which Stern moves from anxious circumspection (What does this Nazi want?) to careful cooperation (How can we benefit?), wifely support ("Herr Direktor, don't let things fall apart, I've worked too hard"), and genuine collaboration (making the list). It's Stern who creates a "list" to begin with, using Schindler's factory as a bridge to relative safety. In the rhythmic urgency of the ghetto registration scenes we see him running interference, organizing papers, protecting individuals, cueing them their lines. Stern is the guardian angel, a guiding force of the kind Schindler only becomes in the endgame of the film, after the decision to move the factory. Schindler accepts this tacitly, and occasionally Stern oversteps the mark (notably with the one-armed machinist), but by Plaszow he's supplying Stern with the means to buy inmates onto his workforce and out of the camp. Certainly Stern is pivotal to the whole operation, a man with a mission. He's the straight man with the mordant and sardonic

THE GIRL IN RED

The emotional pivot of the movie Schindler's List *is the scene in which Schindler sees a little girl in a red coat. In Keneally's book she is called Red Genia, and her presence in the book is based on interviews with people who knew her. She was a real little girl.*

While the scarlet child stopped in her column and turned to watch, they shot the woman in the neck, and one of them, when the boy slid down the wall whimpering, jammed a boot down on his head as if to hold it still and put the barrel against the back of the neck—the recommended SS stance—and fired.

Oskar looked again for the small red girl. She had stopped and turned and seen the boot descend. A gap had already widened between her and the next to last in the column. Again the SS guard corrected her drift fraternally, nudged her back into line. Herr Schindler could not see why he did not bludgeon her with his rifle butt, since at the other end of Krakusa Street, mercy had been cancelled.

At last Schindler slipped from his horse, tripped, and found himself on his knees hugging the trunk of a pine tree. The lines. He's also positioned in a triangle with Goeth as the evil mistress and Stern as the long-suffering but loving wife: they each attract different parts of Oskar. Amidst his bookkeep-erly competence, Stern excels in picking up the pieces, toler-ating the foibles, seeing the goodness underneath. He wins because he's so good in this wifely role—as the knowing-tolerant one, the one who knows himself and also knows Schindler. He gives Oskar the chance to be good and creates Schindler as a possible rescuer and hero.

But Stern is even more important. He is the very first per-son we see in the film (sitting at the station to register the ar-riving Jews), and almost the last (sitting outside the factory at the liberation). He is inserted into the narrative many times: we see him before the storm of the ghetto liquidation (after the parallel shots of Schindler and Goeth shaving); he's a hor-rified bystander of one of the killings; in Plaszow, he passes through the frame as the boy Lisiek is shot; he watches at the birthday party as Schindler gives the incriminating kisses to the Jewish child Nusia Horowitz and the young woman worker; he stands with the Germans at the railhead after the selection, as Schindler hoses down the trucks. These appear-ances, which have no practical function for the action, say

urge to throw up his excellent breakfast was, he sensed, to be suppressed, for he suspected it meant that all his cunning body was doing was making room to digest the horrors of Krakusa Street.

Their lack of shame, as men who had been born of women and had to write letters home (What did they put in them?), wasn't the worst aspect of what he'd seen. He *knew* they had no shame, since the guard at the base of the column had not felt any need to stop the red child from seeing things. But worst of all, if there was no shame, it meant there was official sanc-tion. No one could find refuge anymore behind the idea of Ger-man culture, nor behind those pronouncements uttered by leaders to exempt anonymous men from stepping beyond their gardens, from looking out their office windows at the realities on the sidewalk. Oskar had seen in Krakusa Street a statement of his government's policy which could not be written off as a temporary aberration. The SS men were, Oskar believed, fulfill-ing there the orders of the leader, for otherwise their colleague at the rear of the column would not have let a child watch.

Thomas Keneally, *Schindler's List.* New York: Simon and Schuster, 1983.

something about witnessing—about recording, remember-
ing, being there to tell the tale. Other individuals are used
similarly by the film: Helen Hirsch witnesses Goeth's daily
atrocities in Plaszow, beginning with the murder of the construction engineer Diana Reiter, perhaps the most shocking
in the film, and it is her eyes that record the endless lines for
the gas chambers in Auschwitz, even as the Schindler women
are being saved. Pairing the actors with their respective
Schindler survivors in the film's coda is a way of making this
point in an incredibly moving way, of securing the film's ac-
ceptance as testimony. Stern is the eyes of the film, one might
say. He carries the responsibility of looking—of looking in-
tently, of trying to discern what's going on—which is crucial
to the story and to survival. He is also the film's voice, given
the historically accurate lines to say. He describes clearly the
system's absence of rationality: it may be bureaucratic, tech-
nologized, banal, linked to requirements of the war economy,
and with all the trappings of rationality, but it has no rationality any rational person can decipher, and the Nazis don't
care about production. So *Schindler's List* has a Jewish hero,
after all, we would say.

What does *Schindler's List* tell us about politics? Aside
from the Zionist coda, the answer seems to be very little. The
Nazis' racialized discourse is certainly there—especially in
Goeth's speech on the mission of wiping out the history of
Jewish Krakow or in his monologue to Helen Hirsch and the
ensuing beating, in which sexual desire is trumped by racial
purity. But aside from the radicalism of the SS (their anti-
Semitism is different, the Jews will be exterminated rather
than just restricted, as in the past), the film has no context for
understanding Nazism, or for situating the hostility towards
the Jews. Other targets of Nazi persecution—Communists,
Socialists, homosexuals, other racial categories like Sinti
and Roma, the physically disabled and mentally ill, the socially undesirable—aren't signified in this film (in contrast
to other recent Holocaust pedagogy, like the Holocaust
Memorial Museum in Washington D.C.). Moreover, the politics of the Jews themselves—not just the Jewish resistance
in its Zionist, Bundist, and Communist forms, but the youth
organizations, and the entire subcultural formation of the
ghetto's public sphere—are entirely left out. Other questions
of difference within Jewish communities are also effaced,
and a great deal more could be said, certainly, about gender.

This is different from Keneally's book, where Schindler and the Krakow Jews are given political motivations, and the Zionist underground plays a role.

There are two things to be said here. On the one hand, power is constructed by the film as something beyond popular agency or control, as something coming from the outside, as opaque, uncontrollable, with the force of a natural disaster, and certainly not rational. Moreover, Spielberg does an excellent job of representing the endemic qualities of the tremendous violence of Nazi coercive power, and the paltriness of any human agency of resistance by comparison. He shows the system resting on utter arbitrariness and unpredictability—with the attendant loss of coherence and regularity—and the absence of rules, which meant no one was safe. But the film does this outside any context of political explanation. Politics is a non-existent space, an absence of feasible action, a missing term for whatever the film has to say about survival or optimism for the future.

On the other hand, the film's treatment of childhood does contain a discourse of politics, albeit in an oblique and displaced way. The image of the child—children in danger, children fleeing and hiding, children surviving by their wits, children transported in trucks, children walking to the gas chamber—is extremely potent in *Schindler's List*. Children are an important presence. But apart from the ghetto clearance (a young boy is shot, and children are forcibly separated from parents), the film spares us the brutalizing of small children. Since little else is omitted, it's worth asking how this works. For instance, when the young girls are seized in Auschwitz from the departing Schindler women, the key element is that they are then grabbed back; and when the children are removed from Plaszow, Spielberg chooses—incongruously—an image of innocence, as the children happily wave from the trucks, keeping the trauma for the adults, who riot at the enormity of this loss. Childhood is reserved as a relatively safe place of sentimentality in this way, both by what the film chooses from the catalogue of available horrors not to show, and by what it seems to be saying about optimism and hope. For *Schindler's List* utilizes the imagery of childhood as a sign of possibility as well as horror, in a relation of optimism to possible futures, or futurity per se, as if the only available model for imagining a future is the child's right to grow.

Of course, the most eloquent image is the little girl in red ("Red Genia," as Keneally calls her), whose coat is the film's only element of color aside from the candle flames. She is the child of the film, and she does die, though not in front of us. Indeed, our only frontal view is when she crawls under the bed after escaping the roundup and faces the camera, quite fresh faced and seemingly competent: a survivor, brisk and on her own. She strode confidently and not panicked through the mayhem of the ghetto's liquidation, making her disembodied reappearance on the wagon of corpses later in the film all the more poignant. She is the best counter-example of an un-sentimentalized representation of hope in a way that's genuinely powerful and moving, and a believable device for dramatizing Schindler's moment of recognition as he watches from the hillside, the one that slowly unlocks the capacity for moral choice, for allowing himself to be good. Moreover, that she reappears so fleetingly in the burning of bodies at Chujowa Gozka, in a moment of hell-like representation of mass death, is terribly more wrenching than any other single image might have been. It importantly makes the point that in those circumstances hope and doing good could only be relative and compromised. Optimism could only ever be a traumatized and damaged thing. . . .

What is to be shown in a film about the Holocaust, and can it be shown truthfully, in a way commensurable with the subject's terrible meaning? The Auschwitz sequence encapsulates this dilemma. A film aspiring to narrate the Holocaust couldn't leave Auschwitz out, and the episode was certainly in the Schindler story. The same holds for the controversial shower scene: the gas chambers had to be there, and this was a way to do it that was watchable, didn't break any ultimate taboos, and didn't violate our sense of historical accuracy too egregiously. The scene captures something of our own incredibly complicated, horrified, voyeuristic relationship to the gas chambers. Moreover, our relief at the rescue can't be enjoyed, for the line moving in the other direction is too long, descending unrelentingly to the gas. As in the ghetto clearance, Spielberg cuts and avoids dwelling on the truly unseeable: we are forced to look (typically at the emblematic figure of a small child) long enough to register the knowledge, but not too long. This preserves the distance, positions us as survivors, but leaves the mass reality of non-survival on the screen. There is much here about looking—the light through the slats of the cattle truck picking out the women's eyes, Helen looking back at the death line, the eye of the chamber door, the eyes fixed on the shower heads—and here the film is asking us to keep our witness, renewing Red Genia's injunction as she stared silently from her refuge. The dominant tonalities of this sequence, secured by the slow and mournful music of the Schindler women's Brinnlitz arrival, are of a terrible knowing sadness.

The questions of representability and authorization to speak, in filming the unwatchable can't be resolved, as opposed to being brought into the open, worried over, discussed. But to make a movie is to say, this is not sacred; this is not outside of history; these Jewish victims are not disembodied martyrs; they can be part of discourse. In fact, other movies can be made. Spielberg seems to know this. At the beginning, when we are introduced to Schindler and the Germans in the nightclub, a woman photographer records the evening, with much flashing of light bulbs and framing of shots. This signals how much this is a film about memory and its preservation, about names and faces, about witnessing. But the filmmaker also says: this is my snapshot; it can't encompass the whole of the Holocaust; but this is the story I'll tell. We like its partialities of perspective—those of American Jews, survivors and others, trying to engage with this history and its legacy—because they provide opportunities for opening up the subject. We didn't like all of this film, and hated the conclusion (that is, Schindler's departing speech, and the survivors' march towards the warm glow of the city on the horizon, as opposed to the honoring by Schindler's grave, which we found extremely moving). But we liked the different levels on which the film works. . . . Precisely because *Schindler's List* tells a "real," highly specific, and undeniably exceptional story, it cannot be totalizing, nor claim any final or complete authority. It asserts again that with this history there will be no last word.

DISCUSSION QUESTIONS

CHAPTER 1

1. Compare the Jewish Holocaust with other examples of genocide in the twentieth century, such as the genocide of Armenians by Turks during World War I and the massacre of Tutsis in Rwanda in 1994. Which was the largest in terms of numbers killed? Which came closest to actually causing an ethnic group to disappear?

2. Aside from Jews, which other groups did the Nazis systematically persecute? What reasons did the Nazis give in trying to justify their actions?

3. Nationalism is the idea that each nation is defined by its dominant ethnic group, and that each ethnic group should have its own homeland. This idea was used by the Nazis to justify driving Jews out of Europe. Research other examples of nationalism in the world today. Is the United States a nation defined by its dominant ethnic group?

4. The philosopher Hannah Arendt suggests that the Holocaust was caused by a bureaucratic mentality: basically good people too willing to follow orders. Do you agree? If so, how can we avoid becoming perpetrators of a Holocaust ourselves?

CHAPTER 2

1. How many Jews worked at Emalia? How many Jews did Schindler finally save? How many died on the train from Goleschau? Different sources give different answers. Given conflicting accounts, how can we learn the truth? What should historians do when sources contradict each other?

2. Schindler regularly used lies and bribery to protect his workers, and he allegedly asked a woman to trade sex for the release of female prisoners sent to Auschwitz. Can usually immoral actions sometimes be morally admirable under certain circumstances? Is it possible that Hitler considered the extermination of the Jews to be an action that could be justified "under the circumstances"?

3. Do you think Julius Madritsch made the wrong decision not to join Schindler in moving his factory to Moravia, or do you think his decision can be defended in light of what he knew at the time? Please explain your answer.

CHAPTER 3

1. In the concentration camps, were all prisoners treated alike, or was there a social structure under which some prisoners received preferential treatment? Support your answer with examples.

2. What was the status of children at the Plaszow concentration camp?

3. Was Schindler always successful in his efforts to protect his workers? Explain your answer.

CHAPTER 4

1. How do you explain Schindler's actions? In what ways were his actions consistent or inconsistent with other aspects of his personality?

2. "Virtue theorists," like M.W. Jackson, believe it is better to base moral judgments on questions of character rather than on whether actions conform to moral rules. Given his drinking and womanizing, does it make sense to describe Schindler as having a "virtuous character"?

3. How is a "moral compulsion" different from a "psychological compulsion"? Have you ever experienced a moral compulsion? Can a person who acts on a moral compulsion be said to be acting "of his own free will"?

CHAPTER 5

1. Explain the chain of events by which Schindler's story came to be widely known.

2. View the movie *Schindler's List*. List some points on which the movie is historically accurate. List some points on which it is not accurate. Suggest explanations for these inaccuracies.

3. What is the difference between a film with a historical theme, such as Spielberg's *Schindler's List*, and a documentary? Can the events in a historical film be true? Do documentaries sometimes contain false information? Does the same distinction also apply to historical novels and works of nonfiction?

4. Do you think the movie version of *Schindler's List* distorts history or contributes to the preservation of history?

APPENDIX OF DOCUMENTS

DOCUMENT 1: AN EARLY REPORT FROM POLAND, MARCH 11, 1940

Early reports of the situation of Jews in Germany and Poland were confused. Interested groups, such as the Zionist Organization, did their best to monitor the situation. This report suggests that one reason for the confusion was that the Germans themselves were not very well organized at this point.

11th March, 1940

Dr. L. Lauterbach
The Organisation Department
The Zionist Organisation
P.O.B. 92
Jerusalem

Dear Dr. Lauterbach,

I am sending you some photographs showing Jew's life in Poland. I am also enclosing a report we just received from somebody who left Warsaw on the 2nd March.

You may have seen from previous reports about the situation in Germany and Poland, that the information we receive seems sometimes somewhat contradictory. This is not so much the fault of our informers, but inherent in the situation. The policy of the German Authorities with regard to the Jews is directed from various quarters. The policy of the military authorities in Poland, of the Gestapo-chiefs in Poland and Germany and of the civil authorities is very often influenced by different motives and leading to different methods. Take for instance the case of the Jews of Stettin: they were thrown out of their houses in the night from February 12th to February 13th, all their property was confiscated and they were sent to Poland. But now it appears from various reports that they have been sent back to Stettin as a result of strong protests coming from the German Authorities in Poland who did not know what to do with them.

The same vacillating policy can be observed with regard to the much discussed Lublin scheme. While Eichmann and his group are trying to send Jews from the Protectorate and now also from Germany to this area, the military authorities are trying to check these influx of more Jews into Poland. There is also a tendency to use the Jews on the spot wherever they live as slaves for this or that kind of labour instead of sending them to other parts of the German occupied country.

All these various tendencies in the administration itself make it extremely difficult to find out what the true policy of the German Government is. The only thing which is obvious is, that all these measures have the effect of destroying Jewish property, freedom and life.

Yours sincerely

R. Lichtheim

Reprinted in *Archives of the Holocaust: An International Collection of Selected Documents*, volume 4, Central Zionist Archives, Jerusalem, 1939–1945. Ed. Francis R. Nicosia. New York: Garland Publishing, 1990.

DOCUMENT 2: THE DEFINITION OF A "JEW," JULY 24, 1940

In ethnically diverse Poland it was not easy to know whether or not someone was a Jew. The Nazis were interested in giving the term a racial rather than a religious meaning. The following definition was issued by Hans Frank, the Governor General for German-occupied Poland. In this and other documents, the region under Frank's administration is referred to as the "Government General" to indicate that it was now considered part of greater Germany.

§1

Where the word "Jew" is used in Legal and Administrative Provisions in the Government-General, it is to be interpreted as follows:

1) Anyone who is a Jew, or is considered a Jew, in accordance with the Legal Provisions in the Reich;

2) Anyone who is a Jew, or is considered a Jew, and is a former Polish citizen or stateless person, under §2 of this Regulation.

§2

1) A Jew is a person descended from at least three fully Jewish grandparents by race.

2) A person is considered a Jew if he is descended from two grandparents who are full Jews by race and

a) if he was a member of the Jewish Religious Community on September 1, 1939, or joined such a community subsequently;

b) if he was married to a Jew on the date on which this Regulation came into force, or married a Jew subsequently;

c) if he is the product of extra-marital intercourse with a Jew in accordance with para. 1 and was born after May 31, 1941.

3) A grandparent is automatically considered a full Jew if he was a member of a Jewish community.

§3

1) Where the concept [person of] Jewish *Mischling* is used in Legal and Administrative Provisions of the Government-General, it is to be interpreted as follows:

a) a person who is a Jewish *Mischling* in accordance with the Reich Legal Provisions;

b) any person who is a former Polish citizen or stateless, and is descended from one or two grandparents who are full Jews by race, unless he is considered a Jew under §2, para. 2.

2) The provisions under §2, para. 3 apply similarly.

§4

1) A business enterprise is considered Jewish if the owner is a Jew in accordance with §1.

2) A business enterprise which is owned by a Limited Company is considered Jewish if one or more members who are personally responsible are Jews. . . .

3) A place of business is also considered Jewish if it is in practice under the dominant influence of Jews.

4) The provisions under para. 1-4 also apply to Associations, Endowments, Institutions and other organizations which are not business enterprises.

§5

Legal and Administrative Provisions issued for Jews apply to Jewish *Mischling* only where this is expressly stated.

§6

This Regulation comes into effect on August 1, 1940.

Cracow, July 24, 1940

The Governor General
for the Occupied Polish Territories
Frank

Reprinted in *Documents on the Holocaust: Selected Sources on the Destruction of the Jews of Germany and Austria, Poland, and the Soviet Union,* eds. Yitzhak Arad, Israel Gutman, and Abraham Margaliot. Lincoln: University of Nebraska Press, 1999.

DOCUMENT 5: ORDERS TO IMPLEMENT THE "FINAL SOLUTION," JULY 31, 1941

This is the infamous memo from Hermann Göring to Reinhard Heydrich, head of the Gestapo, ordering the implementation of the "final solution."

To the Chief of the Security Police and the SD,
SS Gruppenführer Heydrich
Berlin

In completion of the task which was entrusted to you in the Edict dated January 24, 1939, of solving the Jewish question by means of emigration or evacuation in the most convenient way possible, given the present conditions, I herewith charge you with making all necessary preparations with regard to organizational, practical and financial aspects for an overall solution of the Jewish question in the German sphere of influence in Europe.

Insofar as the competencies of other central organizations are affected, these are to be involved.

I further charge you with submitting to me promptly an overall plan of the preliminary organizational, practical and financial measures for the execution of the intended final solution of the Jewish question.

Göring

Reprinted in *Documents on the Holocaust: Selected Sources on the Destruction of the Jews of Germany and Austria, Poland, and the Soviet Union*, eds. Yitzhak Arad, Israel Gutman, and Abraham Margaliot. Lincoln: University of Nebraska Press, 1999.

DOCUMENT 4: ORDERS TO CLEAR JEWS OUT OF POLAND, JULY 19, 1942

In this document, Heinrich Himmler, head of the SS, orders the clearance of Jewish ghettos in the Government-General (Poland). Jews were to be "resettled" in "assembly camps" (i.e. concentration camps) including the Plaszow concentration camp, near Krakow.

I order that the resettlement of the entire Jewish population of the General Government be carried out and completed by December 31, 1942.

By December 31, 1942, no persons of Jewish extraction are to be found in the General Government, except if they are in the assembly camps of Warsaw, Cracow, Czestochowa, Radom, Lublin. All other work projects employing Jewish labor must be completed by then or, if completion is not possible, must be transferred to one of the assembly camps.

These measures are necessary for the ethnic separation of races and peoples required in the context of the New Order of Europe, as well as in the interest of the security and purity of the German Reich and the spheres of its interest. Any breach in this proceeding constitutes a threat to peace and order in the entire sphere of German interest, a starting point for the resistance movement, and a center of moral and physical contagion.

For all these reasons, a total cleanup is necessary and is accordingly to be carried out. Anticipated delays beyond the deadline are to be reported to me in time for early remedial measures. All requests from other agencies for alterations or for permission to make exceptions are to be submitted to me personally.

Heil Hitler!
[signed]
H. Himmler

Reprinted in *Fifty Years Ago: In the Depths of Darkness (Commemoration Planning Guide)*. Washington, DC: United States Holocaust Memorial Council, 1992.

DOCUMENT 5: INSTRUCTIONS FOR THE GHETTO CLEARANCES, JULY 22, 1942

Within days Himmler's orders were translated into detailed instructions delivered to the Judenrat, *or Jewish councils, which served as the governing body within the ghettos. This is the text of the instruc-*

tions given to the Warsaw Judenrat. *Similar instructions were undoubtedly delivered to the* Judenrat *in Krakow.*

Orders and Instructions for the Judenrat

The Judenrat is informed of the following:

(1) All Jewish persons, regardless of age and sex, living in Warsaw, will be resettled in the East.

(2) Exempt from resettlement are:

a. All Jewish persons who are employed by German authorities or workshops and can submit proof to that effect.

b. All Jewish persons who are members or employees of the Judenrat (as of the day of promulgation of this ordinance).

c. All Jewish persons who are employed by firms headquartered in the German Reich and can submit proof to that effect.

d. All Jews able to work who have not to date been assigned in the employment process. These are to be segregated in the Jewish quarter.

e. All Jewish persons belonging to the staff of the Jewish hospitals; also the members of the Jewish decontamination squad.

f. All Jewish persons who are members of the Jewish police.

g. All Jewish persons belonging to the immediate families of persons listed in a through f.

h. All Jewish persons who on the first day of resettlement are confined to one of the Jewish hospitals and are not fit to be discharged. Fitness for discharge will be determined by a physician to be named by the Judenrat.

(3) Each Jew to be resettled may take with him as luggage 15 kilograms of personal property. All valuables (gold, jewelry, money, etc.) may be taken along. Provisions for three days should be taken.

(4) The start of the resettlement is on July 22, 1942, at 11:00 A.M.

I. In connection with the resettlement, the Judenrat is charged with the following duties, for the precise observance of which the Judenrat members will be held answerable with their lives: The Judenrat will receive orders having to do with resettlement solely from the Commissioner for Resettlement or from his deputy. For the period of resettlement, the Judenrat may elect a special Resettlement Committee, whose chairman must be the president of the Judenrat, and whose deputy chairman must be the commandant of the Jewish police.

II. The Judenrat is responsible for providing the Jews for shipment each day. For the execution of this task, the Judenrat will utilize the Jewish police (1,000 men). The Judenrat will see to it that each day, beginning July 22, 1942, 6,000 Jews report to the point of assembly by 4:00 P.M. The point of assembly during the entire period of evacuation will be the Jewish Hospital on Stawki Street. On July 22 the 6,000 Jews will report directly to the staging area next to the *Transferstelle*. Initially, the Judenrat may take the required daily contingents of Jews from the population as a whole; later the Judenrat will receive definite instructions, according to which specific streets or blocks of houses are to be cleared.

III. On July 22, 1942, the Judenrat is to clear the Stawki Street Jewish Hospital and to move the inmates and equipment into another suitable building within the ghetto, so that on the evening of July 23, 1942, the hospital will be free to receive the Jews arriving for resettlement each day.

IV. The Judenrat, furthermore, is to see to it that objects and valuable property left behind by the resettled Jews, insofar as they are not contaminated, are gathered and inventoried at collection points still to be determined. For this purpose, the Judenrat will make use of the Jewish police and a sufficient quantity of Jewish manpower. This activity will be supervised by the Security Police, which will give the Judenrat special instructions on the matter. Unlawful acquisition of objects or valuable property in the course of this activity will be punished by death.

V. The Judenrat, furthermore, will see to it that during the period of resettlement Jews working in German enterprises or for German interests will attend to this work. To ensure compliance with this order, it will issue an appropriate announcement to the Jewish population, threatening the severest penalties. The Judenrat must also see to it that enough Jewish food-supply enterprises operate undisturbed in order to secure the food supply both of the Jews at the assembly point and of those remaining behind.

VI. In addition, the Judenrat is responsible for seeing that Jews who die during the period of resettlement are buried the same day.

VII. The Judenrat will immediately, by posters, make the following announcement to the Jewish population of Warsaw: "Upon order by the German authorities, all Jewish persons, regardless . . . (etc., from items 1 through 4).

VIII. Penalties:

a. Any Jewish person who leaves the ghetto after the start of resettlement not belonging to the categories of persons enumerated in numbers 2a and 2c, and not hitherto entitled to do so, will be shot.

b. Any Jewish person who commits an act intended to evade or interfere with the resettlement measures will be shot.

c. All Jews who are found in Warsaw after conclusion of the resettlement not belonging to the categories of persons enumerated under 2a through 2h will be shot.

The Judenrat is notified that if the orders and instructions given to it are not carried out 100 percent, an appropriate number of hostages, who will meanwhile have been taken, will be shot in each instance.

Reprinted in *Fifty Years Ago: In the Depths of Darkness (Commemoration Planning Guide)*. Washington, DC: United States Holocaust Memorial Council, 1992.

DOCUMENT 6: A REPORT FROM THE POLISH GOVERNMENT-IN-EXILE, DECEMBER 10, 1942

Informants managed to get information about the condition of Jews in Poland to the outside world. This report to Allied governments, from the Polish government-in-exile, was issued soon after Schindler's visit to Budapest, Hungary, to deliver information to the Zionist underground. However, this report does not appear to include information from Krakow, which Schindler would have been able to supply.

REPUBLIC OF POLAND   LONDON,
Ministry of Foreign Affairs   *December 10th, 1942*

Your Excellency,

On several occasions the Polish Government have drawn the attention of the civilised world, both in diplomatic documents and official publications, to the conduct of the German Government and of the German authorities of occupation, both military and civilian, and to the methods employed by them "in order to reduce the population to virtual slavery and ultimately to exterminate the Polish nation." These methods, first introduced in Poland, were subsequently applied in a varying degree in other countries occupied by the armed forces of the German Reich.

2. At the Conference held at St. James's Palace on January 18th, 1942, the Governments of the occupied countries "placed among their principal war aims the punishment, through the channel of organized justice, of those guilty of, or responsible for, those crimes, whether they have ordered them, perpetrated them, or participated in them."

Despite this solemn warning and the declarations of President Roosevelt, of the Prime Minister, Mr. Winston Churchill, and of the People's Commissar for Foreign Affairs, M. Molotov, the German Government has not ceased to apply its methods of violence and terror. The Polish Government have received numerous reports from Poland testifying to the constant intensification of German persecution of the subjected populations.

3. Most recent reports present a horrifying picture of the position to which the Jews in Poland have been reduced. The new methods of mass slaughter applied during the last few months confirm the fact that the German authorities aim with systematic deliberation at the total extermination of the Jewish population of Poland and of the many thousands of Jews whom the German authorities have deported to Poland from Western and Central European countries and from the German Reich itself.

The Polish Government consider it their duty to bring to the knowledge of the Governments of all civilised countries the following fully authenticated information received from Poland during recent weeks, which indicates all too plainly the new methods of extermination adopted by the German authorities.

4. The initial steps leading to the present policy of extermination of the Jews were taken already in October 1940, when the German authorities established the Warsaw ghetto. At that time all the Jewish inhabitants of the Capital were ordered to move into the Jewish quarter assigned to them not later than November 1st, 1940, while all the non-Jews domiciled within the new boundaries of what was to become the ghetto were ordered to move out of that quarter. The Jews were allowed to take only personal effects with them, while all their remaining property was confiscated. All Jewish shops and businesses outside the new ghetto boundaries were closed down and sealed. The original date for these transfers was subsequently postponed to November 15th, 1940. After that date the ghetto was completely closed and its entire area was surrounded by a brick wall, the right of entry and exit being restricted to the holders of special passes, issued by the German authorities. All those who left the ghetto without such a pass became liable to sentence of death, and it is known that German courts passed such sentences in a large number of cases.

5. After the isolation of the ghetto, official intercourse with the outside world was maintained through a special German office known as "Transferstelle." Owing to totally inadequate supplies of food for the inhabitants of the ghetto, smuggling on a large scale was carried on; the Germans themselves participated in this illicit trading, drawing considerable incomes from profits and bribes. The food rations for the inhabitants of the ghetto amounted to about a pound of bread per person weekly, with practically nothing else. As a result, prices in the ghetto were on an average ten times higher than outside, and mortality due to exhaustion, starvation and disease, particularly during the last two winters, increased on an unprecedented scale. During the winter 1941–42 the death rate, calculated on an annual base, has risen to 13 percent, and during the first quarter of 1942 increased still further. Scores of corpses were found in the streets of the ghetto every day.

6. At the time when the ghetto was established the whole population was officially stated to amount to 433,000, and in spite of the appalling death rate it was being maintained at this figure by the importation of Jews from Germany and from the occupied countries, as well as from other parts of Poland.

7. The outbreak of war between Germany and Soviet Russia and the occupation of the Eastern areas of Poland by German troops considerably increased the numbers of Jews in Germany's power. At the same time the mass murders of Jews reached such dimensions that, at first, people refused to give credence to the reports reaching Warsaw from the Eastern provinces. The reports, however, were confirmed again and again by reliable witnesses. During the winter 1941–42 several tens of thousands of Jews were murdered. In the city of Wilno over 50,000 Jews were reported to have been massacred and only 12,000 of them remain in the local

ghetto. In the city of Lwow 40,000 were reported murdered; in Rowne 14,000; in Kowel 10,000, and unknown numbers in Stanislawow, Tarnopol, Stryj, Drohobycz and many other smaller towns. At first the executions were carried out by shooting; subsequently, however, it is reported that the Germans applied new methods, such as poison gas, by means of which the Jewish population was exterminated in Chelm, or electrocution, for which a camp was organised in Belzec, where in the course of March and April 1942, the Jews from the provinces of Lublin, Lwow and Kielce, amounting to tens of thousands, were exterminated. Of Lublin's 80,000 Jewish inhabitants only 2,500 still survive in the city.

8. It has been reliably reported that on the occasion of his visit to the General Gouvernment of Poland in March, 1942, Himmler issued an order for the extermination of 50 percent of the Jews in Poland by the end of that year. After Himmler's departure the Germans spread the rumour that the Warsaw ghetto would be liquidated as from April 1942. This date was subsequently altered to June. Himmler's second visit to Warsaw in the middle of July 1942, became the signal for the commencement of the process of liquidation, the horror of which surpasses anything known in the annals of history.

9. The liquidation of the ghetto was preceded, on July 17th, 1942, by the registration of all foreign Jews confined there who were then removed to the Pawiak prison. As from July 20th, 1942, the guarding of the ghetto was entrusted to special security battalions, formed from the scum of several Eastern European countries, while large forces of German police armed with machine guns and commanded by SS. officers were posted at all the gates leading into the ghetto. Mobile German police detachments patrolled all the boundaries of the ghetto day and night.

10. On July 21st, at 11 A.M., German police cars drove up to the building of the Jewish Council of the ghetto, in Grzybowska Street. The SS. officers ordered the chairman of the Jewish Council, Mr. Czerniakow, to summon the members of the Council, who were all arrested on arrival and removed in police cars to the Pawiak prison. After a few hours' detention the majority of them were allowed to return to the ghetto. About the same time flying squads of German police entered the ghetto, breaking into the houses in search of Jewish intellectuals. The better-dressed Jews found were killed on the spot, without the police troubling even to identify them. Among those who were thus killed was a non-Jew, Professor Dr. Raszeja, who was visiting the ghetto in the course of his medical duties and was in possession of an official pass. Hundreds of educated Jews were killed in this way.

11. On the morning of the following day, July 22nd, 1942, the German police again visited the office of the Jewish Council and summoned all the members, who had been released from the Pawiak prison the previous day. On their assembly they were informed

that an order had been issued for the removal of the entire Jewish population of the Warsaw ghetto and printed instructions to that effect were issued in the form of posters, the contents of which are reproduced in Annex 1 to this Note. Additional instructions were issued verbally. The number of people to be removed was first fixed at 6,000 daily. The persons concerned were to assemble in the hospital wards and grounds in Stawki Street, the patients of which were evacuated forthwith. The hospital was close to the railway siding. Persons subject to deportation were to be delivered by the Jewish police not later than 4 P.M. each day. Members of the Council and other hostages were to answer for the strict fulfilment of the order. In conformity with German orders, all inmates of Jewish prisons, old-age pensioners and inmates of other charitable institutions were to be included in the first contingent.

12. On July 23rd, 1942, at 7 P.M., two German police officers again visited the offices of the Jewish Council and saw the chairman, Mr. Czerniakow. After they left him he committed suicide. It is reported that Mr. Czerniakow did so because the Germans increased the contingent of the first day to 10,000 persons, to be followed by 7,000 persons on each subsequent day. Mr. Czerniakow was succeeded in his office by Mr. Lichtenbaum, and on the following day 10,000 persons were actually assembled for deportation, followed by 7,000 persons on each subsequent day. The people affected were either rounded up haphazardly in the streets or were taken from their homes.

13. According to the German order of July 22nd, 1942, all Jews employed in German-owned undertakings, together with their families, were to be exempt from deportation. This produced acute competition among the inhabitants of the ghetto to secure employment in such undertakings, or, failing employment, bogus certificates to that effect. Large sums of money, running into thousands of Zlotys, were being paid for such certificates to the German owners. They did not, however, save the purchasers from deportation, which was being carried out without discrimination or identification.

14. The actual process of deportation was carried out with appalling brutality. At the appointed hour on each day the German police cordoned off a block of houses selected for clearance, entered the back yard and fired their guns at random, as a signal for all to leave their homes and assemble in the yard. Anyone attempting to escape or to hide was killed on the spot. No attempt was made by the Germans to keep families together. Wives were torn from their husbands and children from their parents. Those who appeared frail or infirm were carried straight to the Jewish cemetery to be killed and buried there. On the average 50–100 people were disposed of in this way daily. After the contingent was assembled, the people were packed forcibly into cattle trucks to the number of 120 in each truck, which had room for forty. The trucks were then locked and sealed. The Jews were suffocating for lack of air.

The floors of the trucks were covered with quicklime and chlorine. As far as is known, the trains were dispatched to three localities—Treblinka, Belzec and Sobibor, to what the reports describe as "Extermination camps." The very method of transport was deliberately calculated to cause the largest possible number of casualties among the condemned Jews. It is reported that on arrival in camp the survivors were stripped naked and killed by various means, including poison gas and electrocution. The dead were interred in mass graves dug by machinery.

15. According to all available information, of the 250,000 Jews deported from the Warsaw ghetto up to September 1st, 1942, only two small transports, numbering about 4,000 people, are known to have been sent eastwards in the direction of Brest-Litovsk and Malachowicze, allegedly to be employed on work behind the front line. It has not been possible to ascertain whether any of the other Jews deported from the Warsaw ghetto still survive, and it must be feared that they have been all put to death.

16. The Jews deported from the Warsaw ghetto so far included in the first instance all the aged and infirm; a number of the physically strong have escaped so far, because of their utility as labour power. All the children from Jewish schools, orphanages and children's homes were deported, including those from the orphanage in charge of the celebrated educationist, Dr. Janusz Korczak, who refused to abandon his charges, although he was given the alternative of remaining behind.

17. According to the most recent reports, 120,000 ration cards were distributed in the Warsaw ghetto for the month of September, 1942, while the report also mentions that only 40,000 such cards were to be distributed for the month of October 1942. The latter figure is corroborated by information emanating from the German Employment Office (Arbeitsamt), which mentioned the number of 40,000 skilled workmen as those who were to be allowed to remain in a part of the ghetto, confined to barracks and employed on German war production.

18. The deportations from the Warsaw ghetto were interrupted during five days, between August 20th–25th. The German machinery for the mass slaughter of the Jews was employed during this interval on the liquidation of other ghettoes in Central Poland, including the towns of Falenica, Rembertów, Nowy Dwór, Kaluszyn and Minsk Mazowiecki.

19. It is not possible to estimate the exact numbers of Jews who have been exterminated in Poland since the occupation of the country by the armed forces of the German Reich. But all the reports agree that the total number of killed runs into many hundreds of thousands of innocent victims—men, women and children—and that of the 3,130,000 Jews in Poland before the outbreak of war, over a third have perished during the last three years.

20. The Polish population, which itself is suffering the most

grievous afflictions, and of which many millions have been either deported to Germany as slave labor or evicted from their homes and lands, deprived of so many of their leaders, who have been cruelly murdered by the Germans, have repeatedly expressed, through the underground organisations, their horror of and compassion with the terrible fate which has befallen their Jewish fellow-countrymen. The Polish Government are in possession of information concerning the assistance which the Polish population is rendering to the Jews. For obvious reasons no details of these activities can be published at present.

21. The Polish Government—as the representatives of the legitimate authority on territories in which the Germans are carrying out the systematic extermination of Polish citizens and of citizens of Jewish origin of many other European countries—consider it their duty to address themselves to the Governments of the United Nations, in the confident belief that they will share their opinion as to the necessity not only of condemning the crimes committed by the Germans and punishing the criminals, but also of finding a means of offering the hope that Germany might be effectively restrained from continuing to apply her methods of mass extermination.

I avail myself of this opportunity to renew to Your Excellency the assurances of my high consideration.

L.S. EDWARD RACZYNSKI.

Reprinted in *Fifty Years Ago: In the Depths of Darkness (Commemoration Planning Guide)*. Washington, DC: United States Holocaust Memorial Council, 1992.

DOCUMENT 7: "FACE THE FUTURE": AN EDITORIAL, AUGUST 13, 1943

This is an editorial from an underground newspaper in Krakow titled Fighting Pioneer. *The newspaper was put out by a Zionist youth organization, Akiva. This issue was probably circulated secretly inside the Plaszow concentration camp.*

In view of the tragic existence of the Jews, where the life of the individual depends on chance, and the life of the community as a whole has long been on the brink of cessation, one must, more than ever, see the situation comprehensively. An individual point of view—everyone will surely understand that now—is of no significance today. As individuals, we are all lost. The likelihood of staying alive is minute. Broken and alone—there is not much we can expect of life. Dying together with Polish Jewry we must clearly visualize for ourselves the historic character of this time and tell ourselves with courage that our death does not spell the end of the world. The record of humanity and of the Jewish people will continue at its own speed in the future, even after we are safely under the ground.

The numerical balance-sheet of the Jews will be sad when peace finally comes to the world after the historical blood-bath. This is indeed not the first defeat of a defenseless people scattered over the face of the earth. Slaughter, murders, confiscation of property, and the burning alive of people—all these have been known to us for generations as the essential elements of our martyrology. But there has never been such wholesale extermination. Never did a situation develop like this, where there is no way out. Never before did great numbers of people armed with the most modern technology move against the Jews. Of 16 million Jews in the world, we shall scarcely reach 9 million after the war. And, most important of all, the Jews of Europe will no longer be there, those who up to now made up the healthiest part of the nation. . . .

Nobody held out a helping hand to the Jews who were being destroyed, nobody made any effort to help them to the extent that they could escape from the danger of extermination. They looked on our destruction as on the death of maggots, and not as the loss of a nation with high cultural values. When the question of the Jews came up even the hatred towards the Germans lessened. There was solidarity with the enemy in the joy over the fall of the Jews. Only a few retained any degree of humanity, and even they did not dare to give this public expression. The truth of aloneness was again confirmed.

We shall carry the heavy burden of this isolation until the end of our days, and it points to the fact that the only proper approach is that of self-liberation: We have nobody on whom to depend except ourselves. All other political concepts will lead us astray. We have paid the highest possible price because we were lulled asleep by the prosperity of Europe, or guided by false hopes of rescue that would come from outside. We lost our sense of reality and instead of planning our independence we scattered invaluable forces in alien fields. Who knows what would have been the future of the Jewish people if there were no *Yishuv* (Community) of half a million in Palestine, that built its foundations before the war broke out and which has now reached a million souls? Only this nucleus of a Jewish State now offers assurance for the survival of the people. It makes us believe that an independent Jewish nation will rise again, a well-spring of profound spiritual values, as always. It is easier to die, therefore, in the knowledge that a genuine Jewish life still throbs there, that in that one small corner of the wide world we were not undesirables, lonely victims. There would be no sense in our death but for the feeling that, after we have gone, they will be the only ones who will think about us with genuine emotion.

Therefore, despite certain death, we join them in their struggle for the future. Every one of our deeds paved the way for freedom, and furthers the building of an independent homeland. Our revolt is a protest against the evil that is engulfing the world. To counter the terror that has crushed our people we shall stand prepared for the struggle for justice and freedom that should light up the life of humanity as a whole. We are willing to die in order that the shame of death in slavery shall not burden the future of the Jews, and that these Jews shall not have to recall the Jews of Europe with shame because they allowed themselves to be led unresisting to slaughter, and they had not the spirit and courage to defend themselves against destruction. As we had not been allowed to make our contribution to the creative work of building, we shall at least fulfill our historic duty here: it is we who must raise up the name of the lost people, to wipe away the mark of shame of slavery, and to place it among the ranks of people free in spirit. . . .

Reprinted in *Documents on the Holocaust: Selected Sources on the Destruction of the Jews of Germany and Austria, Poland, and the Soviet Union*, eds. Yitzhak Arad, Israel Gutman, and Abraham Margaliot. Lincoln: University of Nebraska Press, 1999.

DOCUMENT 8: CONCRETE MEASURES TO SAVE SURVIVING JEWS, DECEMBER 26, 1944

Toward the end of the war, Germany began liquidating the concentration camps, consolidating the remaining prisoners in a few death camps. This letter is a plea to the U.S. Secretary of State for assistance in preventing the liquidation of the camps. Although Plaszow is mentioned in the letter, by the time this letter was written, Plaszow had already been mostly disbanded.

AJL   DECEMBER 26, 1944
NIGHTLETTER
EDWARD R. STETTINIUS
SECRETARY OF STATE
STATE DEPARTMENT
WASHINGTON, D.C.

Of the three and one half million Jews who lived in Poland before the war, and of the millions of Jews of all parts of Europe who were deported by the Nazis to Poland, only a very small number survived the terror and extermination unleashed against them by the Nazi hangmen. According to trustworthy sources, from thirty to forty thousand Jews continue to live in the regions of Poland recently liberated by the Soviet armies. In Nazi occupied Poland there are about one hundred fifty thousand Jews interned in special concentration and labor camps. The remnants of our great and old people are hourly in imminent danger of death. Several days ago the Jewish telegraphic agency, as well as the independent Jewish press service, reported that the Jews in five more concentration camps have been murdered. Daily, the number of Jews is diminishing. Sometime ago, we appealed to the American government with three requests: 1: The Jews in the Nazi camps should be recognized as prisoners of war; 2: The International Red Cross should provide these victims with food and other assistance; 3: The American government should again issue a warning to the German government and the Nazi officials against the annihilation of the surviving Jews in Europe. Subsequently, the state department informed us that the requested warning to the Nazis was issued on October 10. We failed, however, to receive a reply to our first two requests. At the end of November we received a cable from the International Red Cross in reply to ours of November 14, asking us to submit a list of the camps for which we had requested assistance and also stating that "on receipt of these particulars, we shall investigate whether responsible authorities will consent to scheme proposed." The Jewish Labor Committee at once cabled a list of the following thirteen such camps: Plaszow near Cracow, Stalowa Wola, Miclec, Pustkow, Czenstochowa, Piotrkow, Radom, Starachowice, Skarzysko Kamienna, Krasnik, Budzyn, Blyzin, Pioniki. Until a few days ago, we had not received any information on our appeal. Last week, however, we received a cable from the Polish government in London advising us that the International Red Cross does not possess adequate financial resources to provide assistance to those in Nazi concentration camps in Poland. We are very much bewildered by this report from the Polish government in exile, especially so because of the new, alarming reports which we have again received concerning the desperate plight of the Jews in the Nazi camps. It is our feeling that these unfortunate victims are being forgotten by the civilized world, as if everything were hopeless and nothing could be done to provide them with some succor. It is indeed painful to put these thoughts on paper, but we can very well imagine that the Jews in the Nazi extermination camps of Poland are most anxiously awaiting our voice—the voice of solidarity and assistance. All they have been receiving, however, is more persecution at the hands of the Nazi fiends. It is our considered judgement that the only great, truly democratic and humanitarian government in the entire world—our American government—and its Secretary of State, must assume the obligation of saving the remnants of our almost extinct Jewish brethren overseas. May we repeat our requests: 1: The Jews in the concentration camps should be declared prisoners of war; 2: The International Red Cross should supply them with assistance; 3: The Nazi madmen should again be warned against the extermination of the Jewish survivors. While we are appealing to you, our hearts are perturbed as to the fate of the Jewish victims of Nazism. A report has reached us that there are still some eighty thousand Jews in the labor camp of Lodz, Poland. We are in great fear that the morrow may bring the annihilation of these internees too. We beseech you to undertake speedy and effective measures. Let our consciences be free of any possible guilt in the death of millions of our Jewish brethren. If you find it possible to receive representatives of our organization to convey to them in the name of the American government words of encouragement and hope we shall be glad to respond to your call.

Jewish Labor Committee, Adolph Held, Chairman; David Dubinsky, Treasurer; Joseph Baskin Secretary; Jacob Pat, Executive Secretary

Reprinted in *Archives of the Holocaust: An International Collection of Selected Documents*, volume 4, Central Zionist Archives, Jerusalem, 1939–1945. Ed. Francis R. Nicosia. New York: Garland Publishing, 1990.

DOCUMENT 9: "WHAT NEXT?": A REPORT ON DISPLACED PERSONS

This document is an extract from a report to the American Friends Service Committee, the Quaker charitable organization, issued just days before the end of the war. This report tells something of the emotional and physical condition of DPs (displaced persons) in Europe at the end of the war.

The end of the Concentration Camp has meant the end of most of the urgent problems of sheer physical survival, but this has only made way for acute and far-reaching long term problems to come to the surface. Everyone of the thousands of ex-internees is asking in German, Polish, French, Dutch, Hungarian or Czeck: "When can I go home?" or in some cases, *"Must* I go home?", "Have I a home to go to?" and "Are my relatives alive or dead?". In this connection we have felt much concerned at the haste with which people have been moved to Transit Camps elsewhere before anything like adequate answers have been found to many of these questions. This does not apply so much to the French, Belgian and Dutch D.P.'s, who so far as we can judge, are comparatively well cared for during transit and on their return home, but it does concern Eastern Europeans, particularly Poles. It applies with special urgency to Polish Jews, very few of whom want to return to Poland, partly for fear of the Russians and partly because of the Anti-Semitic persecution which they had suffered in their own country before the war. Similarly, many non-Jews are reluctant to return to a Russian dominated Poland. Those who, whether Jewish or not, do not wish to return to their own countries, are being given the opportunity to register as "Stateless" and are being sent to a special camp at Lingen. It is apparently hoped that when a sufficiently large number of them have been accumulated, the Allied Governments will decide what is to happen to them next. Some of the Jews want to go to Palestine, but by no means all are Zionists, and most of the others want to go to England, the Dominions or America. It is extremely difficult for these people to decide whether or not to register as Stateless when so many of them are still sick in mind and body, are unable to discuss matters with their relatives, and have so long been shut away from the outside world. To make matters even more difficult in Belsen there was no proper service by which even the small amount of known accurate information could be passed on efficiently to the D.P.'s.

While aware of the complexities of the problem, we feel that if these people are to gain any of that sense of security which is so essential to their recovery, it is urgently necessary that the Governments concerned should at the earliest possible moment make some statement of their policy towards emigrants. We have felt much concerned that people whose future is so uncertain, are already being moved from Belsen into Transit Camps elsewhere. As already mentioned, the Wermacht barracks at Belsen, which have no connection, either physically or in the minds of the ex-internees, with the Concentration camp, are almost ideal as a long term center for D.P.'s; we feel it is most unlikely that conditions in other camps will be as good at the present time. Apart from this, we feel it is most important to avoid pushing displaced people from pillar to post, often separating families in the process, while many of them are still far from ready to cope with frequent changes of environment.

Reprinted in *Archives of the Holocaust: An International Collection of Selected Documents*, volume 2, American Friends Service Committee, Philadelphia, 1940–1945. Ed. Jack Sutters. New York: Garland Publishing, 1990.

GLOSSARY

Aktion: A "police action" directed against Jews, often involving theft and breaking of property, and selection of some people for deportation.

anti-Semitism: Prejudice against Jews, usually based on ethnic rather than religious hatred.

Appelplatz: At the Plaszow concentration camp, the parade ground or square where inspections were held.

Aryan: Caucasians of Indo-European descent. The Nazis used the term to distinguish themselves from other racial groups, such as the Jews. Ironically, the most "Aryan" people of Europe are the Gypsies, who were also persecuted by the Nazis.

Auschwitz-Birkenau: Extermination camp in Poland, about thirty-five miles west of Krakow.

Blochalteste: Female head of a concentration camp barracks.

Brinnlitz, Czechoslovakia: Location of Schindler's munitions factory established as a sanctuary that enabled over a thousand Jews to survive the Holocaust.

Brnenec: See Brinnlitz.

Brunnlitz: See Brinnlitz.

Crakow: See Krakow.

DEF: Deutsche Emailwaren Fabrik (German Enamelware Factory).

Emalia: Informal name by which Jewish workers referred to the Deutsche Emailwaren Fabrik, Schindler's enamelware factory. The word means "the enamelry."

Einsatzgruppen: Squadrons of SS soldiers assigned to harass and kill Jews.

ghetto: A section of a city where people of a single ethnic group are concentrated. During World War II, Jews were forced into ghettos prior to being moved into concentration camps.

Goleschau (Goleszow): A town in Poland, location of a forced-labor mine during World War II.

Gross-Rosen: Concentration and extermination camp located in Poland.

Haftling (pl., Haftlinge): Prisoner.

Hauptsturmfuhrer: German military rank equivalent to captain or commandant.

Holocaust: Literally, "wholly consumed by fire"; a genocide. The Jewish Holocaust of World War II resulted in the deaths of over 6 million of Europe's 9 million Jews. The Jewish Holocaust is also sometimes called the Shoah, which means "whirlwind."

Judenrat: Jewish councils that functioned as local governing bodies inside the ghettos.

Krakow: Traditional capital of Poland under the Polish monarchy. Location of Schindler's Deutsche Emailwaren Fabrak (German Enamelware Factory).

Kreisleiter: A regional administrator.

Kristallnacht: Literally, "crystal night"; "night of broken glass," November 9, 1938, widespread German destruction of Jewish businesses and synagogues.

Mahrisch Ostrau: Regional capital of Moravia, Czechoslovakia.

Mauthausen: Concentration camp in Germany.

Muselmann: The Jewish term for someone reduced to skin and bones by starvation.

Nazi: A member of the National Socialist German Workers' Party, or NSDAP. The head of the Nazi Party was Adolf Hitler.

NSDAP: See Nazi.

Oberfuhrer: A German military rank with no exact English equivalent, between the levels of colonel and general.

Obersturmfuhrer: A German military rank equivalent to first lieutenant.

Ordungsdienst (OD): The Jewish police, held responsible for maintaining order inside the ghettos.

Ostbahn: The eastern branch of the German railway system.

Ostrava: See Mahrisch Ostrau.

Plaszow: Concentration camp near Krakow, Poland.

Podgorze: Suburb of Krakow in which the Jewish ghetto was located.

pogrom: A Yiddish word meaning "organized persecution."

Schindlerjuden: "Schindler's Jews," the name by which the workers at the Deutsche Emailwaren Fabrik, and later the workers at the Brinnlitz munitions factory, referred to themselves.

Schutzstaffel (SS): Literally, "protection squad"; Hitler's personal bodyguard. Working directly for Hitler, the SS operated above the law with duties far beyond merely protecting Hitler. The SS was hated and feared even by other branches of the German military.

Sturmabteilung (SA): Literally, "storm troopers"; Nazi military division eventually replaced by the more radical SS.

Sudetenland: A long-contested region of Czechoslovakia. Before World War II it had a high percentage of ethnic German residents. Oskar and Emilie Schindler were Sudeten Germans.

Svitavka: See Zwittau.

Treuhander: A manager or trustee; in occupied Poland, a German put in charge of a previously Polish- or Jewish-owned business.

Volk: Literally, "folk"; Germans used this term to identify the German ethnic group. Jews were explicitly not members of the Volk.

Wehrmacht: The German war administration under the Nazis, i.e., the German "Department of War."

Zionism: Jewish nationalist movement dedicated to establishing a Jewish state in the Middle East; the Zionists served as a Jewish underground resistance during World War II.

Zwittau: Oskar Schindler's birthplace in Czechozlovakia.

Zyklon-B: A nerve gas used to kill prisoners at Nazi extermination camps, including Auschwitz.

CHRONOLOGY

1908

Oskar Schindler born April 28 in Zwittau, Austria-Hungary.

1914

Austria-Hungary declares war on Serbia; World War I begins.

1918

World War I ends; Zwittau becomes part of the newly formed country of Czechoslovakia.

1928

Oskar Schindler marries Emilie Pelzl on March 6.

1930

In national elections on September 14 Hitler's National Socialist Party (the Nazis) wins 107 seats in the Reichstag to become the second-largest party in Germany.

1933–1934

Appointed chancellor of Germany, Hitler rises in power to become absolute dictator.

1935

Hans Schindler's business folds; Oskar Schindler takes a job as sales manager for Moravian Electrotechnic.

1938

March 14, Germany invades Austria; October 5, Germany takes over the Sudeten regions of Czechoslovakia; November 9, *Kristallnacht*, the Night of Broken Glass; Jewish shops and synagogues destroyed throughout Germany and German-held regions of Europe.

1939

March 14, Germany takes over the rest of Czechoslovakia; September 1, Germany invades Poland one week after signing a mutual nonaggression pact with Russia; September 3, Britain and France declare war on Germany, World War II begins; December, Oskar Schindler opens Deutsche Email-waren Fabrik in Krakow, Poland.

1940

Krakow Jews forced into Podgorze, a suburb of Krakow, which becomes a sealed Jewish ghetto.

1941

Zyklon-B gas is tested at Auschwitz on September 3.

1942

Fall, Schindler travels to Budapest, Hungary, to report on the situation of Jews in Krakow.

1943

March 13, Podgorze ghetto cleared; most Jews are moved to the Plaszow concentration camp; some are sent to Auschwitz; many are shot.

1944

Plaszow concentration camp is closed, including the sub-camp at Schindler's enamelware factory; all residents, except those on "Schindler's list," are sent to Auschwitz or Gross-Rosen; Fall, Schindler opens a munitions factory in Brinnlitz, Czechoslovakia, using workers from the Plaszow concentration camp; December, the Brinnlitz factory receives about 150 Jewish "workers" intended for a mine in Golleshau, Poland; many have frozen to death.

1945

May 8, Germany surrenders to the Allies; Schindler, his wife, and several Jewish friends flee to the American front; May 11, the Brinnlitz munitions factory is liberated by a single Russian soldier on horseback.

1946

Amon Goeth is executed on September 13 for war crimes.

1949

Oskar and Emilie Schindler immigrate to Argentina.

1958

After the failure of a nutria-raising enterprise, Schindler leaves his wife to return to Germany.

1961

Schindler's cement factory in Frankfurt fails; Schindler accepts an invitation to visit Israel.

1962

Schindler is named one of the Righteous Among the Nations by Israel on April 28.

1974

Schindler dies at his home in Frankfurt on October 9; he is buried in the Latin Cemetery in Jerusalem.

1980

Thomas Keneally meets Leopold Page (Poldek Pfefferberg) to have his suitcase repaired; Page convinces Keneally to research and write about Schindler.

1982

Keneally's book *Schindler's Ark* published in England; in the United States it is released under the title *Schindler's List.*

1993

Steven Speilberg's film *Schindler's List,* based on Keneally's book, is released; it wins the Academy Award for Best Picture.

2001

Emilie Schindler dies on October 7 at a hospital in Strausberg, Germany, at the age of ninety-three.

FOR FURTHER RESEARCH

BOOKS AND ARTICLES ABOUT OSKAR SCHINDLER

Thomas Fensch, ed., *Oskar Schindler and His List.* Forest Dale, VT: Paul S. Eriksson, 1995.

Dwight Furrow, "Schindler's Compulsion: An Essay on Practical Necessity," *American Philosophical Quarterly,* vol. 35, no. 3, July 1998.

M.W. Jackson, "Oskar Schindler and Moral Theory," *Journal of Applied Philosophy,* vol. 25, no. 2, 1988.

Ray Jones, "The Economic Puzzle of Oskar Schindler," *American Journal of Economics and Sociology,* vol. 57, no. 1, January 1998.

Thomas Keneally, *Schindler's List.* New York: Simon & Schuster, 1982.

Robert Jay Lifton, "Schindler's Puzzle," *American Health,* June 1994.

Mordecai Paldiel, "Oskar Schindler," *Encyclopedia of the Holocaust,* vol. 4. Ed. Israel Gutman. New York: Macmillan, 1990.

Emilie Schindler, *Where Light and Shadow Meet: A Memoir.* New York: W.W. Norton, 1996.

Herbert Steinhouse, "The Real Oskar Schindler," *Saturday Night,* vol. 109, no. 3, April 1994.

Luitgard N. Wundheiler, "Oskar Schindler's Moral Development During the Holocaust," *Humboldt Journal of Social Relations,* vol. 13, no. 1–2, Fall/Winter–Winter/Spring, 1985–1986.

MEMOIRS BY *SCHINDLERJUDEN* AND OTHER SURVIVORS OF THE PLASZOW CONCENTRATION CAMP

Joseph Bau, *Dear God, Have You Ever Gone Hungry?* New York: Arcade, 1990.

Elinor J. Brecher, *Schindler's Legacy: True Stories of the List Survivors.* New York: Penguin, 1994.

Clark Brooks, "Hand of Fate: He Was Saved from Hell to Tell the World About Unsung Hero," *The San Diego Union-Tribune*, August 16, 1994.

Malvina Graf, *The Krakow Ghetto and the Plaszow Camp Remembered.* Tallahassee: Florida State University Press, 1989.

Ana Novac, *The Beautiful Days of My Youth: My Six Months in Auschwitz and Plaszow.* New York: Henry Holt, 1992.

Lisa Petrillo, "Number 233 on the List: Blessed with Luck, Saved by Schindler," *The San Diego Union-Tribune*, May 29, 1994.

Abraham Zuckerman, *A Voice in the Chorus: Life as a Teenager in the Holocaust.* Hoboken, NJ: KTAV, 1991.

BOOKS ABOUT RIGHTEOUS GENTILES

Per Anger, *With Raoul Wallenberg in Budapest: Memories of the War Years in Hungary.* New York: Henry Holt, 1981.

Wladyslaw Bartoszewski and Lewin Zofia, eds., *Righteous Among Nations: How Poles Helped the Jews: 1939–1945.* London: Earlscourt, 1969.

John Bierman, *Righteous Gentile: The Story of Raoul Wallenberg, Missing Hero of the Holocaust.* New York: Viking, 1981.

Gay Block and Malka Drucker, *Rescuers: Portraits of Moral Courage in the Holocaust.* New York: Holmes & Meier, 1992.

Eva Fogelman, *Conscience and Courage: Rescuers of Jews During the Holocaust.* New York: Anchor, 1994.

Philip Friedman, *Their Brothers' Keepers.* New York: Holocaust Library, 1978.

Peter Hellman, *Avenue of the Righteous.* New York: Atheneum, 1980.

Kazimierz Iranek-Osmecki, *He Who Saves One Life.* New York: Crown, 1971.

Heinz David Leuner, *When Compassion Was a Crime: Germany's Silent Heroes, 1933–1945.* London: Oswald Wolff, 1966.

Samuel P. Oliner and Pearl M. Oliner, *The Altruistic Personality: Rescuers of Jews in Nazi Europe.* New York: Free Press, 1988.

Alexander Ramati, *The Assisi Underground: The Priests Who Rescued Jews.* New York: Stein and Day, 1978.

Carol Rittner and Sondra Myers, eds.,*The Courage to Care: Rescuers of Jews During the Holocaust.* New York: New York University Press, 1986.

Nechama Tec, *When Light Pierced the Darkness: Christian Rescue of Jews in Nazi-Occupied Poland.* New York: Oxford University Press, 1986.

OTHER IMPORTANT BOOKS ABOUT THE HOLOCAUST

Hannah Arendt, *Eichmann in Jerusalem: A Report on the Banality of Evil.* New York: Viking, 1963.

Susan D. Bachrach, *Tell Them We Remember: The Story of the Holocaust.* New York: Little, Brown, 1994.

Michael Berenbaum, *The World Must Know: The History of the Holocaust as Told in the United States Holocaust Museum.* New York: Little, Brown, 1993.

Christopher Browning, *Ordinary Men: Reserve Battalion 101 and the Final Solution in Poland.* New York: Harper-Collins, 1992.

Saul S. Friedman, ed., *Holocaust Literature: A Handbook of Critical, Historical, and Literary Writings.* Westport, CT: Greenwood, 1993.

Martin Gilbert, *The Holocaust: A History of the Jews of Europe During the Second World War.* New York: Holt, Rinehart and Winston, 1985.

Daniel Jonah Goldhagen, *Hitler's Willing Executioners: Ordinary Germans and the Holocaust.* New York: Knopf, 1996.

Robert R. Shandley, ed., *Unwilling Germans: The Goldhagen Debate.* Minneapolis: University of Minnesota Press, 1998.

BOOKS AND ARTICLES ABOUT THE BOOK AND FILM *SCHINDLER'S LIST*

Michael André Bernstein, "The *Schindler's List* Effect," *American Scholar*, vol. 63, no. 3, 1994.

Geoff Eley and Atina Grossmann, "Watching *Schindler's List*: Not the Last Word," *New German Critique*, vol. 71, 1997.

Clifford J. Marks and Robert Torry, "'Herr Direktor': Biography and Autobiography in *Schindler's List*," *Biography*, vol. 23, no. 1, 2000.

Martyr's Memorial and Museum of the Holocaust, *A Viewer's Guide to* Schindler's List. Los Angeles: Jewish Federation Council of Greater Los Angeles, 1992.

Franciszek Palowski, *Retracing* Schindler's List. Krakow, Poland: Argona-Jordan Art, 1994.

Plater Robinson, *Schindler's List Teaching Guide*. New Orleans, LA: Southern Institute for Education and Research at Tulane University, 1995.

INDEX